Reflections on M

The *Bulletin of Latin American Research* Book Series

The *Bulletin of Latin American Research* publishes original research of current interest on Latin America, the Caribbean, inter-American relations and the Latin American Diaspora from all academic disciplines within the social sciences, history and cultural studies. The BLAR/SLAS book series was launched in 2008 with the aim of publishing research monographs and edited collections that compliment the wide scope of the Bulletin itself. It is published and distributed in association with Wiley-Blackwell. We aim to make the series the home of some of the most exciting, innovatory work currently being undertaken on Latin America and we welcome outlines or manuscripts of interdisciplinary, single-authored, jointly-authored or edited volumes. If you would like to discuss a possible submission to the series, please contact the editors at blar@liverpool.ac.uk

Reflections on Mexico '68

EDITED BY
KEITH BREWSTER

This edition first published 2010
Editorial organisation © 2010 Society for Latin American Studies, text © 2010 The Authors

Blackwell Publishing was acquired by John Wiley & Sons in February 2007. Blackwell's publishing programme has been merged with Wiley's global Scientific, Technical, and Medical business to form Wiley-Blackwell.

Registered Office
John Wiley & Sons Ltd, The Atrium, Southern Gate, Chichester, West Sussex, PO19 8SQ, United Kingdom

Editorial Offices
350 Main Street, Malden, MA 02148-5020, USA
9600 Garsington Road, Oxford, OX4 2DQ, UK
The Atrium, Southern Gate, Chichester, West Sussex, PO19 8SQ, UK

For details of our global editorial offices, for customer services, and for information about how to apply for permission to reuse the copyright material in this book please see our website at www.wiley.com/wiley-blackwell.

Library of Congress Cataloging-in-Publication Data

Reflections on Mexico '68 / edited by Keith Brewster.
      p. cm. – (Bulletin of Latin American research book series)
   Includes bibliographical references and index.
   ISBN 978-1-4443-3276-6
   1. Olympic Games (19th : 1968 : Mexico City, Mexico)--History. I. Brewster, Keith, 1956-GV7221968 .R44 2010
   796.48--dc22
                                        2009050978

Set in 10 on 13pt and Palatino
by Laserwords Private Limited, Chennai, India
Printed and bound in the United Kingdom by Page Brothers, Norwich

Contents

Dedication

Dedicated to John and Yveline Rodda

Preface

Reflections on Mexico '68

EDITED BY KEITH BREWSTER

Newcastle University

Bulletin of Latin American Research Book Series

SERIES EDITORS: DAVID HOWARD, JASMINE GIDEON,
GEOFFREY KANTARIS, TONY KAPCIA AND LUCY TAYLOR

The *Bulletin of Latin American Research (BLAR)* has a distinguished history of publishing primary research from a range of disciplines in Latin American studies. Our readers have long been able to draw upon ideas from History, Geography, Politics, International Relations, Anthropology, Sociology, Economics, Gender Studies, Development Studies and, increasingly, Cultural Studies. Many of our articles have addressed thematic topics and debates of interest to all Latin Americanists, such as *mestizaje*, populism or the politics of social movements. This is one of the great strengths of being an area studies journal rather than a discipline-based publication. The current book series thus aims to complement the multidisciplinarity of the journal by publishing original and innovative research from scholars who are working across disciplines, raising new questions and applying fresh methodologies. The series seeks to develop into a major forum for interdisciplinary work in Latin American Studies.

This third volume in the series arose from a conference organised to reflect upon the fortieth anniversary of the Olympic Games held in Mexico City, a significant cultural and sporting anniversary which also marked the chilling commemoration of a violently repressed political protest in the Mexican capital, just a few weeks before the inauguration of the Games. The two events form the framework for a collection of essays, edited by Keith Brewster, that seek to reveal the political, cultural, economic and social legacies not only in the context of Mexican contemporary history, but outwith the country and region as whole. The lively debate presented by the authors spans a range of disciplines and engages with 'Mexico '68' in provocative, surprising and original ways, and will no doubt stimulate further reflections on the contemporary context.

Contributor Biographies

Chris Bolsmann is a sociology lecturer in the School of Languages and Social Sciences at Aston University, Birmingham, UK.

Keith Brewster is Senior Lecturer in Latin American History at Newcastle University, UK.

Claire Brewster is Lecturer in Latin American History at Newcastle University, UK.

Hugh Dauncey is Senior Lecturer in French Studies at Newcastle University, UK.

Chris Harris is Lecturer in Hispanic Studies at the University of Liverpool, UK.

Simon Henderson is a part-time lecturer in US history at Newcastle University, UK.

Ryan F. Long is associate professor of Spanish at the University of Oklahoma, USA.

Hazel Marsh is a lecturer in Spanish at the University of East Anglia, UK.

John Rodda was sports correspondent for *The Guardian* newspaper.

Cover images

The cover shows contrasting images of Mexico '68, a cactus cartoon based on a cartoon by Kambiz, and an Olympic tank, taken from a leaflet handed out during student protests.

Introduction

KEITH BREWSTER

Something unique happened in 1968. For the first time, the world's most prestigious sporting event was entrusted to a Spanish-speaking, Latin American country. The decision by the International Olympic Committee (IOC) to award the Summer Olympics to Mexico City not only stunned the sporting world: it also provoked a wave of criticism from all those foreign commentators who believed Latin America to be too inefficient, too poor and, frankly, too 'unsafe' to assume such a responsibility. It quickly became clear that international reaction to the IOC decision was only partially concerned with sport. More substantively, it pivoted around Latin America's reputation within the global community. Furthermore, Mexico's bid to host the Games and its subsequent preparations suggest that it was willing and able to assume the broader responsibility that the international community had bestowed upon it. In common with all cities staging mega-sports events, a primary motive for doing so was to elevate the international image of the host city and nation. Yet in both rhetoric and action, the organisers of Mexico '68 believed that it offered a great opportunity for the whole continent: for the brotherhood of Latin American countries that shared a common language, a common colonial heritage and, it might be added, a common desire to correct the false image that many casual observers shared of the continent.

Before getting carried away with the rhetoric that surrounds the Games, it needs to be acknowledged that the Olympics means entirely different things to different people. For the IOC, it represents a gathering of the world's youth in a celebration of physical achievement and fraternity. For elite athletes, it is the ultimate competition: a chance to pitch their talents against the world's best. For the global television audience that now watches the spectacle, these two often contradictory sentiments coexist as an appreciation of athletic excellence competes with patriotic pride and, at times, jingoism. The words of the founder of the modern Games, Pierre de Coubertin, that 'the most important thing in the Olympic Games is not to win but to take part', have long been an anachronism. While the IOC might maintain that the medal table is of secondary importance, it remains a media and public obsession and is taken as the ultimate measure of a nation's success. Certainly, for the host cities and countries, the Olympic Games is laden with symbolism, opportunity, and responsibility. A successful Games can reinvigorate reputations, while failure could have adverse economic consequences and might undermine a country's self-esteem. Yet foreign attitudes towards the hosts are rarely complex and frequently short-lived: they often move from intense scrutiny to benign indifference. While, for example, Beijing 2008 fostered considerable debate prior to the Games regarding human rights issues, this quickly subsided once the Games had begun. With almost indecent haste once the closing ceremony of one Olympic Games is over, the attention of athletes, the media and the public swiftly turns to the next.

Yet 2008 offered an excuse to indulge in reflection and retrospection. As the 40th anniversary of a year that had witnessed student riots, civil rights demonstrations and the Soviet invasion of Czechoslovakia, it stimulated frenzied activity in the media and academia as commentators sought to mark and/or measure the significance of those events for future generations. Being an Olympic year, 2008 also provided a good excuse for rummaging around the archives to trace the Olympic movement's trajectory through the modern era to the present day. At such times, perhaps, it is natural for commemorations to dwell on the more familiar. A radio series broadcast by the BBC, for example, featured a 15-minute day-to-day coverage of the developing events from 1 March to 31 August 1968. All the usual suspects were there, including the demonstrations in Washington, Paris, and Prague. In analysing them, the series offered listeners a valuable glimpse of the underlying social, political, and generational tensions of that turbulent period (*1968: Myth or Reality*, 2008). Yet when the series concluded, anyone with even a passing interest in the Olympic Games might have felt a little short-changed that Mexico City 1968 was not deemed sufficiently important to warrant inclusion. To its credit, a separate radio programme specifically dedicated to celebrating the Olympic movement went beyond coverage of great sporting events to mention the developing drama being played out in Mexico City. During the summer of 1968, Mexican students also took to the streets to voice their discontent with local and international affairs. Naturally, perhaps, the commentator drew parallels with student demonstrations elsewhere in the world during that year. There was also mention of the events that took place at the Plaza de las Tres Culturas, Tlatelolco, the square in Mexico City in which hundreds of mainly student protesters were killed by Mexican security forces on 2 October 1968, just ten days before the Opening Ceremony. Unfortunately, in giving the number of fatalities that took place during the Student Movement's bloody conclusion, the programme merely repeated a figure that had been issued by the Mexican government at the time; one that had been discredited almost as quickly as it was published. Casual journalism did much to expose the superficial interest in an event that was a mere detour from the programme's journey along the Olympic memory lane.

It should be recognised that Mexico '68 is remembered less for the location and more for a few iconic moments. As far as the sporting world is concerned these include Bob Beaman's giant leap of 8.90 m in the men's long jump, which smashed the world record and would not be bettered for 23 years. Another US athlete, Dick Fosbury, displayed his revolutionary technique in the high-jump to a delighted world audience. Most of all, Mexico '68 is remembered for the image of US athletes Tommie Smith and John Carlos raising their gloved fists in protest on the victory podium. The majority of academic studies tend to view the Mexico Olympics as the stage upon which acts of greater significance were played out; whether this be the civil rights movement in the United States, the anti-apartheid struggle against South Africa, or the physiological effects of athletes competing at high altitude. Much to the chagrin of the Mexican organisers, when attention is paid to the host city, it tends to dwell less on the Olympic Games themselves and more on the massacre of students at Tlatelolco. In subsequent decades, eyewitnesses, journalists, writers, sociologists, political scientists and historians have sought to understand the origins, details and consequences of the events that led to this tragic episode in Mexican history. Indeed, to the present day, conspiracy theories regularly sustain both academic and popular efforts to apportion blame for the Tlatelolco massacre. The result of focusing on the most dramatic sporting and non-sporting events of Mexico '68 is that the broader context has been lost. In effect, the study of Mexico '68 has become fragmented and compartmentalised, with different disciplines and perspectives rarely engaging with one another.

With the prime objective of achieving a more nuanced appreciation of Mexico '68, a conference at Newcastle University in September 2008 took advantage of the 40th anniversary to bring together a group of academics from different disciplines working on themes connected to the Olympic Games.[1] Rather than forcing an artificial cross-disciplinary approach, the conference papers from which this present volume has evolved reflect an attempt to explore the significance of Mexico '68 from hitherto neglected perspectives. Part of this approach was facilitated by the fact that the Games did indeed represent a step into the unknown. Mexico '68 was different

1 I would like to thank the Society of Latin American Studies and the Faculty of Humanities and Social Sciences at Newcastle University for their generous support of this conference.

because, for the first time in the modern era, a city within a developing nation was to act as host; different, as mentioned above, because it would be the first time that a Spanish-speaking country would stage the summer Olympics; and different because it marked the moment at which the Olympic movement lost its innocence. The consequences of the Student Movement's bloody conclusion, the Carlos and Smith podium protest and the threatened boycott of African nations if apartheid-stricken South Africa were allowed to compete, all combined to burst the apolitical bubble that the IOC had striven to protect throughout the modern era. Such precedents not only serve to place the papers within a specific historical context; they also encourage a broadening of horizons; to step beyond the national boundaries of the host nation in a search for comparisons and parallels to help enrich our understanding of Mexico '68.

Given the objectives of the conference, the choice of John Rodda as keynote speaker could not have been more appropriate. With a long, distinguished career in sports journalism and an unrivalled knowledge of the Olympic movement, Rodda's unique perspective on Mexico '68 alone would have warranted his presence. Yet what made his contribution imperative is the fact that in 1968, Rodda happened to be in the wrong place at the right time. Then a young sports reporter for UK newspaper *The Guardian*, he had specifically been sent to Mexico ahead of the Games because his editor had a hunch that 'something' was happening. In endeavouring to understand what that 'something' was, Rodda had the misfortune of experiencing the horrific Tlatelolco massacre. His harrowing report of the atrocity, published on the front pages of *The Guardian* on 4 October 1968, and his subsequent efforts to ensure that the world beyond knew what had happened have been invaluable in guaranteeing that the Mexican government's efforts to conceal the full extent of the tragedy have failed (Rodda, 1968b).

On 1 November 1968, after he had returned from Mexico, Rodda summarised 'the troubles of Mexico' in another newspaper report in which he astutely prophesied, 'An accurate number of the deaths will never be known'. Nonetheless, leading Mexican intellectuals such as Octavio Paz and Elena Poniatowska have turned to John Rodda's newspaper reports in order to obtain a more reliable number of the casualties.[2] Forty years later, the authority with which he reflects on the suppression of students and the Games themselves is beyond compare.

---

2   Rodda (1968a); Meyer and Sherman, (1987: 670); Paz, (1993: 38); Poniatowska (1971: 170). Meyer and Sherman quote a report in *The Guardian* that recorded 325 deaths. This source was also used by Paz (1993) and Poniatowska has quoted Paz.

As Claire Brewster's chapter reveals, being awarded the 1968 Olympics in 1963 had been both an honour and a concern for the Mexican Organising Committee. Such was the margin of Mexico's victory in the vote that it appeared to have had no problem in convincing the world of its suitability as a venue. However, it is evident that other factors were at stake in 1963 and that Mexico City's overwhelming endorsement was based more on political than practical criteria. This being the case, the organisers of the Games were almost immediately placed on the defensive, incessantly having to justify the faith that the IOC had bestowed upon them. Staging such a major sporting event nonetheless gave Mexico the chance to showcase its achievements on a world stage and to dispel forever the negative stereotypes that had characterised Latin Americans in general, and Mexicans in particular. The nature of foreign criticism and how this affected the manner in which Mexico prepared for the Games reveals much about foreign perceptions of Latin America, and Latin America's perception of itself.

While determined to rise to the challenge presented by foreign cynicism, the Mexican hierarchy was nonetheless concerned that the majority of the Mexican public might somehow 'let the side down' by revealing the less developed aspects of Mexican society. Scepticism both within and outside the country, then, quickly followed Mexico's success. As my own chapter shows, the government consequently embarked upon a huge public education campaign designed to teach Mexicans how to behave, while sweeping aside any aspects and elements that could not be made to conform to the elite ideal. Although the immediate impulse for such a campaign was the Olympic Games, the manner in which it was conducted and the message it sought to purvey reveals something far less transitory. It goes to the very heart of the relationship between the state and the nation in a country that, for foreign consumption at least, purported to be at peace with itself, especially when compared to other Latin American countries. The campaign showed a level of paternalism that barely questioned the state's prerogative to direct thoughts and actions. It reveals a significant degree of mistrust, in which the state became deeply concerned that if the 'true' nature of Mexican emotions were to be revealed, it would cause untold damage to national interests. Given this socio-political dynamic, the events at Tlatelolco assume a more macabre logic.

Mexico City's successful gaining of the 1968 Olympic Games was at the expense of other bidding candidates. Hugh Dauncey's chapter considers the effects of the 1963 vote on Lyon (France's second city), which was placed third out of the four candidates. In doing so, he reveals the national disappointment; feelings that resurfaced in July 2005 when London, rather than Paris, was chosen to host the 2012 Games. Significantly, Dauncey's chapter reveals the tensions that lay behind a bidding process that pitched provincial France against its more illustrious capital. The same rhetoric of civic pride and economic promise that underlay Mexico City's successful bid was evident in its French opponent. For the purposes of the present volume, the chapter is most valuable in what it underlines as having been different about the two bids. Questions of French regional identity and political rivalry were central to the motives for the Lyon bid. The very absence of these issues in the case of Mexico City goes beyond the fact that it was the nation's capital city. It reveals the extent to which Mexico's political system allowed minimal dissent against a centrally driven project. While not all of Mexico City's political leaders may have been in favour of the Olympic project, their incapacity to determine the nature of a bid that had national government endorsement underlines their impotence when compared to their French counterparts. What also becomes clear is that events such as the Olympic Games are deemed to have a disproportionate influence on establishing, consolidating or rectifying a host's international image. For Lyon, the objective was to secure its position as France's second city. In the case of Mexico City, its primacy was never in any doubt. As Claire Brewster's chapter reveals, among the things that Mexico City sought to achieve was to stretch beyond the national boundaries and establish itself as a leading light within the continent.

Despite John Rodda's call for the Mexico City Olympics to be cancelled after the massacre at Tlatelolco, the Games did go ahead as planned. The organisation, if not perfect, was sufficiently good for the Games to be proclaimed the 'best ever'. If the Mexican government had ensured that national political affairs would not jeopardise the smooth running of the Games, it was neither willing nor able to prevent the march of the civil rights movement from reaching the Olympic Stadium. In contrast to the treatment of its own Student Movement, the relaxed manner in which Mexican officials viewed Tommie Smith's and John Carlos's podium protest appeared to vindicate decades of post-revolutionary political rhetoric that had preached tolerance and ethnic harmony. While its own 'successful' civil rights record would not bear close scrutiny, the Mexican state's diplomatic reaction to the podium protest suggests that it was not altogether discomforted by the spectre of its northern neighbour's dirty linen being washed in Mexican public space. Simon Henderson's chapter reveals how the same event was viewed very much differently north of the Mexican border. In placing the protest within the broader context of US society in the 1960s, Henderson moves beyond usual academic treatment of this symbolic act to stress that the protest needs to be understood as something more than the heroic gesture of two athletes. Rather, he argues that by appropriating a space that the IOC had assiduously endeavoured to preserve as apolitical, Smith's and Carlos's protest was able to transmit, in a most effective manner, the many and varied dissident voices that comprised the civil rights movement.

It is a matter of considerable irony that given Mexico's relaxed response to the podium protest, its ability to stage a successful Olympics had been thrown into peril before the Games began over the issue of race. In what has turned out to be an interesting twist of fate, the very country whose apartheid system threatened to jeopardise the Mexico City Olympics would later empathise with the Mexicans' endeavours to overcome international scepticism regarding a developing nation's ability to organise a successful mega-sporting event. Chris Bolsmann's chapter draws parallels between Mexico's hosting of the 1968 Olympics and the debates surrounding South Africa's staging of the 2009 Confederations Cup, as a prelude to the more prestigious 2010 Football World Cup. Bolsmann argues that these major sporting events in South Africa need to be understood against the backdrop of a post-Cold War global political context. In doing so he reveals South Africa's post-apartheid developmental project, its Pan-African agenda, and its aspirations to continental leadership. While such factors obviously locate his focus both in time and space, there are evident links to Mexico '68 and its pro-Latin American agenda. The comparative historical perspective that connects the two countries' plights enriches our understanding of how developing nations are forced to confront barriers that have little to do with economic realities and more to do with overcoming deep-rooted negative stereotypes.

The shadow of the massacre at Tlatelolco, while not completely obscuring Mexico's achievements in 1968, nonetheless occupies the last three chapters of this collection. Rather than take part in the seemingly endless (and ultimately fruitless) endeavours to apportion blame for the deaths of Mexican students, each of the contributors deploys fresh perspectives to analyse how Mexicans have tried to make sense of the tragedy. Chris Harris revisits some of the more crucial literary works that emerged immediately after the massacre: more specifically he compares Elena Poniatowska's (1971) *La Noche de Tlatelolco* with Luis González de Alba's (1997a) *Los días y los años*. For many years, Poniatowska's collection has been regarded as one of the most effective attempts to collate the thoughts and emotions expressed by those affected by the massacre. It has been translated into several languages and remains a best-seller in Mexico and many other countries. Harris's comparative analysis, however, suggests that González de Alba's work offers more promise in encapsulating the 'voice from below' because it was borne from within the Student Movement itself. As such, Harris argues that it should be viewed as an important historical source for producing a new subalternist history of the Mexican Student Movement.

The two texts that form the focus of Harris's comparative analysis are part of a larger genre of literature that relates to the Tlatelolco massacre. In analysing the work of Chilean writer Roberto Bolaño, Ryan Long reveals

Bolaño's unease with the imperative of seeing the tragedy as part of a relentless trajectory towards democracy. Bolaño's (1999) novel, *Amuleto* revolves around a Uruguayan woman who went into hiding within Mexico's national university during its two-week occupation by Mexican troops in September 1968. In common with many witnesses of traumatic events, Bolaño's protagonist, Auxilio Lacouture, suffers periodic flashbacks long after her ordeal is over. Furthermore, as Long argues, the experience not only influences her perceptions of the past, but informs her predictions for developments in the future. Long suggests that this disruption in neat chronological progression represents Bolaño's critique of a literary archive on Mexico '68 that has hitherto isolated the events of Tlatelolco from the broader context, and that has tried to find closure through the perpetuation of a storyline that links the students' struggle to the ultimate triumph of democracy.

One of the final sections of *Amuleto* includes details of a dream in which Lacouture hears a faint but nonetheless audible song: the song of a generation of sacrificed Latin American youth. As Long puts it, these victims 'remain alive enough to sing, as ghosts who insist on the importance of the past'. In the concluding contribution to this collection, Hazel Marsh complements this portrayal by focusing on the lyrics of the Mexican singer/songwriter, Judith Reyes. Already a renowned political activist at the time of the Mexico Olympics, Reyes chose to chronicle the unfolding events of the Student Movement through the genre of *corridos*; re-appropriating this ballad form of music to reveal, as she puts it, 'the other, hidden face of the nation'. Arguing that Reyes's lyrics were untainted by the opposing forces of official and alternative culture, Marsh explores the notion that her songs present a reliable testimony of the past.

In different ways the three studies that focus on the events of 2 October 1968 represent the underlying theme of *Reflections on Mexico '68*. Marsh's analysis of the immediate responses to the Tlatelolco massacre through song lyrics dovetails nicely with Harris's comparative analysis of its immediate impact within testimonial literature. Both insist that these instant reactions have survived and continue to resonate. Long's study of Bolaño's novel reveals the enduring message to be gleaned from this important time in Mexican history; one that serves to inform future generations and helps to understand previous deeds. In a similar way, Claire Brewster's and my own contributions seek to expose more than a sense of how Mexicans viewed themselves and were viewed by others in the 1960s. They argue that such debates had their own history; and that analysing tensions within society in 1968 gives one a better understanding of the developments of society in the preceding decades. The chapters by Henderson, Dauncey and Bolsmann extend the physical and temporal parameters on Mexico '68 in a way that is rarely attempted. The frozen iconography of the raised fists takes on a new meaning when seen through the prism of a multi-dimensional civil rights movement that had begun many years earlier. The focus on South Africa and France offer unique angles for a greater understanding of Mexico '68. The blend of anxieties and aspirations that greeted the IOC decision to grant the Olympic Games to Mexico would be repeated four decades later as the South Africans took on the mantle of displaying the potential of the developing world before a global sporting audience. While Mexico City rejoiced in 1963, Lyon despaired at ever being able to use sport to carve out an identity on the international stage that would distinguish itself from the centralist pull of the French capital.

What makes this collection unique, however, is John Rodda's recollections of Mexico '68. Sports historians are, no doubt, aware of his endeavours to understand the bureaucratic machinery that drives sporting institutions such as the IOC. Yet for any historian of Mexican cultural politics during the 1960s, John Rodda's name is also synonymous with one event more than any other: the Tlatelolco massacre. A hapless coincidence of time and place that resulted in Rodda's witnessing the massacre meant that his career took on a new dimension. Paul Fitzpatrick was in *The Guardian*'s Manchester office the night that Rodda filed 'that extraordinary report from the Square of the Three Cultures' and recalled that although Rodda was already held in 'the highest regard before that terrifying experience, he assumed heroic status afterwards'.[3] John was one of those who survived the massacre. He lived to tell the tale from a unique perspective: that of a professional journalist equipped with the appropriate skills and, above all, the determination to bring what had happened to the world's attention.

The supreme bravery and determination that John displayed that night were again apparent when he accepted my invitation to deliver the keynote speech at our conference. Although diagnosed with a terminal illness, John was determined to override his debilitating condition in order to fulfil the commitment he had made. Typical of the practical approach that all seasoned journalists possess, John suggested that we pre-record his address just in case his illness should prevent him from attending the conference or from delivering his speech. It was that same bravery and determination, matched by that of Yveline Rodda, that ensured that John did indeed make the long journey north. It was a privilege and a great pleasure to all those at the conference that he was able to attend and his presence converted a good occasion into one that was truly memorable. John eventually succumbed to his illness on 2 March 2009. Tributes from former athletes reveal the high regard in which he was held. He was 'quite simply, the doyen of athletics writers', and 'an incredibly knowledgeable man who was very

---

3   Yveline Rodda, email to Keith Brewster, April 2009.

much respected by his peers and athletes alike'.[4] Although various sources have suggested that his commitment to our conference was something that helped him sustain his battle against illness through 2008, I would rather offer a different perspective. It was John's vivid accounts of the events at Tlatelolco that helped to sustain the spirits of all of those who survived the experience, but who were written out of history by the Mexican state-controlled media. It was John's vivid accounts that have sustained, and will continue to sustain, generations of writers and intellectuals who have struggled to overcome state censorship in search of the truth about the massacre. Like the lyrics of Judith Reyes, the words of an English sports journalist have a resonance that reaches far beyond the life of the newspaper within which they were printed. They stand as a stubborn, unyielding testimony that will continue to assist and inform future generations in their endeavour to understand the past.

---

4   Sebastian Coe and Steve Cram quoted in *Guardian* (2009b).

1

'Prensa, Prensa': A Journalist's Reflections on Mexico '68[1]

JOHN RODDA

Forty years on I still get a trembling hand and mild palpitation when I watch the final shots of *Butch Cassidy and the Sundance Kid* (1969). For those of you who missed this classic film, Paul Newman and Robert Redford were a couple of cowboys who turned to train and bank robberies. After one raid on a bank they were holed up in a Bolivian peasant's hovel, to pick off the sheriff's men. But when they peered from their hide-out they saw that instead of a few locals with rifles they were surrounded by half the Bolivian army, bristling with weapons. It was a hopeless position but bravado had marked their style throughout the film; they decided to make a break out shooting their way to freedom, knowing full well that this was the end. When they made the dash the cacophony of rifle fire was identical to the noise I heard as I lay face down on a balcony of the Square of the Three Cultures, Mexico City on 2 October 1968. The reminder was even more emphatic since the film finished with several stills showing dust and gun smoke rising as our heroes fell to the earth. I saw the Butch Cassidy film for the first time in a Croydon cinema in December 1969, a year after it was made, and that final scene set me off shaking violently, which was even more embarrassing, for in those days when the programme ended the screen curtains closed and most of the audience stood for the national anthem. I remember trying to hold one arm with the other against my body to curb this involuntary action.

Anyway, what was a reporter in Mexico to cover the Olympic Games doing lying face downwards on a balcony? 1968 was, of course, the year of student discontent in Europe, in Paris, Prague, Berlin, London, and when there was student action in Mexico many thought it was part of the continuing theme. The verbal protest was originally linked to the Games. Why in a country of such vast poverty was the government lavishing so much money on the event, was the simple question that the students, perhaps in more florid terms, posed.

---

1 This is a transcription of J. Rodda's speech given at the September 2008 'Mexico '68' conference in Newcastle, UK.

That is how it seemed at first, but when tanks arrived outside the university and two students were killed, *The Guardian*, at least, took it seriously. *The Guardian*'s news editor Jean Stead, who was not the first *Guardian* woman to hold that position in the 1960s, called me in and told me to get out there quickly – like tomorrow. This was a bit unsettling, since sporting journalists work to the calendar and rarely did one have to react so sharply – particularly to the prime event, the Olympic Games. A couple of days later I was in the office of Reuters in Mexico City collecting background material and contacts. I learned that while the Olympic Games was the immediate cause, the action went much deeper and the Games was just a very convenient platform to get some international coverage of the country's plight. Other universities around the country were mounting the cause and, in Toledo, they had their own local objective, which showed me that this was more about the 'haves' versus the 'have nots' of Mexico rather than the Olympics. In a village not far from the town there had been a serious bus accident, several people were killed and many injured when a local bus careered off the road and into a steep gully. It was nothing more than mechanical failure in a clapped out vehicle. The bereaved and dependants sought help – some form of compensation from the bus owner – and were told to clear off and not bother the company; the students picked up on this, coordinated the group of dependants who really needed help and sought out the bus owner. He told them to clear off too, but thought better of it when the students pointed out that more buses in his creaking fleet might topple down mountainsides, this time empty, if he did not provide some help for those affected by the accident. I am not supporting such action, merely reporting what happened.

Back in Mexico City, vendors were ordered out of the Cathedral Square on orders from the police as part of the Olympic clean-up. The students went to the police station to point out that these people, particularly at the time of the Games, were what tourists wanted to see. By all means control the numbers, but don't spoil something that is part of the City's fabric as well as helping the economy of the poor; so the vendors were reinstated. These and other incidents showed the influence that the students had, which increased in strength as the academics joined them. I covered several meetings, interspersed with a flow of Olympic copy and at each one there was normally a platoon of the blue-uniformed militia – but not the army and no tanks, which is what I had expected to see.

Normality seemed to be returning, until 2 October, ten days before the Opening Ceremony of the Games, when the students organised a huge meeting in the Square of the Three Cultures. This was bordered on three sides by blocks of flats and a polytechnic, and open on the other side with the high-rise Foreign Ministry building across a road. I arrived just before 5.00 in the evening and found the main balcony where the leaders were showing signs of excitement at the size of the crowd. My interpreter said that this was the largest gathering they had attracted and there were cheers and applause when it increased as a file of several hundred people entered the square from the back with banners at their head. It was the trade unions: 'the first time we have had their support', one of my contacts said. By the time the first speaker began it was estimated that nearly 10,000 people were packed into that square, which gave the operation a huge lift. One of the speakers had just started delivering his message when a green Very light soared up behind the Foreign Office block; it caused immediate agitation in the square below and tension on my balcony. My interpreter went white and said, 'we must leave, it's the military', and I was saying that this was exactly what I had come to see. I think she disappeared down the stair-well, and when people started to drop to the floor I thought I might go somewhere else too. As I turned there was a man in an open-neck shirt and slacks with a white glove on his left hand and a gun in the other that was pointing at me. I said the magic word a couple of times, 'prensa, prensa', which is Spanish for 'press', but he was unimpressed and indicated that I should get on the floor. I repeated the rank I held; he was unmoved but instead of pulling the trigger he deftly flicked the gun over, grasping the barrel and raised it to hit me on the head – I was quicker, turned and flopped down among the bodies already prone. I had only been on the ground a few seconds it seemed, when the firing began. It was so deafening that I could not immediately make out from where it came. But from the cries and screams it was clearly having an effect in the crowded square below. It lasted it seemed for minutes; then came relative quiet before another lead onslaught was unleashed.

To say I was in shock was putting it mildly. After about an hour of this, the lights went out and water started pouring from the floors above – punctures in the water tanks at the top I assumed – and I became saturated. I did work my way a little closer to the balcony wall, which seemed safer. But I could not be sure what was happening. I realised that there must be opposition because, after a short burst of rifle fire, there was a response by a different sort of gun, or guns, in a less disciplined style. What had happened to the man with the white glove? Was he in some way trying to protect those on the balcony by ordering us down?

At this point I thought that the men with guns who had come up the staircase were student supporters, for they were all in civilian clothing, and I believed that we were under siege from the military. These were my horrifying thoughts: that someone would toss a couple of hand grenades or a tear gas bomb into our area or that the military would come up the stairs and just flush out all these bodies lying on the floor. But then I thought there must be students holding the bottom of the staircase, but for how long could they hold out? I took a couple of peeks up and kept saying the word 'prensa', but there was only one man around me who could speak English – and he had only a few words – but turned out to be a Mexican journalist. There was a tremendous amount of shouting up and down the stairs, periods of quiet, and then periods of fierce gunfire all round the square, with bullets embedding themselves into the walls and ceiling. My lowest point came when a machine gunner who I thought was located on a higher level, raked the metal ledge of the parapet top just above my head; it brought a shower of sparks and a reminder of something my father once told me. He spent over three years in the First World War trenches in France and while he talked little of his experiences, I recall him saying that the worst type of shot was the ricochet, which ripped open the body and was far more agonising than a direct hit.

During periods of quiet, I heard vehicles apparently trundling into the square; they seemed to have wheels and tracks. They halted; someone started shouting and then came the crump of bazooka or mortar fire, an explosion and several times the sound of fire burning. They seemed to be picking off flats and open balconies, I surmised, and this confirmed there were two parties involved in combat. I also thought it was only a matter of time before they got round to our spot. I prayed to God to look after my family and make my death instantaneous. I thought, this is going to be it; when they come to our balcony we will just be wiped out. There were only a few of these incidents, but the wait between each seemed to get longer. By then I was sopping wet from those punctured water tanks.

Someone was hit and there was terrible groaning across the balcony floor. A girl was slumped and I saw blood that appeared to be at the side of her temple. I prayed; I put my arm round the Mexican journalist next to me. I kept asking him what was going on and I still had it firmly fixed in my mind that I was with the students who were fighting against the militia.

After about an hour and a half (it was dark by now and I couldn't see my watch) there was a long period of quiet; no firing but a lot of shouting up and down the staircases. The lights went on again and after a while I turned my head to see there was more empty floor space and the man with the white gloved hand was also lying on the floor; they were moving people about. Eventually it was my turn; if you can imagine I was flat on the floor looking ahead and opposite me was this man; we were face to face and not far apart and he had a hand gun pointing at my forehead indicating that I should move across the floor. The idea that I should get to the open side did not appeal because it was so vulnerable; I managed to pull my press accreditation card from inside my blazer pocket, but it had little effect. He motioned that I should go to the staircase and this I did, sliding down the stairs to the relative safety of the mid-floor landing where there was a small group of people. The white gloves seemed to be doing some sorting out, and for the first time in about three hours I began to relax. I heard the word 'prensa' mentioned several times. When I say it was quiet, there was always the background noise of water gushing from the floors above onto our balcony and down the staircase.

The men about me, I now realised, were not students. They were mostly too old and their dress, if it was ragged, was not the raggedness of students. In this little area were other journalists including a man named Dancey of NBC, the American radio and TV broadcaster. I discovered that his interpreter was one of those shot in the back. They got him across the floor and down the stairs to an ambulance.

We were herded into the kitchen of a flat where there were two Germans, one of whom had a tape recorder. A man with a gun made him run the tape. There was nothing on it for, as the German indicated, when the shooting started he had flung himself to the floor and forgot to turn on the tape. I now realised that these men were military and probably wanted to take the tape away. Yet there were several cameramen in our group of nineteen, but there seemed to be no attempt to take their films. We were then ushered into another room of the flat where I saw several bullet holes in the windows, and marks on the ceiling and walls and the highly polished and obviously treasured dining table. By now it was about 8.30 pm and the shooting was only sporadic. We occasionally heard a vehicle driven up and the whine of an ambulance.

Dancey and I had a few words, and I said, 'it's a good thing there are a lot of us here because they can't get us all run over by the cars'. Finally we were told that we were going, and honestly I didn't know what to expect. When we reached the bottom of the staircase the surrounding area was full of troops who stood around shivering. If you examine the few photographs of the soldiers involved in this operation and see the glaze of their eyes, this, together with their shivering, supports the suspicion that they were high on drugs.

Finally one of the white-gloved gunshots, whom by now I suspected were plain clothed militia, told Dancey and me we should leave. He ushered us down the stair-well to the ground, and the first thing I noticed was a pile of bodies, I think between six and twelve, stacked against a wall on my right. Our usher waved us on indicating a pathway through the blocks of flats. I hesitated and said 'No' to Dancey. 'They can just pick us off with a couple of bullets in our backs.' He seemed to agree, and after much gesticulating our minder, bemused at our mistrust, came to the main road, where the traffic was flying through both ways in normal hair-brained Mexican manner – it was uncanny. We hailed a cab and, as one halted, a third person wanted to join us. He turned out to be a Mexican journalist who had little English, but Dancey and I pressed him with the same question. 'How many do you think have been killed?' 'Hundreds, hundreds', he kept repeating.

When we reached the Maria Isabel Hotel I realised what a tramp I looked, dishevelled, soaking wet and wild-eyed. People skirted round me as I went directly to the lift to head for the press centre on the first floor. As the lift doors opened and I went to step out, I came face to face with very man I needed to meet. It was Don Saunders, senior sports writer on the *Daily Telegraph*. I blurted out that I had been involved in the carnage about which some news had filtered through to the press centre. Don was just the person to help me. He never seemed to be a very well man and was sympathetic to other people's plight. He was known as 'Saunders of the liver'. In my circumstances, he was just the man I required. He was the next best person to a medic and there he was ushering me to his room. I discarded my wet clothes and stretched on the bed, relaxing for the first time in about six hours. He called the front desk for a doctor giving a brief reason for the requirement. Within minutes there was a tap on the door; it was not a doctor but an assistant manager. He talked with Don in the doorway about my health and I clearly heard the word 'exaggeration' and it was not Don who said it. A few minutes later a doctor arrived, took a look at me, felt my pulse and then said to Don that he would give me an injection to calm me down. My response was immediate, and I think I ranted a little, saying no way was I going to have an injection. Cynicism is a trademark of journalists and I now had it in abundance towards anything lawful in Mexico; I needed to get on to paper what had happened to me in that square. Don quickly caught on to the nature of my protests and, politely as he could, ushered the doctor from the room suggesting the alternative medication of a whisky or two to make me sleep. The assistant manager was still outside the door.

I needed to get things written and I was in no state to sit and write. Don picked up the phone and within a few minutes Jim Coote, the athletics correspondent of the *Telegraph*, a colleague but a rival, came into the room and sat before a typewriter and bashed away as I poured out the words. Another tap on the door; it was a posse from the British press concerned about my health. They trooped in, crowded round the bed and after the usual pleasantries there was disappointment on every face when I told them that I was not saying a word about what happened until after it had been published in *The Guardian*; they knew that, but they had to try. More words for the typewriter jumbling the chronology a bit. Eventually the dictation was finished and I slept.

When I read my piece the next morning I acted in what today might be regarded as an unprofessional manner. First, I needed to dictate the words to my Manchester office – then I went to the Competitors' Village to seek out Sandy Duncan, the British team commandant and tell him briefly what had happened. There were lots of stories and rumours flying round the camp and I suggested that when *The Guardian* arrived along with all the other British papers in a couple of days, the copies of *The Guardian* should be removed. I think the attitude to competitors by journalists has shifted. In 1968, the participants were there for the honour to be top of their event; it was a competition for amateurs, many struggled just to get on to the Olympic stage with no real hope of a medal. They were dedicated and doing it because they believed the word 'Olympic' raised their status; it was not their job. In that atmosphere, I did not want to be accused of damaging British chances by my dramatic and frightening revelations. An experienced news reporter would have provided a more incisive and rounded report but was unlikely to value the Olympic ethos. Soft, perhaps, by today's standards but that was my view 40 years ago.

I cannot recall whether it was Sandy Duncan or Arthur Gold, a team leader who on my trip to the Competitors' Village suggested I see the BOA (British Olympic Association) Medical officer Dr Peter Massey. That was fortuitous because I spent the best part of an hour with him as he questioned me on every aspect of the previous night's exploits; his probing helped me to remember more and get things into a tidier chronological order, but as I came to realise later, this was what today we call counselling. I met him again on a couple of occasions and remember giving my belated thanks for his services over some Pimms at Henley Regatta.

My first reporter's task was the follow-up, which took me to the Hotel Camino Real where the International Olympic Committee Executive Board was in session. These meetings are held in private. I sent in a message to speak to Lord Killanin who was then Chef de Protocol and a former Fleet Street journalist. He saw my state and asked me to send a note to Avery Brundage (president of the IOC). I did so in brief terms and concluded with the view that the Games should be cancelled. The following morning, by which time my tome had been published, I did a live interview on the BBC's *World at One* programme with William Hardcastle. I could see the $64,000 question looming: 'Do you think the Games should go on?' 'No', I said. I was not surprised that the IOC ignored or rejected my similar recommendation and instead issued a statement that this unrest had nothing whatsoever to do with the Olympic Games. It was only a couple of years later that I learned that this statement purporting to come from the Executive was only under the name of Brundage because several other members did not concur.

By now the rumours were piling up. There were plenty of figures: 35 killed, the official one, to 500, just guesswork, which was closer to the estimate of the Mexican journalist we encountered in the square. Then there were the repeated stories of the large pieces of paper bearing a daubed red cross stuck on the doors or windows of houses. They were apparently indications that if some one was missing from this address don't bother the authorities with your enquiries. Two young girls who were missing never to be seen again, were members of small corps of press stewards in the Media Centre. Most of the missing were university students and pretty well all of them from middle-class and wealthy families. I had always heard that life was cheap in Latin America and here was an example straight in front of my face.

As I ploughed into my Olympic reporting, there were constant reminders of the square. The rumours about paper fixed to a front door or window daubed with a red cross hardened with evidence of sightings. The number of my contacts dwindled from about half a dozen to two. Some may have been killed, others imprisoned. More rumours, too, about planes flying out over the Gulf of Mexico to dump weighted bodies. When the athletic programme of the Olympic Games began, next to my seat writing a column for *The Times* was the athlete Roger Bannister, by then the only four-minute miler who was also a specialist in neurological malfunction. He was interested in the violence of my jerking body every time the starter fired his gun, an affliction that only diminished after about four days of athletic competitions.

I kept in contact with my remaining Mexican links on my return to London and was told that through a slow and careful operation some form of valid figure for the dead and injured of 2 October would be reached. In the following January or February, I published a short piece in *The Guardian* giving the number of deaths at 267 and the injured at around 1200. These figures were compiled through doctors and staff at the City's hospitals who had been presented with bodies and those who died in their care. The Mexican Ambassador in London, acting on behalf of a government sticking to its original figure of 35, was incensed; he had to be. The original Mexican figure was pathetically wrong; mine, too, was inaccurate but closer to the truth because many bodies were disposed of without the aid of hospitals or mortuaries. I prefer to use my figure, as it is a calculation by professionals involved in the carnage. But the guesswork of the Mexican journalist who shared the cab taking us away from the square – 500 – was probably closer to reality.

This was 1968, 40 years ago, when it was a rare occurrence that journalists were involved in such risk; in fact one of us, an Italian woman reporter (Oriana Fallacci) was injured on my balcony. Since then, many of my profession and that of radio and television have been killed, injured or taken hostage. We tend to hear only about the British, but there are others – from our allies and the other side. In 2007 worldwide, 171 journalists were killed because of their job, only six less than the previous year.

Looking back, I suppose I should have returned to Mexico to gather material for a book. But I was athletics, boxing, rowing and Olympic correspondent for *The Guardian* as well as throwing in some coverage of rugby football. I was too busy and frankly did not have the confidence, I suspect, to change course in my career. Anyway, my output from this Mexico memory dwindled to an occasional anniversary piece – about every five years. Of course, in one respect my instant judgement was wrong. Had the Games been cancelled then, they may not have survived – they would have been halted in Munich four years later after the Israelis were assassinated in the Competitors' Village, the Moscow boycott 1980 would probably have succeeded, and that in Los Angeles four years later would have had greater impact. Its dogged resilience in the face of political interference, demonstration and intimidation is the bedrock of Olympic survival – but that's another story.

One of the rumours circulating around the IOC hotel in the days after the shootings was the suspicion that Brundage had sent a message to the country's president, Gustavo Díaz Ordaz about the consequences of the student troubles spilling over into Olympic arenas. It was suggested that Brundage told the president that the Games would be halted in such an eventuality. Only nine years ago did I have confirmation that this was a fact – and, in my estimation, a crucial one. I helped a man called Arthur Takac write his life story. Takac was a significant figure in the backrooms of the sporting world. He had been a Yugoslav Davis Cup tennis player, ran the 800 m on the track internationally and was the country's team manager at the 1948 Olympic Games in London. He was sometime coach to Red Star Belgrade soccer team and was the country's top athletics official. He moved to the IOC headquarters in Switzerland and then on to the organising committee of the Olympic Games in Montreal, and was a key witness in the subsequent corruption trials. He also worked for twelve months to train and put together the team of officials that operated at the athletics programme of the Games in Mexico. During the Games, he was an aide to Brundage and told me that he delivered the message to the president of the country, a message in which Brundage said that should there be trouble on any Games site, the celebration would be cancelled. Apparently this was sent around the middle of September and it strengthens my suspicion that the government cooled its attitude to protests, which thus mounted, and when the big rally was held on 2 October that was the time to smash them. From the government's point of view, it was a successful outcome; the brutality of that night snuffed out any possible further action; there was not even a shout of protest, just the soft sound of weeping.

Ten years ago, the Paris correspondent of the Mexican magazine *Proceso* came to my home, just outside Taunton, together with a photographer to interview me about 2 October 1968. She had combed through newspaper files in several European cities and found my piece in the British Library at Hendon. She was very excited about it and wanted to quote large chunks and add some of my reflections. Her magazine, a weekly, had a circulation of 25,000 and they were planning to lift this to 30,000 because this seemed to be a subject very few people knew much about, including those who might have been affected by the loss of a relative; they had always wanted to know more. On the Thursday they published, the entire print was sold in four hours and they only stopped reprints on the Sunday when they had passed 100,000. It had, she subsequently told me over the phone from Paris, lifted the cover off a piece of Mexican history that until then had, not surprisingly, been largely suppressed.

Apart from the initial shock and horror of the Square of the Three Cultures on 2 October 1968 was my bemusement that with a vast contingent of the world's media, not all of it sporting, the story disappeared so easily. Forty years ago there was no 24/7 reporting, satellite broadcasting was in its infancy and we were a long way from laptops and mobile phones. In part, I regret lacking the skill of a Norman Mailer or Alistair Cook who surely would have made the world sit up and take more notice.

About five years earlier, the late Chris Brasher writing in UK newspaper *The Observer* quoted a Swedish coach saying 'There will be those who will die . . .' referring to the Games. No, this was not foresight of brutality but an opinion of what might happen when Olympic sportsmen pitch themselves against one another on a track 7000 feet above sea level. When the Games were awarded to Mexico City at the IOC session of 1963 in Baden Baden, some members asked questions about the effect of altitude and were assured, during Mexico City's presentation, that after a couple of days you would become acclimatised. The question was about the athletes; the answer probably referred to the effect on IOC members, though at their age they should have taken greater caution. In fact, the problem of altitude only unfolded slowly when those with experience made their point. Ultimately the IOC acknowledged the difficulty when they called on the British Olympic Association to send a team of athletes to Mexico City in 1965 to undertake some scientific research. Sadly, this was only a cursory stab at the problem, for the team included a lot of expertise: the majority of the guinea pigs were international athletes of experience and the scientific input was led by Griffith Pugh who had taken part in Edmund Hilary's successful conquest of Everest in 1953. The team came up with the recommendation that a period of acclimatisation should be undertaken well before the Games and, after considerable debate and opposition from Avery Brundage, who thought any suggestion of training camps had a professional smell, it was announced that Olympic teams could train at altitude for a period of six weeks a year before the Games and arrive in Mexico City a little earlier than would be normal. This turned out to be wholly inadequate as the results indicate, and there were painful and bizarre scenes in the arenas. Death came close: four Swiss oarsmen, who collapsed at the end of their opening race, were taken to hospital and flew home before the end of the Games seriously ill. One British competitor suffered similarly. Maurice Herriott, one of the world's leading 3,000 m steeplechasers who had taken the silver medal four years earlier in Tokyo, ran his heat over a minute slower than his normal time and collapsed needing oxygen, like Ron Clarke of Australia, a world record breaker at 10,000 m. Herriott returned home and stayed in hospital for about six weeks while his blood, which had been severely damaged, was washed out and replaced. This was an event I failed to cover properly in Mexico, but many years later I caught up with Maurice Herriott, who unfolded the experience. Fortunately the Olympic Games in Mexico was the penultimate one of Brundage's straightjacket twenty-year reign as president.

If awarding the Games to Mexico is regarded as a mistake, the aftermath fulfilled the spirit of the Olympic Movement in another way. Altogether Kenyans, Ethiopians and Tunisians won twelve medals in the track events, which was a resounding triumph because they had won in these events only four medals in all their previous games. Prior to the Games, Kenyans had begun to make an impact in distance running accompanied by newspaper stories that the key to their success came from their early school years when they ran to and from school every day. The tabloids occasionally embellished the story by having the runner fleeing from wild animals. That daily running played a key part as it had done for Spiridon Louis, winner of the first Olympic marathon in 1896. He was a multi-faceted Greek, being a postman, shepherd and water carrier. Every day he went the 2.5 miles from his village to Athens taking fresh water in barrels strapped to the backs of a couple of donkeys. Therefore, on the inward journey to town he had to run alongside the animals, but he could, if he wished, ride home again. Doing this every day, twice, presumably on Sunday as well, was a good base on which to run 40 km.

Prior to Mexico, sea-level distance runners never had it so good. The men from the mountains have since been catching up, as the results of the post-Mexico Games indicate, in events on the track from 5000 m upwards and the way they have scooped up the cash in international events of these distances. Sea-level competitors have cottoned on too, and many now live or spend a lot of time training at altitude.

While running any distance over 400 m at the Mexico Olympic Games became a pain for the sea-level athletes, there were records in all the explosive events; the most emphatic advantage that the thin air provided came, of course, in the long jump where American Bob Beamon leapt to a world record, a performance in which he obliterated the previous mark by more than a metre. He was hailed worldwide for this phenomenal leap, including by his fellow Americans. Not all Olympic champions were feted and the event that at the time achieved the widest publicity was in absolute contrast – that of Beamon's US team mate Tommie Smith, winner and world record breaker in the 200 m. His time of 19.83 was another jaw dropping sensation in Mexico's thin air. It was eleven years before his world record was surpassed – on the same track. But there was greater newsworthiness to come. At the medal ceremony, Smith and his colleague, bronze medal winner John Carlos, stood on the podium with one hand in a black glove, their bare feet a symbolic reminder of America's treatment of its black population. The demonstration produced an angry response from the IOC whose Executive Board ordered the US Olympic Committee to take action; the athletes were promptly sent home. Smith and Carlos, both students at San José College, California, were members of the Olympic Project for Human Rights, an organisation demonstrating the way in which US athletes treated their black competitors. Smith and Carlos were sent home and suffered. It was not until 1984, in Los Angeles, that Smith came back to the Olympic family – as an official at the Los Angeles Games. This was, of course, not the first time that American Olympic competitors suffered from being coloured. Jim Thorpe, a Native American, was welcomed home a hero after his victories in the 1912 Olympic Games in Stockholm with a ticker-tape parade in New York, but the following year an investigative journalist discovered that Thorpe had, prior to the Games, been paid about $25 a week for playing in junior baseball. He was stripped of his medals and disqualified from athletics. It took the Native American community years of campaigning before his medals were officially restored in 1983. I saw Muhammad Ali win his gold in the light heavyweight division in the Rome Olympic Games of 1960. But he quickly became a disillusioned young man when, soon after arriving back home in Louisville, he and a friend were thrown out of a restaurant that did not serve blacks. Realising that being winner did not change his life, he stood on the Ohio River Bridge and threw his gold medal into the water below.

In spite of the fundamental principle 'No discrimination ... is allowed against any country or person on grounds of race, religion or politics', the IOC had a long and uncomfortable relationship with apartheid, but the sentence they effectively delivered on Smith and Carlos was extreme. However, earlier in 1968 they had withdrawn South Africa's invitation to take part, under pressure from the Mexicans who feared a boycott by many countries because of South Africa's apartheid policy. Two years later, the IOC kicked out South Africa from the Olympic Movement, which was to help, in a small way, the ending of that country's divisive policy.

That however is another story. In the history of the Olympic Games, there is still much to be unearthed in the chapter 'Mexico '68'. But this weekend, when some of the questions will be put and some answered, may come to be remembered as the time when the events of 2 October in the Square of the Three Cultures took on their full shape and meaning within Mexico's past.

2

Changing Impressions of Mexico for the 1968 Games

CLAIRE BREWSTER

Newcastle University, UK

In October 1963, Mexico City was chosen as the first venue in a developing nation to host the Olympic Games. Not surprisingly, perhaps, almost immediately afterwards a wide range of concerns were voiced about its ability to stage such a prestigious event. Avery Brundage, president of the IOC, gave an indication of the extent of the apprehension on 7 October 1968, just five days before the Olympic Games opened. Addressing an IOC meeting, he stated: 'When the Games were granted to Mexico City ... in Baden-Baden, there was a flood of criticism from all over the world.' He then listed the main concerns:

> Why were the Games awarded to a city at an elevation of 7349 feet above sea level?
> How can Mexico, with its limited experience, organise properly an event of the size and complexity of the Olympic Games?
> Latin America is the land of 'mañana': how can one expect that the facilities will be ready on time?
> What about the 'curse of Moctezuma'?
> Will there be adequate protection against the numerous Mexican bandits?
> What about sunburn from solar radiation at such an elevation?[1]

The obvious question, then, is why was Mexico City chosen? In this chapter I consider the motives of the leading figures who were instrumental in putting together Mexico City's proposal and argue that the decision to bid for the Games was a top-down, elite project in which members of the Mexican Organising Committee had a firm idea of the image of Mexico they wanted to present to the world. I also explore some of the issues behind the Olympic selection process that acted in Mexico's favour in 1963. Having gained the vote, I examine how the prospect of staging the 1968 Games was reported

---

1   Archive of the International Olympic Committee (hereafter IOC/HA): Box 246. Folder, IOC, 67th International Olympic Committee session, Mexico City, 7 October 1968.

within Mexico; I then assess the role that Mexico intended to adopt as the host country and how it sought to confound its critics.

The Men Behind the Bid

Mexico City's success in obtaining the 1968 Olympics was largely due to the efforts of three men who enjoyed considerable political influence and who had for some time been pushing for Mexico's increased profile in international sports. The first was Adolfo López Mateos, president of Mexico from 1958 to 1964 and a keen sportsman in his youth. The second, José de Jesús Clark Flores, had become a member of the IOC in 1952; he also led the Mexican Olympic Committee from 1952 to 1965.[2] The third, Marte R. Gómez, had been elected to the IOC in 1934. Both Clark Flores and Gómez were respected, influential members of the IOC. In particular, Avery Brundage saw Clark Flores as one of his more loyal supporters.

Ties with Brundage were extremely important in the early 1960s. Christopher Hill describes him as 'a man of ruthless authoritarian and reactionary opinions, [who] ran the [IOC]... almost as a private hobby from 1952 until his retirement at the end of the Munich Games' (Hill, 1996: 61). There can be no doubt that Brundage was favourably disposed towards Mexico as a venue for the Games. Back in 1950, as president of the United States Olympic Association (USOC), Brundage had suggested holding an IOC meeting in Mexico City 'to help boost sport and also let IOC members appreciate how developed Mexico City now is'.[3] Brundage had also been president of the Pan-American Games Association, which had its headquarters in Mexico City. This gave him the opportunity to see Mexico's sports administrators in action, and a strong working relationship flourished between them. In 1955, Mexico City had hosted the Pan-American Games and Brundage would have witnessed first-hand its ability to stage a major international sports competition. By the time of the Baden-Baden vote in 1963, Brundage had been president of the IOC for eleven years and it is clear that his opinions carried considerable weight with the IOC executive board. In turn, the opinions of the executive board played an important part in influencing committee members to favour one bid over another. This being the case, any bid with Brundage's unofficial backing stood a good chance of succeeding.

---

2   Roberto Casellas suggests that Clark Flores was the main instigator of the drive to win the Olympic Games for Mexico City (Casellas, 1992: 18–19).

3   IOC/HA: Notice no. 0099075 Correspondence NOC for Mexico and IOC 1932–1972. Letter dated 13 March 1950 from Brundage to Taher Pacha.

Indeed, a letter from Brundage to Clark Flores in August 1962 suggests that the IOC president had been central to Mexico City's decision to launch a bid for the 1968 Games:

> As you know, Mexico has already applied for the Olympic Games ... and I think [that] if the city authorities are interested, another invitation should be submitted at our meeting next year ... So far as I know, the situation is wide open with no one city having a priority. Even if you are not successful it ... will increase your chances of getting the Games in the future.[4]

After unsuccessfully bidding for the 1956 and 1960 Games, the discouraged Mexicans had not attempted to obtain the 1964 Games. Secure in Brundage's private backing, however, in 1963 they decided to put forward a third bid. After the vote, Brundage reflected: 'I understand that I have been criticised in certain quarters for leaning too far in the direction of Popocatepetl, but I don't think any harm was done' (cited in Zolov, 2004: 164).

The Baden-Baden Vote

During the first half of the twentieth century, the Western world dominated the IOC. In 1963, the only cities from the developing world to have made a bid for the Olympic Games were Buenos Aires and Mexico City.[5] Moreover, with the exceptions of Melbourne, Tokyo and Sapporo (all of which would eventually host the Games) these two Latin American cities were the only candidates outside of North America and Europe to make a bid during the modern Olympics era. This indicates the difficulties developing countries have experienced when competing with wealthier nations in making a credible bid. Indeed, it could be argued that little has changed: Mexico City remains the only city from the developing world to have hosted the Olympic Games.

Given the widespread concerns voiced immediately after Mexico City was awarded the Games, it is surprising that such had been the margin of the city's victory over its rivals in the first round of voting in Baden-Baden that a second was not needed. As Brundage reflected: 'I must say that there are

---

4 Avery Brundage Collection (hereafter ABC): Box 139. Folder COM 1961–1969. Letter from Brundage to Clark dated 2 August 1962.
5 Buenos Aires had shown much interest in hosting the Olympic Games throughout the twentieth century, but this was only the second time that the city had reached the election stage. For a discussion of the many efforts made by Buenos Aires to stage the Games, see, Torres (2007).

many who are ... stunned... at the success of Mexico' (cited in Zolov, 2004: 164). Mexico had certainly enjoyed Brundage's support, yet although he was undeniably influential within the IOC, were other factors at play in Mexico's success? In considering this issue the complex procedures behind the choice of venue for major international sporting events are revealed.

The overwhelming endorsement for Mexico City's bid makes remarkable reading. The result of the first round of votes was as follows:

Mexico City	30
Detroit	14
Lyon	12
Buenos Aires	2

To judge the strength of Mexico City's bid more accurately, it is necessary to consider the quality of the opposition. Counting slightly against Lyon, perhaps, was the fact that the Olympics had already been held twice before in France, albeit in Paris. As Hugh Dauncey's chapter in this volume explains, the result of the failed bid for the 1968 Games had a considerable impact in France. Similarly Detroit, which had tried unsuccessfully to gain the Games on several occasions, could have been penalised because the United States had already hosted the Games in St Louis and Los Angeles. Yet the wide margin of Mexico City's victory nonetheless suggests that more fundamental issues had gone against the competing bids.[6]

Details of the way in which each IOC member votes are unsurprisingly shrouded in secrecy, but contemporary international events might help to shed light on their deliberations. As IOC members gathered in Baden-Baden, the Cold War atmosphere was distinctly frosty, especially as it pertained to Latin America. The Cuban Revolution had triumphed on 1 January 1959; in April 1961, the US-backed Bay of Pigs invasion had occurred, while a few months later, the Berlin Crisis led to the construction of the Berlin Wall; in October 1962, the two superpowers came to loggerheads during the Cuban Missile Crisis. These tensions were reflected in the sporting world when US and French officials refused to issue visas to East German athletes and prevented them from competing in their countries. Within such an environment, IOC members from the Soviet bloc were extremely unlikely to support any bid from a NATO country. Certainly, if newspaper reports of Soviet reactions to the Baden-Baden vote are accurate, the visa issue was a major factor against Lyon; while, officially at least, Detroit was disregarded

---

6   ABC: Box 71, Minutes of Meeting of Exec Board 5 June 1963–Lausanne. Two other cities, West Berlin and Vienna, also submitted bids but they were received after the deadline and were not considered.

because the United States had already hosted the Games (*El Universal*, 1963). Yet this rationale does not explain why Grenoble, France, was chosen to host the admittedly less-prestigious 1968 Winter Games. Ideological tensions may well have been a significant factor, but other issues must also have been at play.

One aspect could have been Mexico's position as a developing nation and the stated aim of the IOC to encourage the expansion of sport in Third World countries. President Sukarno of Indonesia was among those who were far from convinced of the latter, and in 1962, in retaliation for what he viewed as the discriminatory pro-Western practices of the IOC, he announced a plan to host the world's first Games of the New Emerging Forces (GANEFO Games) in Jakarta.[7] With the financial and moral backing of China, the Games were promoted as an act of Third World solidarity against imperialist oppressors. The inaugural GANEFO Games was held in Jakarta from 10 to 22 November 1963. Teams from 48 out of a possible 68 countries attended, which made these Games a credible threat to the IOC monopoly of world athletics; in particular competitions concerning Third World countries (Guttmann, 1984: 227–229). Was it merely a coincidence that IOC delegates voted for Mexico City to host the 1968 Olympics just one month before the first GANEFO Games began? While there may not have been any overt link, the looming spectre of a Third World rival to the Olympics may have swayed some IOC members to avoid a possible split within the organisation by choosing a host from the developing world.

If the IOC was concerned about encouraging participation from developing and Third World countries, the Baden-Baden voters were left with just two possibilities: Buenos Aires and Mexico City. On sporting criteria alone, Buenos Aires should have been a strong contender. It had only narrowly lost the bid to host the 1956 Games to Melbourne and had hosted the first Pan-American Games in 1951. But its position was severely weakened by

---

7 Indonesia had been temporarily suspended from the IOC in 1962 after President Sukarno moved to prevent Israel and Taiwan from attending the IV Asiatic Games held in Jakarta in September 1962. This took place against a background of Arab diplomatic pressure against Israel, and the People's Republic of China's boycott of the 1956 Olympics due to the inclusion of a nationalist Chinese team from Taiwan. Although the Indonesian Olympic Committee explained that President Sukarno's intervention was a political decision and not the work of sports administrators, the IOC ruled that the committee had transgressed rules concerning free access to all nations. That the IOC was being unduly harsh on Indonesia is underlined by the fact that it made no sanctions against the US and French Olympic Committees for refusing visas to East German athletes and thus preventing them from competing in their countries during that same year.

the state of Argentine politics during the period leading up to the Baden-Baden vote. If ever confirmation of negative Latin American stereotypes was needed (such as political instability, high inflation and military dictatorships), in 1963 the IOC needed to look no further than Argentina. In the preceding year President Arturo Frondizi had been overthrown by the military and replaced by José María Guido. Factionalism within the armed forces led to heated conflict in September 1962 and in April 1963 the navy rebelled. Presidential elections were held in June that year, bringing the minority government of Arturo Illia to power. This latest Olympic bid from Buenos Aires representatives could not have been more badly timed; they left behind them a country in considerable political and economic turmoil. Furthermore, as far as the Eastern bloc was concerned, Argentina's staunch support of US foreign policy towards the Cuban Revolution would have made Buenos Aires an unpalatable choice as host for the forthcoming Games.

There were therefore several issues behind the overwhelming endorsement for Mexico City's bid. Selecting Mexico City was not necessarily a vote of confidence in the Mexican nation, nor in its people. Cold War politics and the need not to isolate non-aligned countries made Mexico City a more expedient option. I would argue that rather than being a willing choice, most IOC members felt compelled to make history by selecting Mexico City. And, if this assessment is correct, it helps to explain why there was so much scepticism about Mexico's ability to deliver immediately after its landslide victory.

Mexico '68: International Concerns

What were the origins of the widespread pessimism regarding Mexico City's ability to stage a successful Games and were such sentiments valid? Indeed, in many respects, such attitudes seem unfounded: the city had already hosted international sporting events; moreover, most cities that host the Olympic Games do so for the first time and thus have no direct prior experience. Yet as the first Latin American host, Mexico City was the target of multiple prejudices regarding the perceived lack of organisational skills in Hispanic countries. Despite the organisers' best efforts to allay fears and to provide reassurance, as Brundage's statement quoted at the beginning of this chapter reveals, a general attitude persisted that their plans were way behind schedule and that the lives of sportsmen and women would be at risk by competing in Mexico City. Mexico was not the only recipient of such anxieties: members of the IOC had voted for Mexico City as a venue and needed to defend their decision. Brundage consistently pressured the Mexican Organising Committee to develop a more efficient communications system that would send out regular 'good news' stories to counter the negative rumours.

Among the most commonly expressed concerns regarding Mexico City's hosting of the Games were the hazards of competing at high altitude and its dangerous levels of pollution.[8] In order to counter such views, the Organising Committee[9] offered scientific evidence to demonstrate that competing at 7400 feet would not cause damage to competitors and it invited international scientists to conduct on-site tests to confirm this. Several bodies, including the British Olympic Association, took up this offer and undertook physiological investigations in Mexico City (Killanin and Rodda, 1979: 160). Despite these measures, international newspaper coverage continued to use the altitude as an excuse to question the wisdom of holding the Games in Mexico City. In 1966, Brundage was still having to deal with questions from critical journalists, including one who 'wanted to transfer part of the Games to Montreal because of the great danger due to the altitude'.[10] Brundage clearly believed that the Organising Committee needed to do more to transmit positive messages to the international media. As a partial response, perhaps, the president of the Mexican Federation of Sports Medicine, Dr Gilberto Bolaños Cacho, was commissioned to undertake specific tests on pollution levels in Mexico City and to assess the possible danger to athletes. Among his findings was that: 'Smog (the fusion of fog and gases) does not exist in Mexico City. What does exist is atmospheric pollution.' In concluding that this atmospheric pollution would neither cause damage to health nor adversely affect the performances of athletes, Bolaños Cacho underlined that Mexico City's pollution levels were not as high as those of London, Tokyo and Los Angeles, all of which had successfully hosted the Games. Moreover, he explained, the setting of Olympic Villages in the south of Mexico City was beyond the pollution zone.[11]

Yet concerns over the altitude could not be so easily abated. There was no shortage of critics who raised fears for the safety of athletes; an attitude that would continue throughout the duration of the Games. Indeed, as John Rodda's chapter in this volume testifies, the experiences of Ron Clarke, Maurice Herriott and the Swiss oarsmen vindicate these misgivings. In defence of the IOC decision to use Mexico City, Brundage emphasised: 'the Olympic Games belong to the world – North and South, East and West, hot

---

8 IOC/HA: P. V. Sessions 1964–1966, CIO session in Baden-Baden 16–20 October 1963, pp. 5–6.
9 'The Organising Committee' refers to the Mexican Organising Committee that was established to plan and coordinate the 1968 Olympic Games. It was a separate committee from the permanent Mexican Olympic Committee.
10 IOC/HA: File 0100624, Correspondence 1966. Letter from Brundage dated 26 July 1966.
11 Archivo General de la Nación, Comité Organizador de los Juegos Olímpicos (hereafter AGN, COJO): Caja 128, 7 August 1967.

and cold, dry and humid, high and low'.[12] The British Olympic Association's scientific report on the effects of competing at altitude concluded that provided a period of acclimatisation took place there should be no danger to athletes. The IOC then circulated the following guidelines to all national Olympic committees:

> To achieve fairness as far as possible between competitors, no athletes, other than those who usually live or train at such heights shall specially do so at high altitudes for more than four weeks in the last three months before the opening of the Games. The IOC points out that to break this rule would be a gross breach of good sportsmanship and it is sure that no-one connected with the Olympic Movement would wish in any way to be guilty of taking an unfair advantage over the other competitors.[13]

Several countries nonetheless invested considerable money in giving their athletes a period of training well in excess of this prescribed limit. Yet even so, most of the endurance events at the 1968 Olympics were won by athletes from the poorer countries of Africa – all of whom lived at altitude.

The most vociferous criticism levelled at the Mexican Organising Committee, however, were charges of incompetence and disorganisation. In a vicious cycle of rumours, unease voiced by international sports administrators led to increased media speculation, which in turn put more pressure on the Organising Committee. Were these fears justified or merely being fuelled by the prevailing derogatory stereotypes? One of the major sources of negative foreign press coverage was the plan to construct rowing lanes in Xochimilco on the southern outskirts of Mexico City. This episode reveals the cultural differences between Mexico (and, perhaps, much of Latin America) and the Western world. The original scheme had been to remodel the existing canals to a standard suitable for Olympic competition. An IOC report from July 1966 confirms approval of this proposal.[14] This was in spite of the fact that the President of the International Rowing Federation, Thomas Keller, had proclaimed the water in the lanes to be dangerously contaminated (Casellas, 1992: 27). Yet in late 1966 the plan to use Xochimilco was abandoned in favour of a new purpose-built rowing venue in nearby Cuemanco.[15] Appalled by the lack of progress, Keller wrote to Brundage predicting that the installation

---

12   Frederick J. Ruegsegger Papers, 1928–1978. Folder 22: September to December 1967. See drafts of speech made by Brundage.
13   ABC: Box 71. Circular from Westerhoff to NOCs dated 27 May 1966.
14   ABC: Box 71. Letter from Brundage to IOC members, NOCs and Federations dated 4 July 1966.
15   IOC/HA: Brundage Microfilm Collection, reel 101, box 178. Letter from Ramírez Vázquez to Keller dated 22 December 1966. See also letter from Ramírez Vázquez to

could not possibly be built in time for a trial that had already been scheduled for October 1967. He went on to point out that construction work on the regatta course for the Munich Games in 1972 was already more advanced than Mexico's.[16] Although one might sympathise with Keller, his attitude reveals a widely held misconception regarding Mexico's preparations for the Games. In Munich the process of planning permission, appeal procedure, possible industrial disputes, and then the preparation of the site might well have meant that six years was a necessary construction period. In Mexico City, however, other customs and practices were at play. As Pedro Ramírez Vázquez, chairman of the Mexican Organising Committee, pointed out to Keller, comparisons with Munich were false because 'the construction industries of Mexico and Germany differ greatly'.[17] With wages in Mexico low, huge numbers of labourers were set to work on the construction project ensuring that the facilities at Cuemanco were ready for the trial regatta in October 1967.[18] As Ramírez Vázquez later underlined: 'German engineers said that if they had 2000 workers, they could build the rowing lanes at Cuemanco in two years. We did it in eight months, using local labourers' (Alvárez del Villar, 1968). The point to be taken from this example is not so much that the Mexicans did produce the goods on time, but that in the years leading up to the Games few beyond Mexico were willing to accept the reassurance of the Organising Committee.

Yet the question of Mexican competence went much deeper than that of leadership. In March 1967, an article in the *Auckland Star* quoted a US citizen living in Mexico who maintained that the Olympic Games were 'doomed and destined to be a dismal failure'. While the credentials of the 'special correspondent' and the veracity of these claims were immediately challenged, the article contributed towards the generally pessimistic assessment of the Mexicans' ability to deliver.[19] In a more sinister vein, an article by Siegfried Kogelfranz in *Der Spiegel* in early 1968 caused an outcry in Mexico (*El Nacional*, 1968; Zea, 1968). Drawing on themes reminiscent of Social Darwinism, Kogelfranz

---

Brundage dated 9 January 1967 in IOC/HA: Brundage Microfilm Collection, reel 102, box 178.

16 IOC/HA: P. V. Sessions 1964–1966, CIO session in Madrid 6–9 October 1965, 9; IOC/HA: file 0100624, correspondence COJO 1963–1967. Letter dated 7 December 1966 from Keller to Brundage complaining about lack of preparation for rowing lanes and suggesting a switch of country for the trial regatta to be held in October 1967.

17 IOC/HA: Brundage Microfilm Collection, reel 101, box 178. Letter from Ramírez Vázquez to Keller dated 22 December 1966.

18 IOC/HA: file 0100624, correspondence COJO 1963–1967. Letter dated 28 November 1966 from Brundage to Ramírez Vázquez; see also Casellas, 1992: 29.

19 AGN, COJO: Caja 403, 154. Letter dated 21 April 1967 from Charles Guptill discussing this article.

referred to the mixed race of Mexicans and questioned both their capacity to organise the Games and their ability to win medals. While Mexicans dismissed Kogelfranz as a racist, his comments struck a raw nerve. Thirty years earlier, Mexico's own sports administrators had pointed enviously towards the widespread enthusiasm for sports in Western Europe (including Germany) and concluded that only by embracing such an ethos would Mexicans develop the necessary characteristics to improve their racial stock and thus help the country to advance.[20] That such racial inadequacies were still being identified in 1968 would have done little to quell Mexican self-doubts.

Mexico '68: National Celebrations and Concerns

As the reaction to Kogelfranz's article indicates, scepticism about Mexico's ability to stage a successful Olympic Games was not confined to foreign observers. Winning the bid to host the Olympics was a massive coup, but it was also a tremendous challenge for Mexico to prove that it was as advanced as the elite believed or, perhaps more accurately, wanted others to believe their country to be. For them, Mexico was on the brink of obtaining First World status and was hence fully capable of competing with the Western world on equal terms. During Mexico's so-called 'economic miracle' years of the 1940–1960s, industrialisation had taken place largely funded by revenue from Mexican oil and huge US investment. But it created an unequal society: Mexico was, and remains, a polarised society of 'haves' and 'have-nots'. While the Mexican elite may have had confidence in themselves, from the time that Mexico City won the bid to host the Games, the Mexican elite displayed a distinct lack of trust and confidence in their countrymen.

On hearing the news of its successful bid, the Mexican nation as a whole was nonetheless euphoric. The national press reflected this joy. Journalist Alejandro Campos Bravo declared that staging the Olympics, 'confirms, yet again, the international prestige of our country'. He directly cited President López Mateos, who underlined: 'It is world recognition of the effort of the Mexican people, . . . in having elevated its international position not only on the sports field, but also through its economic and political stability.' To this a delighted Minister of Internal Affairs, Gustavo Díaz Ordaz added: 'Mexico is going to be a great amphitheatre for sportspeople throughout the world. . . . It will be a magnificent testing ground for Mexico. The campaign will be important for both tourism and the economy.' Campos Bravo's article also included supporting sentiments from other leading figures in the political and economic

---

20   AGN: Lázaro Cárdenas 532.2/1. Document dated September 1935. See details of the speech made by Senator David Ayala.

spheres, all of whom expressed their pride and underlined the economic benefits of staging the Games (Campos Bravo, 1963). Yet beneath such jubilation was the very real fear in some sectors of Mexican elite society that with the eyes of the world upon them, the behaviour of some of their compatriots would reveal Mexico's aspirations to First World status to be fraudulent.

Preparations for the Games were also adversely affected by the fact that there was a presidential election in Mexico within a year of securing the bid, an occurrence that traditionally instigates a change of personnel at most levels of bureaucracy. Reflecting on the events in an interview published in *Detroit News* in January 1965, the executive secretary of the USOC, Art Lentz, cast serious doubts over Mexico City's readiness to stage the Games. Referring to the election of the incumbent president, Gustavo Díaz Ordaz, Lentz warned: 'The problem this time, like it is so often when you try to count on Latin-American countries, is a shift in the government. Mexico has a new president and from what we can gather, the guy who was promoting the Olympics in Mexico, Gen. José Clark Flores, is now out in left field someplace and things are really messed up.'[21]

Initially, however, the change of presidency did not unduly affect the Organising Committee. In recognition of López Mateos's personal commitment to the project, President Díaz Ordaz appointed him as chairman of the Organising Committee in June 1965. Yet in November 1966, López Mateos was forced to step down because of ill-health and Díaz Ordaz appointed Pedro Ramírez Vázquez to replace him. In many respects, this was a logical appointment as Ramírez Vázquez, an architect of world renown, had held the position of vice-chairman of the committee with responsibility for overseeing construction projects. His expertise had already led to numerous prestigious new building projects around the world. As Lentz had predicted, and much to Brundage's chagrin, there was no place for Clark Flores in the new-look Organising Committee. In a telephone conversation with Marte Gómez, Brundage voiced his anxieties regarding the turn of events, privately describing the departure of Clark Flores as 'a catastrophe for Mexican sport'.[22] But in public, in the interests of presenting a calm facade perhaps, Brundage bowed to the inevitable and endorsed the change of leadership to the IOC as follows: 'Architect Ramírez Vázquez has an international reputation and is an excellent organiser. We can expect that the facilities will be adapted and ready

---

21 IOC/HA: Brundage Microfilm Collection, reel 102, box 178. Letter from Brundage to Flores Clark dated 20 January 1965 enclosing copy of Lentz's article.
22 IOC/HA: Brundage Microfilm Collection, reel 131, box 52, 1, Clarke Flores, Gen. José de C; details of telephone call from Brundage to Gómez quoted in letter dated 25 October 1966, from Gómez to Cristina Mújica, secretary and translator for Brundage.

in time'.[23] Having chosen Mexico City to host the Games, the IOC had to adhere to its decision and give its full backing to the Organising Committee.

The Public Image of Mexico '68

The Organising Committee, now led by Pedro Ramírez Vázquez, comprised a microcosm of elite society who paradoxically liaised with foreign experts in a project that was designed to portray the 'true' face of Mexico and its people; a face that had fundamentally elitist features. One of the underlying principles guiding the Organising Committee was that the Olympic Games should present a positive, lasting impression of Mexico. Yet precisely what image of Mexico should this be? One that emphasised its indigenous roots; its rich colonial heritage; or the confident, modern nation that Ramírez Vázquez and his colleagues wanted to promote?

The logo for the 1968 Games perhaps offers the best and certainly the most fitting symbol of the vision of Mexico that the Organising Committee intended to promote. Ramírez Vázquez decided that the emblem needed to represent a combination of past and present. He singled out the pre-Columbian artistic designs of the Huichol ethnic group for particular attention (Figs. 1 and 2). Its stark black and white patterns engage directly with the Op Art movement that was sweeping across the Western World during the late 1960s. The concentric lines were harnessed by the Organising Committee and became the internationally-recognised logo 'Mexico 68'. It is made clear in the *Official Report of the Organising Committee* that this symbol was also deliberately intended to be a visual portrayal of the country's successful integration of its ethnic past to the modern world (Ramírez Vázquez, 2001).[24] Yet as far as Ramírez Vázquez was concerned, there were strict limits to the extent to which Mexico should be seen to be drawing on its history. The remodelling or the construction of the various sports installations made no concessions whatsoever to the pre-Columbian or colonial past. In inviting tenders for the designs of the new stadia, he emphasised the need for innovation, creativity, and, conscious of possible criticism, economy.

From the outset, the underlying tenor of official messages was that the Games would add to the Mexican treasury rather than drain it. In his first annual presidential report after the Olympics, Díaz Ordaz emphasised that the overwhelming majority of the 2.2 billion Mexican pesos of government investment in the Games had been spent within Mexico and, hence, ploughed

---

23   AGN, COJO: Caja 401, 'Comité Olímpico Internacional', Letter from Brundage to all members of the IOC and National Olympic Committees dated 22 November 1966.
24   See also, Rivera Conde (1999).

Figure 1. Huichol Artistic Design
Source: AGN COJO (unnumbered box). *Official Report of the Organising Committee of the XIX Olympiad.*

back into the domestic economy for the benefit of all citizens (Díaz Ordaz, 1969). Evidence of economic constraint can be seen in the decision to use existing stadia wherever possible rather than embark on an unnecessary construction programme. For example, the National Stadium situated within Mexico City's university campus, built in the early 1950s, was chosen to hold the athletics competitions. The facilities were updated and for the first time

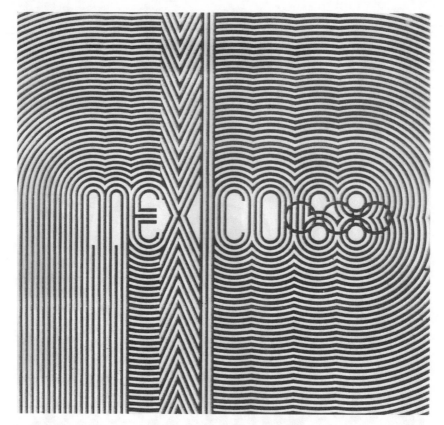

Figure 2.   Logo of the 1968 Olympic Games
Source: IOC/HA *Official Report of the Organising Committee of the XIX Olympiad.*

in Olympic history, a *Tartan* synthetic track was laid. Mexico City's Aztec stadium, designed by Ramírez Vázquez, in which the football matches would be played had already been under construction when Mexico City won the Olympic bid and was inaugurated in May 1966. The new buildings that had to be constructed were deliberately modern in design. For example, the sports palace in which the basketball competitions were held was constructed with an inventive use of steel and concrete (Fig. 3). The competitors' apartments in the Olympic Village were based on contemporary designs used in Europe (Fig. 4). In the interests of recovering some of the costs, after the Games these were converted into residential complexes and sold on the open market.

The project for Mexico '68, then, was well defined: to forge a lasting impression that Mexico was a modern progressive country that was comfortable with its past. In May 1968, the Organising Committee's public relations director, Roberto Casellas, underlined this imperative in an address to the British/Mexican Society:

Figure 3.   Palacio de Deportes (Sports Palace), Mexico City
Source: Author's photograph.

Figure 4.   Competitors' Apartments in the Olympic Village, Mexico City
Source: Author's photograph.

On this occasion [the Olympic Games] Mexico wishes to show its true image to the world. We want to do away with the picture of the Indian sleeping his eternal 'siesta', and with the dramatic representation of a country plagued by revolutions. While both of these images may have been representative of Mexico's past, they are no longer true in the present. We want to make known our progress in the fields of science and technology. We want to show the inspired works of our artists, the charm of our cities, the great natural beauty of our countryside and our achievements in modern architecture.[25]

This quote amply illustrates Mexico's preoccupation with correcting its international image and that the Organising Committee was on a mission to change forever the negative stereotype. Hence, as illustrated in Keith Brewster's chapter in this volume, the beautification of the capital city would include the removal from sight of any elements of society that were deemed to be undesirable, and the Mexican government sponsored public information campaigns to teach basic standards of civility and decency to Mexican citizens.

Mexico also intended to use the 1968 Olympics to underline its position within the Spanish-speaking world. As Ramírez Vázquez pointed out in 1967:

> Our responsibility in hosting the Olympic Games is one we share with Latin America and the entire Spanish-speaking world, because we know that the rest of the world will judge the Spanish-speaking world by how the Olympic Games proceed. But with the full cooperation that we are receiving from all Mexicans, we are confident that we will be able to meet our great responsibility.[26]

In June 1968, a series of 100 'radio chats' was broadcast throughout the continent with the explanation:

> Mexico's commitment is, in reality, a commitment made by all countries who speak Spanish, especially those in Latin America. That's why the committee wants as many Americans as possible to give a demonstration of what they can do through Mexico. Hence, the Olympic committee wants American radio stations to take a few minutes to inform their listeners about what's happening in Mexico and thus to show the organising efficiency and capacity of Latin Americans.[27]

It is clear both from Ramírez Vázquez's words and the opening address of the radio series that Mexico was using the Olympic Games to assume the role of leader of the Spanish-speaking world. Such an attitude had extra significance because at that time Mexico had no diplomatic relations with Franco's Spain and had offered asylum to many Spanish refugees, including the Republican

---

25 AGN, COJO: Caja 403, 154, tomo IV, 14 May 1968. Roberto Casellas to the British/Mexican Society.
26 AGN, COJO: Caja 300, 40, Co-presidencia. See text of speech by Ramírez Vázquez to the Society of Architects, 15 November 1967.
27 AGN, COJO: Caja 403, Charlas Radiofónicas, Nos 1–104. 'American' in this sense refers to all countries of the American continent.

government (Ramírez Vázquez, 2001).[28] A dominant theme in the radio series was the fraternity among Latin American countries, a brotherhood that the Mexican Ministry of Sport reinforced by offering training facilities and financial support to help less wealthy Central American countries prepare and compete in the Games.[29] In keeping with its promotion of the Spanish language, after the Games a Mexican delegation proposed (without success) that Spanish should be adopted as the third official IOC language.

Another way in which the Mexican Organising Committee carved out an international identity for itself was by using the Olympic Games to underline Mexico's foreign policy of neutrality and non-intervention. During a period in which the Cold War conflict was affecting all corners of the globe, the Organising Committee chose reconciliation as the theme for the Games. The white dove of peace appeared on all official publications. These were to be the 'Peaceful Games' and the Mexican national congress passed a motion that 1968 would be designated the 'Year of Peace'.[30] As the chapters by John Rodda, Chris Harris, Ryan Long and Hazel Marsh in this book reveal, the students of Mexico City would experience the bitter irony of this slogan (see also Hellman, 1983 and C. Brewster, 2005: 35-68).

There are several possible motives for Mexico wanting to make the most of its non-aligned, international position. At face value, it made sense to emphasise the Olympic Charter's apolitical ethos within a context of global conflict. Beyond this symbolic message, however, was the very practical aspect that the Organising Committee wished to avoid any chance of the Mexico City Games being marred by the Cold War. The emphasis on peaceful coexistence also spoke directly to the nations of the Non-aligned Movement, the majority of which were from developing and Third World countries. This was particularly important because following the wave of de-colonisation, the 1968 Games were the first to which many of the newly formed African nations were invited. Ironically, this aspect of international politics forced the Mexicans to abandon their role as welcoming hosts when the inclusion of South Africa threatened to instigate a widespread boycott by other African nations. Faced with this situation, President Díaz Ordaz added considerable

---

28 The cooperation of the Spanish Republican government in exile proved to be crucial in averting an awkward issue concerning Spain's participation in the Games and the possible hostile reception by the Mexican public. In the event a team from Spain did attend the Games and suffered no adverse consequences. See correspondence betweeen the Spanish delegation, the IOC and Ramírez Vázquez in late 1967: AGN, COJO: Caja 403, 152, tomo III, Control of Installations.

29 AGN, COJO: Caja 142, 39–200. See details of interview between Ramírez Vázquez and Julio A. Millan of *La Prensa Gráfica* of El Salvador.

30 Carlos Armando, 'A la Comisión de Relaciones Exteriores', *Diario de los Debates*, año I tomo, 27 December, 6.

weight to the Mexican Organising Committee's demand that the invitation to South Africa be withdrawn.

Given its lack of experience on the world stage, it is perhaps surprising that Mexico chose to make such a determined stand. It was certainly a high-risk strategy by Mexico, as almost all Western countries were adamant that the Olympic Charter demanded South Africa's right to participate. As Douglas Booth points out, during the 1960s, South Africa relied on its old ties with white-dominated international sports bodies to support its stance regarding racial segregation (Booth, 2003: 477–493). The IOC was no exception and displayed considerable support for South Africa. After a long debate, it was eventually agreed that the IOC would withdraw South Africa's invitation because of 'the international climate'.[31] The wording deliberately avoided any direct reference to apartheid. South Africa's exclusion from the 1968 Games averted a major catastrophe for the Mexican organisers, and probably for the Olympic Movement itself.[32]

Mexico's unwavering stance and its intense lobbying in support of South Africa's exclusion lent much credence to its image as a defender of the dignity of Third World countries. Yet was this sufficient reward for the Mexicans to have gambled so much by supporting the nascent African nations? One reason may well have been a genuine sympathy with their situation. The Mexican government portrayed its own revolution (1910–1917) as a movement through which the country had banished all forms of colonial racism; hence it would not want to be seen to condone such attitudes elsewhere. More pragmatically, if up to 32 African nations had boycotted their first Olympic Games, it would have been a considerable blow to Mexico City's reputation as a host (*Excélsior*, 27 February, 1968b, *El Nacional*, 29 February, 1968a).[33]

A more speculative reason for Mexico's defiant attitude relates to the thoughts of Octavio Paz, that Mexicans believed themselves to be inferior to other races. In his assessment of *pachuquismo* (Mexicans who had settled in the United States), Paz noted that although 'they have lived in the [United States] for many years, wearing the same clothes, speaking the same language as the other inhabitants, ... they feel ashamed of their origins. ... They act like persons who are wearing disguises, who are afraid of a stranger's look

---

31 For an overview of the debate, see: Quick (1990).
32 IOC/HA: Commission Executive 1968. See minutes of Executive Board meeting dated 20–21 April 1968. It is not possible to ascertain how influential Brundage's Mexican secretary, Cristina Mújica, was in making him take a more conciliatory posture regarding the Organising Committee's pleas. Casellas suggests that her influence may have been crucial (Casellas, 1992: 144).
33 See reaction to the vote on 26 February 1968, by the African Supreme Sports Council to boycott the Games.

because it could strip them and leave them stark naked' (Paz, 1961: 5). While Paz may not have included himself among such people, his findings help to explain the paradox facing Mexican society after being awarded the Olympic Games. Despite the genuine wish by the organisers to host a major world sporting event, the fear that some of their compatriots would be exposed as somehow lacking when under the critical glare of close foreign scrutiny was never far from the surface. The need to prove themselves on the international arena weighed heavily on the Mexican elite. Mexicans had already blamed the failure of their 1956 Games bid on an 'English-speaking' voting bloc. In addition, as criticisms of Mexico City's preparations increased in the Western media, US officials had suggested that one of their cities would be ready to take over the hosting of the Games if it proved to be 'too much' for the Mexicans. The United States had joined other English-speaking delegates to demand South Africa's inclusion in the 1968 Games. As the nations of the IOC marshalled their forces on either side of the apartheid issue, Mexican pride perhaps took over and the Organising Committee determined that it would not allow Mexico's Games to be hijacked by international heavy-weights (Ramírez Vázquez, 2001).[34] If this supposition is correct, Mexico's hosting of the 1968 Games can be seen to have a sub-plot: to defend the dignity of nations from the developing and Third World and by doing so to attempt to uphold Mexico's credibility.

This same philosophy of championing nations from the developing world can be seen in Mexico's decision to resurrect the Cultural Olympics: a year-long programme of events that were designed to emphasise the rich cultural heritage that each country could offer through its ancient and contemporary folklore. It is fair to acknowledge that the Cultural Olympiad did indeed provide a celebration of the world's diverse traditions of art, music and dance, and its technological and scientific achievements. The full extent of the cultural programme fills a complete volume of the *Official Report of the Organising Committee of the XIX Olympiad* (see Mexican Organising Committee, 1969: Vol. IV). In fact, Mexico's plans soon became so extensive that some IOC members began to doubt the wisdom of re-introducing this element to the Games. Ignoring the non-competitive dimension that the Mexicans so emphatically stressed, the president of the British Olympic Association, Alexander Duncan, expressed fears that the programme would turn into a mini-Olympics in which each country tried to outshine the rest.[35]

---

34   In this important matter, Latin American countries showed their fraternity by rallying to Mexico's position.
35   IOC/HA, file 0100677, Correspondence 1965–1971. Letters between Duncan and Johann Westerhoff, Secretary General of the IOC dated 15 July 1968 and 19 July 1968.

Even Brundage, who had initially been a keen supporter of the cultural events, admitted, 'Mexico is going a little too far'.[36]

The Cultural Olympics was clearly an extensive undertaking, but Ramírez Vázquez defended its resurrection precisely because so many poorer nations would be attending the Mexico Games. Unlikely to win many medals because of their inferior training facilities, he maintained that each and every competing country, no matter how impoverished, would be able to make a valuable contribution through its unique, rich cultural heritage (Ramírez Vázquez, 2001). These worthy aims should not be dismissed and, indeed, it is clear that such aspects were an integral part of Mexico's overall plan to highlight the achievements of the smaller nations of the world. Yet the emphasis on culture may also have been a defence mechanism that reflected Mexico's own position in the sporting world. One of the major domestic criticisms levelled at Mexico after it had won the bid to stage the Games was that its national team would be ridiculed when competing against the sporting world's elite. So worried were Mexican sports administrators that they made excuses for the poor showing expected of their athletes *before* the Games.[37] This was a realistic prediction; after all, Mexicans had hardly distinguished themselves at previous Olympic meetings. So weak had been their performance at the 1948 London Olympics that one Mexican politician had offered the explanation, 'Mexicans are not athletes, they're poets' (Velasco Polo, 1978). Similarly, after the 1964 Tokyo Games, officials rationalised Mexico's meagre performance by suggesting that the republic was 'a nation of artists' rather than sportsmen and women (*Siempre*, 1964). Hence, the realisation that Mexicans might not win many medals but could 'do culture well' was, in itself, a valid reason for resurrecting the Cultural Olympics. Moreover, it would be of great financial benefit to the tourist trade as the Cultural Olympics took place throughout 1968, rather than the two weeks of sporting competitions.

---

36 IOC/HA, file 0100624, Correspondence COJO 1963–1967. Letter from Brundage to Lord David Killanin dated 17 July 1967. This largely accounts for the scaling-down of overseas contributions to the Munich Cultural Programme and its concentration upon diverse aspects of German culture.

37 *El Universal*, 20 March 1965 reports on the findings of the trainer Bud Winter, who blamed an inadequate diet and a consequent weak physical condition for Mexico's expected poor performance at the 68 Games. AGN, COJO: Caja 401, 18 December 1967. A report given by Dr Josué Saenz, the president of the Mexican Olympic Committee, underlined that Mexicans were 'not a strong race'.

Mexico '68 - The Test

When asked what he felt had been the main failures of the 1968 Olympic Games, Ramírez Vázquez highlighted just two areas: inadequacies in transport had led to delays in getting the public away from events; and technical difficulties had prevented results from being transmitted to the foreign press as quickly as he would have liked (Suárez, 1968). After the Closing Ceremony, Brundage, in keeping with Olympic tradition, declared the Mexico City Games to have been the 'best ever'; and it should be said that there were few dissenters. There were neither any further student protests, nor brutal acts of repression by government forces for the duration of the Games. Moreover, contrary to all expectations Mexico won nine medals (three gold, three silver and three bronze) and was by far the most successful Latin American country at the XIX Olympiad.

In contrast to the dire predictions of Mexico's inability to stage a successful Games criticism of Mexico was far more muted afterwards. Peter Wilson of the *Daily Mirror* drew attention to the lack of organisation and reflected that, 'Mexico, despite colour and exuberance and a determination to prove that it had truly come of age, was not properly geared up to staging this modern unwieldy extravaganza of sport'.[38] An article in *The Honolulu Star* on 22 October 1968 noted that things were going badly in Mexico, and predicted that the student riots would resume once the Games had finished. It stressed that there were many reasons for Mexico's failure; primarily that it could not afford the expense. It pointed out that foreign visitors were unimpressed by what they had seen and that the anticipated boost in tourist trade would not happen. It underlined the economic disparity between the high-tech facilities for the athletes, and the dirt tracks and decrepit transport that most Mexicans had to endure.[39]

Not all foreign reporters were so disparaging. One Spanish publication refuted each of the previous criticisms of Mexico in turn. First, it pointed out that concerning the one aspect that was beyond the Mexicans' control – the high altitude – they had done all they could to ease the problem by laying on successive competitions in the years leading up the Games to enable athletes and trainers to analyse the effects of the thin air. Regarding the threatened African boycott, the article praised the Organising Committee's swift actions in pressuring the IOC to resolve the issue. In respect to the

---

38   The comments of both reporters were highlighted by an unidentified US newspaper. IOC/HA: Brundage Microfilm Collection, reel 102, box 177: US Press Clippings.

39   AGN, COJO: Caja 403, 154, tomo V, Relaciones Públicas – copy of article dated 22 October 1968.

African-American podium protest, the article stated that although the general feeling was that it had not been the right thing to do, the Mexican press had refrained from criticising the athletes and had treated the affair with understanding and respect. Most significantly, the article argued that despite the many fears voiced concerning Mexico's ability to stage the event, the organisation had been excellent and that not one sporting event had been delayed because of any lapse in administration.[40] J. L. Manning of the *Daily Mail* was equally encouraging, concluding 'the Games overcame unprecedented problems of size, numbers, organisation and competition. They defeated continuous political onslaught and withstood cruel defamation. That must be considered a remarkable success for Mexico and the movement'.[41]

Conclusion: A Transformation of Mexico's International Image?

In considering the choice of venue for the 1968 Games, a good case can be made for arguing that the decision of IOC members in Baden-Baden to endorse Mexico City was both logical and supportive of a new climate of inclusion within the Olympic Movement. Questions may have been raised about the wisdom of staging the Games in a developing country, but if this step were not taken then the Olympics would be destined to remain in the First World in perpetuity. As one of Latin America's strongest and most stable countries, Mexico was a fitting destination for facilitating the IOC's step into the unknown. Yet, as has been illustrated, there is sufficient circumstantial evidence to propose that the success of Mexico City's bid was more to do with global and regional politics than with Third World solidarity or Mexico's deliverance from it. The level of international scepticism aimed at Mexico immediately after the selection process implies that the developed world was unconvinced by Mexico's professed maturity.

Paradoxically, given the confident public announcements of the Organising Committee and the Mexican government, many members of the Mexican elite were still unsure where their nation really stood on the international stage. The politicians, diplomats and international sporting officials behind the bid frequently travelled abroad and understood the customs of the international circuit. Yet they knew less about the culture and people of their own country. Few of them had much experience of the lives of 'ordinary' Mexicans, as

---

40 IOC/HA: Articles de Presse 1968–1968, Notice no. 0105829. 'Una sorpresa para muchos: la perfecta organización'.

41 The comments were highlighted by an unidentified US newspaper. IOC/HA: Brundage Microfilm Collection, reel 102, box 177: US Press Clippings.

their paths barely crossed: they lived in exclusive neighbourhoods, had been educated in private schools and many had never travelled on public transport. Although such people might shrug off international stereotypes of Mexicans, these images could not be fully dismissed from their own consciousness. Within their protestation that Mexico had achieved modernity and prosperity and hence should be respected internationally, lay a deeper unease concerning the true character of the Mexican people. As Keith Brewster's chapter in this volume shows, the degree of international scepticism concerning Mexico City's suitability to host the Olympics would have direct domestic consequences.

The Mexican Organising Committee wanted to use the 1968 Games to showcase its cultural, political and economic progress; to stand before the world as a nation very much in development; to promote Mexico as a great location to visit; a viable place in which to invest; a model of Latin American achievement and stability; a champion of Third World, non-aligned countries; the representative of the Spanish-speaking world; and, above all, a peaceful country that was at ease with itself. That the members of the Mexican Organising Committee were able to confound all the dire predictions made from Baden-Baden onwards was a credit to their organisational abilities, the support they received from political and sports authorities, and the goodwill of their own countrymen. In an effort to make sure that Mexico's international image not only remained untarnished but actually improved as a result of hosting the Games, the Organising Committee deployed everything at its disposal to stage-manage all aspects. Mexico had made considerable advances in the twentieth century. Certain sectors of society could, with some truthfulness, claim to have achieved First World status. Provided one did not dig too deeply, Mexico could claim to be a country that enjoyed good race relations; especially when compared to its Northern neighbour. Mexico City undoubtedly put on a good show for the duration of the Olympic Games. International impressions of Mexico did change, albeit only while the Olympic flame was burning in the national stadium. But as John Rodda has testified, the brutal suppression of the Student Movement revealed that the portrayal of Mexico as a peaceful country at ease with itself was nothing more than a thin veneer.

3

Teaching Mexicans How to Behave: Public Education on the Eve of the Olympics

KEITH BREWSTER

Newcastle University, UK

The imperative for Mexicans to put on a good show was at the heart of all policy decisions regarding Mexico City's preparations for the 1968 Olympics. Yet as is noted in Claire Brewster's chapter, the degree of international surprise following Mexico's success at Baden-Baden was swiftly matched by international scepticism over the city's ability to stage a successful Games. At its most optimistic, the Mexican response to such misgivings was a bullish confirmation that its efficient hosting of the Games would leave no doubt that Mexico was well on the way to accomplishing its transition to a First World, modern country. This chapter explores the notion that, simultaneously, a more pessimistic sentiment took hold that provoked Mexico's elite to question whether the image of modernity that they had created could actually withstand close scrutiny. If it could not, the imperative would be to shore it up sufficiently to prevail during the two weeks of international competition and, thereby, to save Mexico's face on the international stage.

In analysing the ways in which Mexico sought to sustain its positive image, it is vital to understand the dynamics within Mexican society. This chapter suggests that despite decades of social reforms, the Mexican elite had fundamental doubts about the capacity of their 'socially inferior' compatriots to uphold an image of modernity and sophistication. By sustaining this argument, I revisit a recent historiography of post-revolutionary Mexico that generally accepts that an ongoing process of negotiation and compromise between the state and nation over the fundamental issues of nationhood and national inclusion produced a relatively stable and unified Mexican society. While I do not call into question the existence of such processes nor query the consequences for society that are ascribed to them, I argue that the current emphasis on bottom-up perspectives has had the effect of deflecting attention from the concerns of the very group that initiated the process of state – nation dialogue; namely the Mexican elite.

What I intend to offer in this chapter, therefore, is a close analysis of the elite project to stage a successful Olympic Games in order to obtain a better impression of how members of the elite viewed their compatriots in 1968. After more than 40 years of socio-cultural reforms that had been designed to incorporate all Mexicans beneath the civilising, unifying umbrella of patriotism, to what extent did elite actions in 1968 portray a measure of confidence in the success of these projects? Obtaining an insight into the psyche of the Mexican elite is notoriously difficult because patriotism demanded that all official rhetoric needed to underline the success of the Revolution in creating a unified people. Certainly all official publications and utterances coming from the Mexican president, politicians and the Olympic Organising Committee presented a united front in projecting Mexican confidence in the commitment it had made to the world. It is for this reason that I supplement more 'traditional' methodological approaches with one that rarely troubles the historian, namely public broadcasting. Specifically, I analyse a series of television propaganda films sponsored by the Organising Committee featuring the famous Mexican comedy figure, Cantinflas. In doing so I consider them from a historian's perspective rather than that of a cultural critic. This is partly because of my own training, but mainly because any analysis devoid of historical context risks presenting a partial, and thus potentially false, interpretation. In following a cultural history approach, my focus is less on 'those from below' and more on what the actions of their 'superiors' shows us about the relationship between different social groups.

It is this underlying objective that helps to link the present focus on 1960s Mexico to the developing social dynamics of other countries of Latin America. The wide disparity of wealth that contributed to the Mexican elite's sense of isolation from its own people was (and still is) a common phenomenon in many countries of Latin America. As Latin America's disparagers would swiftly rush to point out, such isolation did not result in any lack of control: repression, electoral fraud, corruption, and patronage were tools commonly deployed to steer a country in the desired direction. The use of culture, in this case the humour of Cantinflas, offered an alternative, more subtle, option. While recent historiographical trends suggest that the potential of cultural politics is now firmly in our sights, the analysis that follows aims to expose how rich, and sometimes quirky, this potential can be.

An 'Age-old Humility'

As Claire Brewster points out in this volume, Octavio Paz was the Mexican who most famously commented on Mexico's sense of inferiority in its relations with the rest of the world. For the purposes of the present chapter, it is fruitful to dwell on his belief that Mexico's peculiar history has meant that it lacks confidence in its own roots. He suggests that being dominated by the descendents of European colonisers, Mexicans have found it hard to embrace origin narratives that are rooted in pre-Columbian history. Simultaneously, the nationalistic political rhetoric of post-revolutionary Mexico has made it equally difficult to embrace its Spanish colonial ties. As such, Mexicans have engaged in a constant search for a definition of what it means to be Mexican, borrowing foreign cultural values and ideas in an attempt to sustain an element of civilisation that moves beyond the country's indigenous roots. This lack of self-identity, Paz continues, has fostered an innate sense of subordination in Mexico's dealing with the rest of the world, especially the developed nations of Western Europe and North America.

It should be noted that Paz's notion of inferiority was written over a decade before preparations for the Mexico Olympics began and there is scope to suggest that this pessimistic reflection on Mexico rapidly became out of date. In his own study of Mexico City's preparations for the Olympic Games, for instance, Ariel Rodríguez Kuri uses a range of official publications to argue that Mexico went into the Games as a nation that was comfortable with its place within the international community and confident in its ability to sustain such an image during the two-week celebration of sporting prowess (Rodríguez Kuri, 1998: 108–129). Certainly, two decades of unprecedented economic growth had done much to support the view that Mexico was indeed emerging from the shadows of underdevelopment and was taking its first tentative steps towards first world status. In his study of Cantinflas, Jeffrey Pilcher's portrayal of Mexico and its people in the 1960s falls largely into line with that of Rodríguez Kuri. Moreover, Pilcher questions the findings of commentators such as Samuel Ramos who, in 1967, reiterated Paz's belief that Mexico was still suffering under the weight of an inferiority complex in the area of international relations (Pilcher, 2001: 39–41).

Yet the evidence to sustain this new, confident image of Mexico is far from conclusive. As Rodríguez Kuri admits, the limitations of any analysis that uses official rhetoric for its evidence is that it is intrinsically laced with patriotic boosterism. Pilcher refers to, but does not cite, 'numerous' authoritative voices that dismiss the notion of a Mexican inferiority complex (Pilcher, 2001: 39–41). Newspaper editorials at the time Ramos was making his observations, however, reveal that such confidence was not as embedded as Pilcher suggests. In May 1967, for example, the editor of the daily newspaper *El Nacional* published a piece entitled 'A Mature People' in which he referred to the humble posture that Mexicans had previously adopted in their dealings with the rest of the world. In suggesting that Mexicans were now coming of age the article concluded by affirming:

The Olympiad will confirm to us that we are now young adults; that it is now time to abandon our short-trousers mentality. This is not only because the world is not as terrible as we thought, but also because we have matured, and that it is good to make ourselves aware of this and the responsibilities that it brings. (*El Nacional*, 1967)

An article in *Excélsior* one year later followed a similar line by pointing out that for too long, both foreigners and Mexicans had been content to designate Mexico as under-developed:

Worse still, our patience, our terrible age-old humility, has produced an innate lack of confidence which has meant that we automatically question our ability to comply with the responsibilities [that staging the Games] confers upon us (Alvárez del Villar, 1968).

It is highly significant that such rallying cries of reassurance were issued at that time. A superficial reading would appear to corroborate Pilcher's depiction. Yet if Mexicans were so confident of their own abilities, why was it necessary to issue such reassurances? By July 1968 most of the major construction projects had been completed and there was little danger that Mexico City would not be ready to host the Games. Yet this retrospective sigh of relief gives a sense of the strains that had enveloped the nation in the preceding years: strains that had been borne through an innate lack of confidence. Even as Mexico prepared for the football World Cup in 1970, President Gustavo Díaz Ordaz chose to reflect on how the Olympics had confirmed Mexico's serene self-assurance:

We have moved away from the timid provincialism that fostered an inferiority complex; but we have not moved to the vain glory shown by those who feel themselves to be superior to others. Mexico displays its enthusiasm for sport in a discreet, but resolute manner (*El Nacional*, 1970).

Given that such comments were made well after the relatively successful Olympic Games, the fact that Díaz Ordaz nonetheless felt it necessary to refer to a past in which 'timid provincialism' had created a sense of 'national inferiority' underlines how deeply pervasive this sentiment must have been.

I believe that this reveals a more complex outlook than has previously been suggested. I have no doubt that the social and political elite were totally confident in their ability to hold their own in the developed world. There is certainly little evidence that they viewed themselves to be inferior. However, it is far less clear-cut that the elite shared the same degree of confidence in their compatriots. Decades of state paternalism that had, at its heart, an assumption that Mexicans needed to be directed and guided meant that on the eve of hosting the world's premiere sporting event in Mexico, many members of the elite were concerned that if left to their own devices, their compatriots would fall short of the standard expected of 'civilised' behaviour. Ensuring the readiness of installations for major sports events was a demanding task, but one towards which the elite's organisational skills could be channelled. Ensuring the readiness of the Mexican people for such events, however, was an entirely different proposition because much of the success of this project was out of the hands of the elite: it demanded the cooperation of the rest of society. There is convincing evidence to suggest that not only did such a scenario raise considerable alarm among the elite, but that it governed the way in which the Organising Committee prepared their country and countrymen for the arrival of visitors.

It should be acknowledged straight away that any host of the Olympic Games engages in an enormous amount of window dressing. In this respect, Mexico City was no exception. As Ron Butler, a correspondent for the *Seattle Post Intelligencer*, reflected:

> Apart from the Olympic sites, Mexico City itself, always impressive, has been remarkably spiffed up and polished in preparation for the Games. New fountains and plazas have been built, baroque palaces and churches have been restored. French and American hippies have been tossed out of the country as public nuisances. (Butler, 1968)

Yet if one were to take the *Official Report of the Organising Committee* at face value, then it was not only the physical landscape that had changed:

> In the not too distant past, a great variety of peddlers, hawkers, and pitchmen – never difficult to spot because of the large crowds they attracted – made their living in Mexico City's many plazas and parks. These elusive itinerants are now only found at small town fairs and circuses, and today people fill the plazas and parks in search of public attractions of a different nature: plays sponsored by the National Institute of Fine Arts, poetry readings, concerts, ballets, recitals, painting exhibitions, and lectures – things that enrich the cultural life of Mexican people (Mexican Organising Committee, 1969: Vol. I, 189).

The important question here is that if these changes actually had taken place, was it through popular demand or an imposition from above? If it was the latter, it suggests that there was still a niggling doubt that Mexicans could measure up to the cultural sophistication the elite wished to bestow upon them. As John Rodda's contribution to this volume makes clear, the 'great variety of peddlers, hawkers and pitchmen' had not disappeared because of public apathy; rather it was as a result of official attempts to rid the cityscape of elements that did not 'enrich the cultural life of Mexican people'. My argument for insisting that an inferiority complex did play into Mexico's preparation for the Games relies on more than evidence gleaned from national newspaper editorials. It stems from the actions of the elite as seen through the Organising Committee; more specifically, the actions that reached above and beyond those expected of any host city or nation when staging an international sporting event of such prestige.

Why might the Mexican elite have felt particularly nervous about the behaviour of their compatriots in 1968? There are several reasons, of which the most obvious was the fact that the Olympic Games would attract the largest influx of foreigners into Mexico City in the republic's history. Equally important, however, was that the state's prerogative to guide Mexican thoughts and actions had, for over a decade, been challenged by a rebellious youth. While the more detailed consequences of this challenge in 1968 will be explored in later chapters, its relevance at present is that it placed another pressure upon those who were concerned about the type of image that Mexico would project during the Games. Third, the portrayal of Mexico City as a sophisticated modern metropolis had been undermined by recent mass migration from the countryside. As observed by Oscar Lewis, with such migration came an influx of rustic customs and practices, practices that contradicted elite portrayals of the city and its people (Lewis, 1964). My objective in this chapter, therefore, is to focus less on attempts to improve the physical landscape and more on the nature of a public education campaign that was designed to improve the human landscape.

Making Mexico Fit for Foreign Consumption

A year before the Games began, the Mexico City government passed by-laws prohibiting street selling in certain parts of the city, predominantly tourist and sports locations. The mollifying aspect of this policy was that the authorities aimed to find vacant stalls in existing market places for those who were temporarily displaced by such measures.[1] John Rodda's observation that students were still protesting against the removal of such individuals only days before the Olympic Games began suggests that official attempts to compensate those affected had been either inadequate or incomplete. For those Mexicans who simply could not be taken out of sight, another approach was adopted. Back in 1965, a report from the Confederación Deportiva

---

1 Archivo histórico del Distrito Federal (hereafter AHDF): Memoria del depto. del DF (1967–1968); AHDF: Gaceta Oficial del Depto del DF. 20 October 1967.

Mexicana (Mexican Sports Confederation) proposed that the Organising Committee should use all modern means of communication at its disposal to accomplish the 'difficult and arduous task' of educating Mexicans to become good hosts (Confederación Deportiva Mexicana, 1965: 203). This task would call for the combined efforts of national and local governments, sports bodies and the Mexican Organising Committee, which deemed it necessary to launch a huge media campaign designed 'to establish a sense of national responsibility' and 'to awaken the natural hospitality of Mexicans towards foreign athletes and visitors' (Estrada Nuñez, 1965).

Soon afterwards, newspaper articles reflected on stereotypical weaknesses among Mexicans. In June 1966, the daily newspaper *El Día* expressed hope that 'in the two years we have left before the Olympics, there will be an intense campaign to instil within the public a sense of punctuality, so that by the time the Games begin it will have become a habit' (*El Día*, 1966). At around the same time, an editorial in *El Universal* suggested that although the world might falsely believe that all Mexicans 'leave things until tomorrow', it would be equally wrong to deny the fact that there is 'much talk and little action among us. Whether it be in construction projects, training our athletes, or providing sufficient hotel spaces, we need to make progress now – it is a question of honour for all Mexicans to get this right' (*El Universal*, 1966).

A sense of the scale of this programme can be gleaned from local government documents. In the final year of preparations alone, the Mexico City authorities spent 24 million pesos renovating squares within the city. 200,000 leaflets were distributed offering advice on various aspects of being good hosts, while 700 radio broadcasts and 144 television broadcasts pushed the message home.[2] Similar efforts were being conducted by national and state government authorities. If, as has been suggested, Mexicans were completely confident of their own abilities, it seems strange that so much effort and money should have been invested in modifying their behaviour in preparation for the influx of foreigners. In order to understand more about this apparent contradiction, I will now focus on one particular aspect of the Organising Committee's own campaign. It helps to bear in mind that this took place within the context of an unprecedented challenge to decades of state-driven paternalism: a challenge provoked by growing concerns that new influences (both from overseas and migration from the Mexican countryside) were changing the social dynamics within Mexico City in ways that the authorities could not determine.

What follows is an analysis of four two-minute television broadcasts that were sponsored by the Mexican Organising Committee. By scrutinising the

---

2   AHDF: Memoria del depto. del DF (1967–1968).

choice of situations depicted and the demeanour of the characters involved, these clips reveal much about persistent tensions within Mexican society. Before doing so, it may be useful to offer a few words about the main character. Cantinflas was one of most enduring, popular characters played by the actor Mario Moreno. By the 1960s, a generation of Mexican cinema-goers had grown up with comical exploits of Cantinflas. Studies on Cantinflas suggest a common theme; one in which the *pelado* (a bumbling innocent) stumbles his way through life, but with quick wit and an even quicker tongue he nonetheless manages to point out the absurdity and pomposity of officialdom. Cantinflas is simultaneously subversive and compliant, as he is seen to be the critical voice of the people while never channelling such criticism in a way that might threaten the system. Yet John Mratz suggest that by the 1960s an important change had taken place in this public image. Cantinflas (reflecting the politics of Moreno himself) had become more of an establishment figure, less critical of bureaucracy and more supportive of attempts to re-establish a sense of order in an increasingly rebellious society (Mratz, 2001: 43). Indeed, as Pilcher points out, by the early 1960s Cantinflas's political and professional ambitions coincided as he appeared in an increasing numbers of films in which his screen image represented a man who sought to uphold a nostalgic sense of national ideology, professional probity, and social responsibility in the face of a counterculture of non-conformity manifest in foreign imports such as The Beatles and Che Guevara (Pilcher, 2001: 195–197). Cantinflas's deployment by the Organising Committee, therefore, represented a further step along the line of conformity; espousing elite and middle-class values from within the personification of working-class Mexico. There can be no doubt that the spectre of the Mexican people being placed under foreign scrutiny on an unprecedented scale meant that the frivolous, even childish antics of the *pelado* needed to change. As the article in *El Nacional* underlined 'it is now time to abandon our short-trousers mentality' (*El Nacional*, 1967).

The broadcasts sponsored by the Organising Committee portray Cantinflas in the guise of Patrolman 777, a character who had been given a first outing in the film *El gendarme desconocido* in 1941, and one who had been revived in another film *Entrega inmediata* in 1963 (Pilcher, 2001: 191). Thus, Patrolman 777 was already established in 1960s contemporary culture, but he also stimulated nostalgia for older generations. It is certainly the case that in Patrolman 777 the Organising Committee was depicting a version of Cantinflas that no longer exposed the absurdities of the middle classes but the failings within the poorer classes. Almost without exception, the targets of Cantinflas's often pompous admonishments were to be found among the popular classes. In some cases adapting scenes out of *El gendarme desconocido* (Pilcher, 2001: 81),[3] Patrolman 777 brings into the local police station a series of characters and situations that foreign visitors should not have to encounter during the Olympic Games: a taxi driver who has overcharged an attractive female tourist from the United States; hooligans caught fighting at a football match in the Aztec stadium; a housemaid who has thrown rubbish onto the street; and a hippy who has caused a nuisance in a tourist area. In each case, the message was clear: Mexicans needed to modify their behaviour to create a good impression, to present Mexico in the best possible light, and to lend dignity to the Mexican nation.

Before going into the detail of these shorts, it is worth making a few general comments. It is important to note that the original public education campaign envisaged by the Organising Committee had not contained humour and was more formal and direct, in line with the tone adopted by many official broadcasts of that time. Pedro Ramírez Vázquez, president of the Organising Committee, claims that he was able to persuade colleagues that humour might be a more effective way of convincing people to accept the campaign's underlying messages (Ramírez Vázquez, 2001).[4] This, in itself, shows a level of sophistication and confidence by those devising the nature of the campaign. They were able to move away from the straight, serious posture often associated with Mexican officialdom to reveal a more relaxed approach. Even so, this was nonetheless picking up on a trait within Mexican humour that had been associated with Cantinflas for many decades. The vital difference in these shorts is that those who were on the receiving end of Cantinflas's tongue were not the bureaucrats but the masses. There can be little doubt that the result was a top-down imposition of values that exposed the nature of elite concerns.

A second general observation is that the shorts ostensibly portrayed a familiar social dynamic. Upon conveying various characters to the police station, Patrolman 777 brings them before a suited bureaucrat in the form of a police chief. The advancing age and slightly unprofessional manner of the latter (depicted by his tendency to eat his lunch behind the public

---

3   Pilcher describes a scene in *Gendarme Desconocido* in which Patrolman 777 exudes a breathtaking gasp of cold steel: a consequence not only of not possessing a holster for his gun, but of having no underpants. The same scenario is included in the short of the housemaid discussed below.

4   Original footage of the Cantinflas shorts can be viewed at the Filmoteca Nacional, Mexico City. The degree to which Ramírez Vázquez can claim sole credit for this more humorous approach to public education is debateable. As early as February 1965 (before he became chairman), it was reported that Cantinflas was considering a request to become involved in the Organising Committee's campaign. See Segura Procelle, 1965.

desk) suggests that the police chief has limited abilities and, perhaps, limited ambitions. Nonetheless, this representative of Mexican officialdom contrasts starkly with the fast talking, scruffy Cantinflas, whose often dishevelled appearance is obviously meant to identify with the majority of the Mexican working class. Yet from the way that Cantinflas addresses his subjects, it is clear that any supposed empathy is used to re-establish the state's prerogative to modify and correct behaviour. For a character such as Cantinflas, renowned for sending confused messages, this takes on different meaning as he attempts to act simultaneously as the people's fool and the people's teacher.

The short concerning the taxi driver overcharging a foreign tourist goes to the heart of official concerns regarding Mexico City's hosting of the Olympics. As Patrolman 777 admonishes the taxi driver for trying to cheat his attractive, young passenger, he uses comedy to reiterate the message being promoted by the Mexico City authorities (who had launched huge campaigns designed to ensure that all taxi drivers and bus drivers were registered and aware of their patriotic duty to create a good impression).[5] The taxi driver, suitably ashamed of his actions, offers no defence and simply stares at the floor, submissively accepting his reprimand. Yet even as he implores the taxi driver to be honest so that foreigners will think of Mexicans as 'gentlemen', Patrolman 777 deftly slides his hand down the tourist's back towards her backside. Cantinflas then deploys his famous play on words by stressing that the tourist is from Dallas. This is an overt reference to the Mexican expression 'da las nalgas' which means 'to offer oneself' or 'to be licentious'. The actress playing the tourist in this short had been voted Miss California 1964 and during the mid 1960s she appeared in several Mexican films as a sexy dumb blonde. In broken English, Cantinflas then offers to make amends by showing her some of the city's sights: 'I would like to show you the Mexico City, the cathedral and something else if you don't mind, eh . . .'. His gestures and the obvious sexual innuendo of his parting remark confirms that machismo was alive and well in Mexico and certainly not seen as a failing to be corrected. Would it be too far to suggest that the short also takes a slight dig at Mexico's northern neighbour? In emphasising the vulnerability of a North American visitor who is inappropriately dressed and neither speaks Spanish nor knows Mexican ways, there may be at least a hint that the sophistication of the so-called developed world is lacking. Certainly, the compliant, smiling way in which the young woman accepts Patrolman 777's invitation suggests naivety and/or promiscuity.

---

5   See for example AHDF: Memoria del depto. del DF (1966–1967); AHDF: Memoria del depto. del DF (1967–1968).

The short concerning the arrest of hooligans at the Aztec Stadium reflects a familiar story: legitimate passions concerning crucial decisions on the football pitch become inflamed by excessive alcohol and lead to fighting among rival fans. Patrolman 777 explains to his boss that as he intervened to restore order, he was drenched by the contents of a beer glass 'that didn't smell of beer, jefe'. Undeterred, the urine-soaked agent of law and order forcefully conducts the miscreants to the police station to be punished for their unruly, uncivilised behaviour. In reporting the facts to his superior, Patrolman 777 alludes to an accusation made by one of the men that he had stolen money from the accuser's pocket. His explanation is as simple as it is feeble: believing the pocket bulge to be a gun, Patrolman 777 had 'confiscated' the contents. On finding it to have been a wad of peso notes rather than a gun, Cantinflas defends his actions by suggesting that the hooligan could have bought a gun with the money involved. A conspiratorial glance between Patrolman 777 and his boss suggests that few questions will be asked and that the money will later be shared between them.

Showing a demeanour similar to that of the taxi driver, the two hooligans offer no explanation for their behaviour. Rather they stare at the floor as they receive a verbal onslaught from the self-righteous preserver of decency and decorum. Patrolman 777 expresses the underlying concern 'If this sort of thing can happen at a local football match, what's going to happen at the Olympic Games?' Such disquiet was not merely rhetorical. In 1966, the president of the IOC, Avery Brundage, had written to the Mexican Organising Committee sending copies of Associated Press articles reporting fighting and rowdiness in the crowd during a boxing match in Mexico City. Brundage sought and received assurances that such behaviour would not happen during the Olympics.[6] Within this context, the use of Cantinflas in this short can be seen as one of the practical steps taken by the Organising Committee to ensure that their promises to Brundage would be honoured. Yet, at another level, the admonishment of drunken behaviour is tempered by the confiscation of money; tacit recognition of the popular perception that Mexican police were corrupt. As in the previous scenario where Mexican machismo was unofficially sanctioned, in trying to mask or to rectify certain aspects of Mexican behaviour, the creators of the shorts appeared to acknowledge that some things were beyond their powers to change.

Concern regarding hippy culture reflected a trend that began in the 1950s in which Mexican adolescents had begun to question the right of the state to control their lives. This challenge found form in the adoption of alternative

---

6 IOC/HA: File no. 0100624, Correspondence COJO 1966. See letter dated 28 November 1966.

cultures (Zolov, 1999). Part of this was a direct import, manifest in the popularity of such 'corrosive elements' as Elvis Presley, The Beatles and The Rolling Stones. Yet, as Hazel Marsh explains in her chapter in this volume, some was home-grown, as perceived by the way in which Mexican hippies sought an affinity with rural indigenous cultures that offered a more appealing range of values and world views. For the Mexican authorities, this alternative youth culture represented a serious challenge to the paternalistic pattern of the past, a challenge they viewed as imported, un-Mexican, and that would lead to decadence and disorientation. The Cantinflas short of the hippy illustrates all these concerns.

A hippy is brought into the police station for the apparently tame excuse of making a nuisance of himself in the Zona Rosa, a commercial tourist area of Mexico City. The physical appearance of the hippy reveals several significant factors. His long curly hair and round-rimmed glasses cannot mask the fact that he is pale-skinned. In contrast to the distinctly mestizo characteristics of all the other miscreants previously considered, the hippy could be taken for a foreigner or, more likely, the son of an elite family. The hippy's dress, too, suggests recognition of overseas fashions: his glasses and multi-buttoned tunic are reminiscent of the attire donned by The Beatles during this period. Drawing his boss's attention to the youth, Patrolman 777 refers to the latter as 'a hairy being', evidently at a loss as to how best to describe him. This confusion continues as Patrolman 777 reports that the youth describes his nationality as 'hippy'. Cantinflas proffers the thought that he might be from the Mexican town, Jilotepec (an obvious confusion with 'hippy') but that he might equally be Comanche or Chamulan. In each case, this appears to allude to the rural, non-urban affectations of someone who is clearly not indigenous, and who might not even be Mexican. Indeed, the 'hippy' nationality suggests the influence of an imported culture and the feared loss of Mexican identity. The other significant issue raised in this short is Patrolman 777's interpretation of the hippy's attempt to give him a flower as being a bribe. When his boss states that such a gesture was not a bribe, Patrolman 777 assumes it to be a love token, 'which is even worse'.

It is important to emphasise that the inclusion of this scenario with the collection of shorts was not a response to the Mexican Student Movement. The making of these shorts predated the movement and adds weight to Zolov's claim that the movement was merely the latest symptom of long-standing tension caused by a generational challenge to state paternalism. The importance of the short is more in the way in which Patrolman 777's preoccupations and preconceptions reflected those shared by authorities and parents concerning recent developments within Mexican youths. Patrolman 777 voices sympathy for the hippy and states that he believes he has the potential to be a good Mexican citizen: 'I want to state that deep down he is a good person, but how can you see deep down when you can't get beyond his eyes?' In an obvious allusion to the clouded, wayward gaze of the drug addict, it is clear that this hippy, like so many of his peers, seems to be intent on wasting his potential on decadent, un-Mexican behaviour. Patrolman 777 warns his boss against getting too close to the hippy because of the smell. For a generation of Mexicans brought up on government campaigns that emphasised personal hygiene as an essential aspect of civilised behaviour, the fact that this hippy evidently prefers not to wash would not have gone unnoticed to the viewing audience. In common with all other shorts, it concludes with a monologue from Patrolman 777 in which he berates the hippy's demeanour and reminds him of his duty as a Mexican in the forthcoming Olympics. Yet the hippy obviously has a large degree of self-confidence. In stark contrast to the mestizo taxi driver and drunken football fans, when being admonished he looks straight at Patrolman 777. The seemingly confident manner of the youth again suggests an educated, middle or upper-class background and can be seen as a reflection of the growing willingness of this sector to challenge old structures of respect and control.

As with the other shorts, the hippy episode represents a plea for decorum, decency and respect. Perhaps more than any other, however, is the endeavour to return Mexican youths back to a righteous path. It might be slightly misleading to suggest that this rebellious confrontation between authority and Mexican youths was universal. For the most part, Mexican youths, both in Mexico City and beyond, had not embraced what authorities viewed as the excesses of a libertine life. They remained, by and large, respectful of their parents and diligent in their studies and work. The thing that most vexed authorities, and indeed parents, was the example that an influential element within Mexican youth society might set for the country's younger generation as a whole. For several decades, a much more desirable role model had come in the form of youth groups such as the Pentathlón.[7] A quasi-military youth group, the Pentathlón was a common sight in patriotic celebrations. With an emphasis on clean living, physical fitness and respect for the family, authority and the flag, the Pentathlón appeared to uphold a sense of discipline and worthy Mexican values. At a time when youths appeared to be rejecting the paternalistic control of the state, the Pentathlón offered a familiar hierarchical structure that would prevent them from being led astray. Its emphasis on masculinity and physical vigour contrasted starkly with the effeminate portrayal of hippy culture.

7   The author would like to thank the British Academy for funding the research that informs the study of the Pentathlón.

Figure 3.1. Rebels without Helmets
Source. Pentathlón Deportivo Militar Universitario (PDMU) Archive, unidentified newspaper

As can be seen in the cartoon by Pámanes (Figure 3.1), the Pentathlón could be seen as a beacon of hope during a time when society was desperately searching for solutions to counter the disaffection of its youth ('Rebeldes sin casco' – 'rebels without helmets' – is an obvious allusion to the 1955 US film, *Rebel without a Cause*).[8] No doubt reflecting a greater debate concerning state – youth relations and how best to curb wayward behaviour, Pámenes suggests that persuasion rather than coercion would be more likely to achieve

---

8   PDMU Archive: unnumbered file, circa 1965. The cartoon appears with neither details of the newspaper nor the date on which it was published. The depiction of rebellious youths, however, reflects the rise of youth culture during the 1950s and 1960s.

positive results. Cantinflas's exchange with the hippy can be seen as one more attempt to persuade Mexican youths not to follow the ways of the 'rebeldes sin casco'. The events of 2 October 1968 would represent a more forceful method of removing the role model.

The fourth short of an indigenous housemaid reprimanded for throwing household rubbish onto the street caused great indignation when I recently showed it to a Mexican audience. After escorting the housemaid to the police station, Patrolman 777 admonishes her for treating the street outside her employer's home 'as if it were her own pigsty'. At one level, the message is clear: 'don't throw litter onto streets' – 'keep Mexico City tidy'. As such this was no different from similar campaigns in Britain during this time. However, the indignation of my Mexican audience was partly brought on by a shared sense of embarrassment at the language used by Cantinflas. Specifically they were shocked by the disrespectful, intrinsically racist manner in which Patrolman 777 addresses the maid. The maid's clothes and skin colour combine to affirm her indigenous roots. The fact that she is seen to close her eyes while being admonished reflects a sign of embarrassment, awkwardness and subordination when faced by a person of authority. At one point, Patrolman 777 refers to her as a 'gata sicodélica'. A literal translation would be 'psychedelic cat', a phrase commonly used in 1960s. This is one way of interpreting it, but the demeanour and appearance of girl do not reflect this. 'Gata' or 'gatita' were (and sometimes still are) used among members of the white, upper and middle classes to refer to servants and/or housemaids. The full force of the meaning is not easy to express. Rather than 'cat', the nearest English terms to conveying the correct sentiment might be 'dog' or 'mongrel'. Certainly it is a term of casual disrespect by one class to another. Similarly, admonishing her for being lazy also fits a common dominant-class perception of the so-called lower orders. 'Sicodélica' (psychedelic) is more problematic and my thesis here is more speculative. It obviously does not refer to the maid as psychedelic in the hippy sense. Rather it might be alluding to the maid's short fringe, that is out of keeping with the central-parting usually associated with indigenous hair styles. It may, therefore, be a jibe that although she is trying to be modern and trendy, by adopting an inappropriate culture she can never escape the fact that she is an innocent 'Indian' in the big city. That she is berated for throwing rubbish onto the street and treating it as if were her *own* pigsty, overlooks the basic truth, of course, that the rubbish she has discarded is not her own but comes from the middle-class household in which she is employed.

Broader Implications

What can we make from a study of Cantinflas's participation in the Olympic preparations? In earlier decades the 'lovable fool' that Cantinflas often played was allowed to adopt the role of people's champion, albeit on the understanding that his threats against the established order were frivolous, light-hearted and restrained. Yet the years of encouraging the act of *pelado* had a price to pay in the relative immaturity of the Mexican people (at least in the eyes of the state). By the 1960s, however, the 'lovable fool' had become the system's voice; one who conveyed the message that Mexicans had to change their ways. The impending Olympic Games gave new impetus to this initiative. No longer could Mexican society act the *pelado* in the knowledge that a paternalistic state would set them back on the right path. In October 1968, this convenient, fundamentally domestic arrangement would be interrupted by the close proximity of a critical foreign gaze. In these circumstances, it was imperative that irresponsibility or unreliability were replaced by cordiality and efficiency.

The salient messages evident in all these shorts are the need for cleanliness, dignity, patriotism, honesty and good manners. In this respect, they are consistent with the messages coming from other forms of communication. Exactly how such qualities were to be instilled among the Mexican population reflects the time-honoured system of carrot and stick. This can be seen in the demeanour of Patrolman 777 towards the various characters. In the case of the housemaid and the hippy, the police officer shows considerable compassion and leniency. Rather than roughly escorting the housemaid into the station by the arm, he guides her by the elbow. Similarly, while pointing out the hippy's obvious deficiencies, Cantinflas is at pains to stress his basically good character. In addressing both characters, his tone is conciliatory and measured. In the case of the taxi driver and drunken hooligans, however, a much more robust approach is taken to crimes of drunkenness, violence and dishonesty. He is much more aggressive in bringing them into the police station and admonishing them. Indeed, his frustration with one of the hooligans provokes him to hit out at the man. In both these cases, he suggests that they should be fined and/or detained for their actions 'so that they can be taught a lesson'. The one approach suggests persuasion, the other imposition. While it might be a slightly glib observation to make, in clearing Mexico City's streets of undesirables, the authorities showed both approaches. 'Peddlers, hawkers, and pitchmen' were encouraged to move on with the promise of temporary market stall locations in other parts of the city. When protesting students showed no signs of heeding calls for rational responsible behaviour, a much more robust and, eventually, tragic solution was found.

What I believe this reveals is a fundamental lack of trust by the Mexican elite concerning the capacity of their own people. It shows a reversion to a form of state paternalism reminiscent of social reforms from the 1930s to 1950s during which the 'lower orders' were deemed to be unclean, drunken, violent and unpatriotic. At this time, schools, cultural brigades and other state actors had been sent out into the provinces to wrest the wayward peasants from their perceived superstitious and slothful ways. In their stead, lessons of personal hygiene, suitable forms of physical activity and instructions on morality were deemed as the most effective way of bestowing an air of urban civility on all Mexicans.[9] That such lessons were continuing to be made in the run-up to the Mexico City Games suggests several things. Importantly, it implies that the elite were less than confident that the decades of revolutionary reforms had achieved their underlying objectives, and that such attempts may count for nothing if the Mexican people were placed under international scrutiny. Class tensions, fuelled by the inward migration of rural Mexicans to the capital city, had underlined the considerable gaps that still lay between different sectors of Mexican society. It exposed the fact that the elite were deeply concerned that when the world came to Mexico, their depiction of the country as modern and sophisticated would be exposed as fraudulent; that instead of a refined society, foreigners would focus their attention on the Third World squalor that was a daily reality for many of those living in Mexico City. Above all else, it exposed an elite that were torn between two irreconcilable emotions. Patriotism and pride demanded that they should defend Mexican honour and contribute towards making the Olympic Games a success. Class-driven prejudice, however, meant that they were not only aware of derogatory foreign stereotypes of their country and its people, but that many of them shared such views of their compatriots.

---

9 For fuller discussion of this thesis see K. Brewster (2004, 2005); K. Brewster and C. Brewster (2010).

4

Lyon '68: The Games that Weren't, or the Intermediate Event-zone of a Non-Olympics

HUGH DAUNCEY

Newcastle University, UK

Although the French press and French academics interested in sport have contributed to the interest shown worldwide in the 40th anniversary of the Mexico Olympic Games, underlining the significance of the first Olympics held in a developing country, analysing the politics of the Black Power protests and of the staging of the Games themselves, and celebrating the enduring athletic achievements of competitors, 2008 also marked an important sporting anniversary for France, namely that of the 1968 *Winter* Olympics held in and around Grenoble! As the editor of this volume has demonstrated elsewhere, the Summer Games of 1968 were staged by a country with an uncertain national identity and about whose abilities to organise an event of this scale there were significant doubts (C. Brewster and K. Brewster, 2006), but France, a 'First World' nation in the full flush of Gaullist modernisation and confidence only succeeded in hosting the Cinderella competition of the Winter Games. 'The Games that weren't' of Lyon '68 show how French politics and French attitudes towards sport undermined a bid that was doomed to failure in Baden-Baden in 1963.

France's Olympic Bids

France in the late 1960s was strongly marked by the Winter Olympics of 1968, which were successfully hosted by the French provincial city of Grenoble and the surrounding Rhône-Alpes region. National self-confidence in sport and in general was boosted by the organisational abilities demonstrated by the city and by the Games management, and the skier Jean-Claude Killy (now a member of the IOC) became a national hero by winning three gold medals. The 1968 Winter Olympics were a success story for France, illustrating the country's ability to be 'la France qui gagne' (France as Winner) on the sports field and in the international system: President de Gaulle's ambition to restore French grandeur through stable domestic politics, strong foreign policy and pride in French culture found a convenient illustration in the Grenoble Games, as the new Fifth Republic (created in 1958) emerged from the aftermath of bitter disengagement from Algeria and the years of political instability suffered under the post-war Fourth Republic.[1]

The Rhône-Alpes region again organised the Winter Games in 1992, this time around Albertville, and these two sporting 'mega-events' form a strong thread in France's narrative of sporting excellence during the Fifth Republic. What is much less celebrated and well-known is obviously the French *failure* to win the honour of running the 1968 Summer Olympics, Lyon's bid being eventually quite lowly placed in the final decisions made in 1963 at Baden-Baden. The principal focus of this volume is, of course, the Mexico Games themselves, but this present chapter hopes to provide something of a counterpoint to considerations of how and why Mexico won the right to organise the Games and how the Games reflected and changed Mexican society and politics. Despite the obvious contrasts between France and Mexico in the 1960s in terms of socio-economic development, standing in the international system and even athletic/sporting prowess, the ambitions behind Lyon's unsuccessful campaign to host the 1968 Summer Games and the mechanisms of the bid's elaboration shed intriguing comparative light on why and how cities and countries stand as candidates to stage sporting 'mega-events'.

This chapter sets out the sporting and political complexities of what still remains a little-known episode in France's Olympic history, discussing the failed bid for the 1968 Summer Games within the context of the strong (but sometimes confused) encouragement given to sport (elite and/or mass) by governments of the early Fifth Republic, rivalries between Lyon (France's second city) and the capital Paris, which also hoped to bid at one stage of the selection process, and the contemporary infrastructure-development issues of Lyon and the Rhône-Alpes region. What this study attempts to do is to throw some light on the domestic politics of 'Lyon '68', placing the unsuccessful candidacy of France's second city within the framework of government perspectives on sport, as well as locating these 'official' attitudes within the wider field of social and cultural attitudes towards sporting activities as leisure and competition. It is also important to understand some of the ways in which the bid for Lyon '68 inter-related with agendas of economic modernisation and regional development in the rapidly changing context of France in the 1960s.[2]

---

1 De Gaulle's famous and repeated assertion that 'France is not herself without Grandeur' found expression in a wide range of policy fields during the 1960s. A classic interpretation of the concept of 'grandeur' in de Gaulle's primary field of interest – foreign policy – is given by Cerny (1980).

2 France during the 1950s and the 1960s was undergoing a period of rapid socio-economic modernisation aptly described by Jean Fourastié as 'les trente glorieuses'

France, the Olympics and Sports 'Mega-Events'

The initial starting point for any analysis of Lyon's bid to host the 1968 Summer Games has to be an understanding of France's (special) relationship towards the Olympics and to other sporting mega-events such as the football World Cup. French involvement with the International Olympic movement has of course always been strong, since the central importance of Pierre de Coubertin in the creation of the modern Olympics in the late nineteenth century, and France has similarly been a key player in the running of other international sporting organisations such as the Fédération Internationale de Football Association (FIFA). Unlike countries such as Mexico, for example, France exercised a founding influence on the development of international sport, and France has thus traditionally enjoyed strong representation within the international management structures of sport. In part because of the privileged role played within these organisations by French personalities and officials, from the running of Universal exhibitions to the staging of international sporting competitions, the French state from the nineteenth century onwards, has been keen – almost 'exceptionally' keen – to use the power of world trade fairs or sports contests to showcase France, French abilities and French values to the world community.[3]

Building on Coubertin's catalysing role in the mid 1890s, which led to the 1896 Games held in Athens, it was France that staged the 1900 Olympics as a 'hybrid' games held in conjunction with the famed Exposition Universelle. In 1924, France played host to the Summer and Winter Games, organised in Paris (interestingly enough at the expense of Lyon) and in Chamonix (which later was involved in the 1968 Winter Games), but since this early period, although France and French cities have repeatedly been candidates to host the Summer Olympics, they have always lost out to competitors more favoured by the IOC: Parisian hopes to host the 1992 Barcelona Games, the 2008 Beijing Games and, most recently and most bitterly, the 2012 London Games have all been crushed, leaving France with only the memory of the 1924 Summer Games and the 'consolation prizes' of the 1968 and 1992 Winter Games. In contrast, Britain hosted the London Summer Games of 1908 and 1948 (Dauncey, 2004, 2008) and is currently preparing the Games of 2012, which many in France feel was 'stolen' from Paris by British chicanery in

---

(the 30 glorious years of economic growth between the end of the Second World War and the onset of the oil crisis in the mid-1970s (Fourastié, 1979)).

3   The notion of French 'exceptionalism' is often used to describe how France either 'does things differently' or simply 'is different'. Often tied to the nature of French 'Republicanism' or to the Gaullist desire to maintain independence of all forms in the international system, it has recently been thought to be evolving (Chafer and Godin, 2009).

the bidding process. French interest in the hosting of the Olympics has been matched by her keenness to organise the football World Cup as a showcasing of France to the world, both in 1938 (Tumblety, 2008) and in 1998 (Dauncey and Hare, 1999), and the 2007 Rugby World Cup similarly came to France, but repeated failure to secure the Summer Games has led to feeling that France is unlikely to be a candidate again in the foreseeable future for the Olympics, although in March 2009 the French Olympic Committee selected Annecy as France's candidate for the 2018 Winter Games.

Just as in Singapore in 2005 when Paris lost out to London 2012, the failure of the Olympic bid by Lyon for the Games of 1968 in Baden-Baden in 1963 was also taken badly; for a variety of reasons the Gaullist state of the new Fifth Republic was particularly keen to harness the prestige of the Olympics and the developmental impetus of preparations for the Games to the transformation of French society and infrastructures. When the Winter Olympics were awarded to Grenoble for 1968 (in January 1964 in Innsbruck) it seemed almost a consolation prize for losing out to Mexico, and these Winter Games were soon to be described by the then sports minister Maurice Herzog as 'les Jeux de la France' (the Games of France), who was told by President de Gaulle that he could have a billion Francs to make the event a national and international success. However, various studies have subsequently assessed the 'balance sheet' of the Grenoble Games (and, comparatively, those of Chamonix '24 and Albertville '92), progressively revising initial impressions and municipal, regional and national propaganda about their success in accelerating the development of Grenoble and its region (Terret, 1990; Arnaud and Terret, 1993; Kukawka, 1999). Were Lyon to have hosted the 1968 Games instead of Mexico City, similar doubts might have been raised in following decades, but the decision in Baden-Baden in 1963 came as a heavy blow both to the coalition of decision-makers and stakeholders in Lyon itself and in government.

So, despite her early leading role in the renaissance of the Games in the modern era, France's relationship with the Olympics in the contemporary period since the Second World War has been somewhat unsatisfactory. It is perhaps an example of France's difficulty in coming to terms with a world in which – for all her influence – she is no longer a prime-mover of international sporting organisations and competitions, as she was in the late nineteenth century, and with an international system in which Europe no longer has any unquestioned right to privilege, for example in hosting 'mega-events' such as the Olympics.

Lyon '68: National Pride, Regional Development and Sport

A key moment in France's post-war development came ten years before Mexico '68, when in 1958, the ailing Fourth Republic (born in 1946) was replaced by de Gaulle's Fifth Republic. The new regime, with a Constitution providing for more effective government, and ultimately the presidential style of government that has characterised French politics since the election of de Gaulle as President in 1965 by universal suffrage, brought a radical transformation of the state and of French attitudes towards France's 'place in the world'. Gaullism attached high importance to French 'grandeur' and independence in all fields, and elite sport soon came to be seen by the new Gaullist administration as an instrument of French national prestige. It was as part of this new emphasis on sport as an element of French 'grandeur' that Lyon's unsuccessful rivalry with Mexico City was played out. Lyon as well as France during the late 1950s and early 1960s was undergoing a period of political change, as a 'generational shift' occurred among key personnel such as the mayor, the prefect and the president of the regional council, facilitating new thinking and supporting ambitions to accelerate the development of the city and its region (Benneworth and Dauncey, forthcoming). The new drive at the level of the state to instrumentalise elite sport in support of national prestige coincided with new networks of new agents of governance in Lyon that were keen to meld central-government 'sports policy' and municipal/regional development.

The institutional history of French 'sports policy' is complex and tortuous, as various studies attest (Callède, 2000; Chifflet, 2005), but one date is always prominent in any analysis of the meanderings of state interest in sport, leisure, physical exercise, youth and health: in September 1958, the new Gaullist government of Michel Debré created a junior ministry of Haut Commissariat à la Jeunesse et aux Sports (High Commission for Youth and Sports), headed by the famous mountaineer, Maurice Herzog (he conquered Annapurna in 1950, becoming a minor national hero of a France that was lacking in confidence). Throughout the little-loved Fourth Republic (1946–1958), state interest in sport had been somewhat dormant, as governments had struggled with other priorities in rebuilding the economy, decolonising France's Empire and managing the often painful processes of socio-cultural modernisation that accompanied the first decade or so of France's '30 glorious years' of prosperity from 1945 to 1975. However, the renewed preoccupation with sport of early governments of the Fifth Republic actually continued institutional initiatives that had first appeared in 1936 under the Popular Front, when the Left had promoted sporting activities for all, as part of a drive to provide a right and access to leisure for the working classes. It also echoed and built upon more problematic government attitudes and structures that had been developed by the collaborationist Vichy Regime between 1940 and 1945, when sport and physical exercise had been harnessed to the reactionary social and political goals – 'Travail, Famille, Patrie' (work, family, homeland) – of the Etat Français. Between the Liberation and 1958,

French sports policy remained in the doldrums, partly because government intervention in sport was tainted by memories of Vichy, and partly because the parlous situation of public finances during the Fourth Republic did not really allow the significant expenditure that would have been needed. Plans for improving the country's sporting infrastructures within the framework of the five-year national planning system came to nothing, as priority was repeatedly given to education rather than sport and leisure. Any desire governments of the Fourth Republic had to promote sport were vitiated by these problems of finance, conflicting understandings of 'sport' as elite or mass, professional or amateur, and a reticence to 'direct' civil society.

For sport to be taken seriously by government again, it needed the change of regime in 1958 and a new Gaullist emphasis on sport as necessary both for 'le prestige de la Nation' (national prestige) and for 'la santé de tous' (the health of all), which attempted to resolve the elite/mass dichotomy by suggesting that success in international competition would foster grassroots fitness. Thus, it was only the Fourth Plan (1962–1965) – preparation for which was ongoing as Lyon's Olympic bid was being drawn up, and that was to have helped lay some of the bases for Lyon '68 – that really began to address the needs of sport and physical education, with an ambitious programme of infrastructure development intended to encourage mass participation in sport and, crucially, the production of an elite group of sporting champions who would represent France in international competition. Emphasis on elite sport was the defining feature of thinking in the late-1950s and early-1960s and, arguably, it has been interpretations of sport as contributing to the 'prestige of the nation' through success in international competitions – the Olympics especially – that have come to dominate the French state's attitude towards sport during the Fifth Republic. This created much resentment amongst those politicians of the Left and left-wing analysts of sports policy who see the emphasis on success in medals tables as a detraction from investment in 'sport for all' as leisure and health for the masses, in the tradition of earlier French thinking on 'éducation physique' creating a fit and healthy population.[4] France's bid – through Lyon – for the '68 Games was an instrument of national prestige through the staging of a sporting mega-event, glory through anticipated sporting victory, and (for Lyon) the creation of sporting infrastructures for the general public.

This 'Olympic turn' in French state thinking on sport appeared most strikingly after the 1960 Rome Olympics, when the French team returned

---

4   The foremost French critic of the Olympics has been the sociologist Jean-Marie Brohm, who over a period of many years has produced a number of scathing analyses – academic and more polemical – of how the Games distort sporting activity (see for example Brohm, 1981; Brohm, Perelman and Vassort, 2005).

home humiliated by a meagre haul of medals. In the new climate of national pride and confidence engendered by the decisive, dynamic and active Fifth Republic, and in the context of an ideology of 'French grandeur' developed by President de Gaulle, representatives of French sport were required to perform successfully in international competition, in contribution to the hoped-for Gaullist 'rayonnement' (radiation, like the rays of the sun) of French culture and expertise in the international system. France's total tally in 1960 was only five medals and not a single gold, prompting one of the most famous of all newspaper cartoons (drawn by Jacques Faizant for the newspaper *Le Figaro*) involving a sullen General de Gaulle, incongruously attired in tracksuit and plimsolls setting off to compete himself, under the grumbling caption 'Dans ce pays, si je ne fais pas tout moi-même . . .' (Do I really have to do everything *myself* in this country?). This satire underlined just how much the athletes and the organisational structures in place to identify and support them seemed to have failed the nation, or at least Gaullist interpretations of how sport could be used to shore up France's 'prestige'.

The Olympic debacle of 1960 reinforced the Gaullist state in its view that government needed to be as *dirigiste* (interventionist) in sport as it was inclined to be in other fields: in 1961, a special General Delegation responsible for preparing France's participation in the Olympics was set up under Colonel Marceau Crespin (Laget and Mazot, 2000: 29–32), and Herzog's 'High Commission' was – in June 1963 – transformed into a minor ministry, administering closely the relations between the state and French national sporting organisations in all sports (known as sports federations) in the French model of sport as 'service public'. Against this ideological and organisational backdrop, the first programme-law developing sporting and educational infrastructures invested some 600 million Francs in public and private sports facilities between 1961 and 1965 as part of France's Fourth National Plan. Between 1960 and 1965, 1,000 swimming baths and 1,500 stadia and playing fields were created, and this significant investment was continued in the second programme-law of 1966–1970 with the construction of some 2,000 more sports grounds and 1,500 gymnasia.

It was also during the early 1960s that debate resurfaced about the need, in Paris, for a 'national' sports stadium, capable of seating 100,000 spectators and suitable for hosting the largest national and – crucially – international competitions. This need was only finally answered during France's infrastructural preparation for the 1998 World Cup, with the building of the famous 'Stade de France' in Saint-Denis, just north of Paris (Dauncey, 1997) as the central, capital element in the renovation of stadia across the country (Dauncey, 1998). But the timidity with which Paris and successive governments approached the vexed dossier of the 'national stadium' during the 1960s, 1970s and 1980s contrasted with the overall success of infrastructural improvements achieved in the 1960s by the state in partnership with municipal authorities and private sports clubs (about 30–40 per cent of costs were subsidised by central-government funding). France in the 1960s was in full 'modernisation', as volontarist, *dirigiste* policies attempted to catch up on the perceived failures of the Fourth Republic in adapting French socio-economic structures to the realities of the modern world, and sport, in various ways, but perhaps most noticeably in terms of 'equipment' (and discourses) was at the forefront of the process. This, in outline, was the 'politics of sport' that formed the backdrop to Lyon's ambitions to host the Games of 1968.

Maurice Roche (2000, 2006) has developed a theoretical framework for the analysis of large-scale sporting and other festivals (what have come to be termed, mainly following Roche, as 'mega-events'), in other words Trade Expos, World Cups, Olympics Games, and so on. 'Mega-events' have become a focus of much study in recent years (Horne and Manzenreiter, 2006) and can help inform this study of 'Lyon '68', even as a 'failed' bid. Sociologically, Roche's analysis hinges on three distinct temporal dimensions: event core, intermediate event zone and event horizon. Analysis of the event core involves examination of the dramatological content, that is to say, the various 'ritualistic and theatrical features which contribute to the charisma, aura and popular attraction' of the mega-event. The intermediate event zone includes the pre- and post-event processes; for all intents and purposes, local and national politics and national and international economics. The event horizon investigates the long-term causes, motivations and effects of mega-events; here the focus for Roche is more generally the structural conditions of modernity. Other chapters in this volume focus variously on different aspects of the 'event core' of Mexico '68, the 'intermediate event zone' of the Games and indeed their 'event horizon', but here, in this analysis of how France failed in her ambition to stage the Games, we are trying to build an understanding of Lyon '68 as a case-study of an 'intermediate event-zone', both in terms (principally) of pre-event processes and also (although this is work that will be developed in further publications, for example, Benneworth and Dauncey, forthcoming) post-event changes in urban governance.[5]

As well as the 'politics of sport' during the early years of the Fifth Republic, discussed in outline above, another crucial contextual element of a proper understanding of the 'pre-event processes' of Lyon '68 is the

---

5   This work uses the concepts of 'governance capacity' and 'urban festivalism' to investigate how far and in what ways *failed* bids to host mega-events also impact on the cities that elaborate them. Studies of mega-events and festivals have always tended – quite naturally – to focus on the processes around, and results of actual competitions, expos and other happenings, but attention paid to 'non-events' can also be instructive.

relationship between Lyon and Paris. Lyon is France's second city, vying with Marseille for the silver medal in the French urban hierarchy. Provincial cities in France have traditionally entertained a strained relationship with the capital, in France's highly-centralised, concentrated, 'Jacobin' administrative and territorial system. Lyon in particular has always struggled to maintain its identity and 'independence' in the face of Parisian dominance, but until 1977 at least, when President Giscard d'Estaing allowed Paris to regain full municipal existence with a mayor, Lyon benefited from the advantage of a strong tradition of local/regional politics, and made the most of the advantages brought by strong mayors, often important national politicians, who were able to defend Lyon's interests in, and against, Paris. When the French candidate for the 1968 Games was being chosen, Parisian 'identity' was thus somewhat diffuse because of the lack of an elected mayor, and the movement to present Paris as the proposed host, although making the most of links with central government, lacked the advantages of tight municipal/regional definition and backing, a precise geographical identity, and strong, experienced 'champions' to lobby for it. In contrast, Lyon's principal champion of the Olympic bid was the Radical mayor Louis Pradel, a surprise victor in the municipal elections of 1957 and 1959, who succeeded the extremely long-serving and nationally famous mayor Edouard Herriot, also a radical, three-times Prime Minister in the 1920s and 1930s, and minister under the Fourth Republic. Herriot was mayor of Lyon from 1905 until the Second World War, then again from 1945 until his death in 1957, and did much, during his long tenure, to attempt to develop the city's sporting infrastructures and traditions. Pradel, as well as having a strong interest in sport, was ambitious to redevelop Lyon's urban infrastructures. It was under Herriot in the late 1940s and 1950s that the Municipal Council set up a committee responsible for the encouragement of sporting and leisure activities, ultimately headed by Pradel before his elevation to the mayorship in 1957, and as early as the First World War, Herriot had used his visibility and influence at the national level to lobby in favour of Lyon's sporting interests. Pierre de Coubertin visited Lyon during the First World War, inspecting its sporting facilities in general and, particularly, the major omni-sports stadium being built on the insistence of Herriot in the Gerland area of the city (now the Stade Gerland of the football club Olympique Lyonnais). In what amounted to more or less a private correspondence with Coubertin[6] Herriot negotiated that Lyon should be considered for hosting the 1920 Games (if Antwerp should decline) or the 1924 Games (eventually awarded to Paris, after Lyon

---

6   Archives Municipales de Lyon, reference 1 II 0249 1, Edouard Herriott, Personal Correspondence with P. de Coubertin.

withdrew). Thanks to Herriot's political acumen, he was able to increase the 'visibility' of Lyon; Lyon's bid for the 1968 Games was thus – as for Mexico City – its third attempt, even though the pre-eminence of Paris (as evidenced by the attribution of the 1924 Games to the French capital) was still obvious.

The new-found political enthusiasm at national level for sport that arose during the very early years of the Fifth Republic provided welcome catalysing support to initiatives that had already been put into action in Lyon during the later 1950s under the guidance of Mayor Louis Pradel. As well as a general encouragement given to sporting activities in the city and region, the idea of Lyon being able to stage the Olympics centred around the building of teams of individuals able to produce the bid itself and the building of actual facilities. Much of the process centred around Pradel himself and his lieutenant Tony Bertrand, whose expertise in organising large-scale sporting events led to his involvement in a number of major competitions in the Francophone world during the 1960s (Bertrand, 1994: 50–52). Against the backdrop of Presidential wishes for 'une France qui gagne' (France as winner) in international sporting competitions, Pradel was increasing the urban governance capacity of Lyon through the motivational project of bidding for the Games, and simultaneously renovating urban infrastructures of all kinds.

The link between the bid for the Olympics as a mechanism for rejuvenating the city and its management can be seen in one of the earliest of Pradel's major initiatives, the holding of a large-scale 'festival' to celebrate Lyon's 2,000th anniversary as a city. Held in 1958, the bi-millennial celebrations of the founding of Lyon included a wide range of cultural and political activities and a substantial programme of sporting events, based on the work during the late 1940s and early 1950s of the Office municipal de la jeunesse et des sports (initially set up in 1946, and building on some structures left by Vichy) in favour of sport in the city and appropriate facilities. The bi-millennial celebrations attracted many visitors to Lyon, almost as a dress-rehearsal for future large-scale events, and the planning of the 'festival' required a shake-up of the procedures of the city administrators, which had suffered some drift during the later years of Herriot's mayoralty. Louis Pradel had been in charge of municipal sports policy under Herriot, and on election as mayor he appointed his collaborator and friend Bertrand to the responsibility, and it was this central partnership that from 1958 concentrated attention and resources on the development of sports infrastructure in the city and surrounding region, and from about 1960, piloted most of Lyon's Olympic bid. With the open support of the regional prefect of the Rhône-Alpes area, Alain Ricard (attributed with the original idea for bidding for the Games and an example of the 'generational shift' in decision-makers that had occurred in 1957–1960), and the more implicit backing (from Paris) of national High Commissioner for Youth and Sports, Maurice Herzog (born in Lyon and hoping to obtain a seat as a Gaullist deputy in Lyon in the 1962 legislative elections), Pradel and Bertrand rapidly constructed a coalition of support for the Olympic bid.

After a visit to Lyon on 27 January 1961 by Herzog that led to considerable discussion in the Municipal Council meeting of 20 February about the city's ongoing preparation of a bid (Conseil Municipal, 1961) during which Pradel was able to answer the minor concerns of a variety of critics, Lyon's intention to be a candidate was officially declared to the French Olympic Committee and in turn passed on to the IOC in Lausanne, but nationally, the city's ambition caused some jealousy and gave rise to some scepticism. In reflection of the steep urban and political hierarchy in France, Lyon's bid was judged by some in the capital as 'pretentious', but there seemed to be little ambition in Paris – at least at that moment – to consider organising the Games in the City of Light. Despite rumbling Parisian criticisms, in April 1962, a visit to Lyon by Colonel Marceau Crespin, the influential national official appointed to be in charge of France's 'Olympic preparation', resulted in declarations by him in support of Lyon (Vourron, 1962a), and in July, Armand Massard, vice-president of the IOC, municipal councillor in Paris and president of the French Olympic Committee, similarly produced an open backing of Lyon's ambition, enthusiastically reported in the regional newspaper *Le Progrès de Lyon*, which was one of the major players in Pradel's coalition of support for the Games (*Le Progrès de Lyon*, 1962). Massard's endorsement of Lyon was perhaps surprising: although he had a *national* responsibility for Olympic matters in France and might thus be expected to be impartial, he nonetheless also held elected office in Paris. In early August 1962, the head of the Paris Municipal Council, Pierre-Christian Taittinger, announced that Paris would also be a candidate to host the Games, thereby placing the French Olympic Committee in the uncomfortable position of having to choose between the rival cities (*L'Equipe*, 1962). In late November 1962, however – after the mid-month legislative elections in which both Taittinger in Paris and Herzog in Lyon were involved – the Parisian candidacy disappeared as the French Olympic Committee decided by nineteen votes to five to give Lyon the right to represent France at Baden-Baden in October 1963, and attention began to focus on just how Lyon's bid could be adequately financed (Vourron, 1962b). Thus the short-lived Parisian bid reflected both long-standing issues of centre – periphery rivalry and more short-term contingencies of party politics and election campaigning. One of the rare studies of Lyon's failed bid for the 1968 Games emphasises very strongly the difficult relationship between Lyon as France's second city and the capital (Terret, 2004). Yet other more general studies of the mayoral career of Louis Pradel stress how he struggled to balance the political parties of his coalition support and was sometimes obliged to make concessions to Gaullists at either national or local level in order to maintain control (Sauzay, 1996, 1998). One of Pradel's weaknesses was his lack – in comparison with Herriot – of experience and influence in politics at the national level, and although he benefited from a network of contacts and 'fixers' who facilitated direct access to various ministries and officials in Paris, his administration occasionally had to make compromises to avoid antagonising Gaullists in local and central government.

The final details of the bid were presented to the Lyon Municipal Council on 28 April 1963, and after a short debate, agreed with little serious opposition (Conseil Municipal, 1963). Again, *Le Progrès de Lyon* eulogised about Mayor Pradel's plans for rejuvenating the city (*Le Progrès de Lyon*, 1963a, 1963b) but elsewhere, minor protests were voiced. What opposition there was seemed to surface mainly in the city's monthly cultural news magazine, *Résonances*, which published a summary of how the bid had come about (Dériol, 1963) and in which a short series of articles during the spring and summer of 1963 confronted supporters and detractors of the mayor's ambitions. The discussion in *Résonances* centred principally around fears that the financial cost of staging the Olympics would outweigh the wealth the operation would create and the government subsidies promised by what was criticised as a recently-created and doubtless impermanent Ministry of Youth and Sport. Concern was voiced at the financial deficit made by the 1960 Games in Rome, but criticism of the feared costs tended to neglect completely, or at best discount as intangible or immeasurable, the secondary benefits of hosting the Olympics, above and beyond the mere balance sheet of preparation and the weeks of competition (Berthet, 1963).

Rather than being 'pretentious' (as the Parisian elite preferred to view it), the elite of Lyon saw the city's bid for the Games as an 'audacious' attempt to protect and enhance Lyon's status nationally as France's second city, internationally, within the developing context of the recently created Common Market, and even globally (Pradel, 1963; Delfante, 1963). The global scale of the Olympics was a way of refocusing attention on Lyon not just as an also-ran to Paris, but as an important and successful contemporary centre of industry and business located at the centre of European transport corridors. The issue was described in terms of Lyon remaining either just 'une petite ville de Province' (a small provincial city) or aspiring to the role of a major European metropole. The official bid document itself rather naively stressed Lyon's geographical position at the crossroads of Europe, Africa, East and West:

> If one looks at a map of the world, the city of Lyon holds a privileged position. It is situated mid-way East to West, between Japan and Latin America; North to South between Finland and Black Africa. It is the link between Northern and Southern Europe, an advanced post of Central

Europe and a point of junction with the Mediterranean and Africa. Regional capital and second city of France through its radiative power and expansion, Lyon takes its place among the great European Metropoles . . . the Capital of Gaul rich with a past over two thousand years old is proud to be the most modern of old cities (Ville de Lyon, 1963).

The promotional film that was made to help mediatise the campaign was boldly entitled 'Lyon, grande ville européenne'. In retrospect, Lyon's bid-planners should have anticipated the attractiveness of the 'risky' choice for the IOC of awarding the Games to developing Mexico, and elaborated a narrative of Lyon's place in the world that was stronger and more persuasive.

Since the late 1940s, the French state had been increasingly concerned about the over-concentration of economic activity, wealth and power in Paris and its surrounding region of Ile de France. A famous study published soon after the birth of the Fourth Republic had described France as being Paris, surrounded by a desert of declining agricultural activity, rural depopulation and small provincial towns (Gravier, 1947) and posited the need for policy to redress these spatial inequalities. Thinking about regional development during the late 1950s and early 1960s led in 1963 to the creation of the national regional development planning delegation (DATAR), which aimed to rebalance regional disparities, but Lyon's political and business elite was aware that beyond this domestic national planning perspective, their city needed to aim at becoming more than just the regional capital of Rhône-Alpes. Lyon's past prosperity as France's second city had long been based on traditional industries, but as France's economic modernisation proceeded apace during the second half of the French economy's 30 glorious years of growth between 1945 and 1975, moving the working population increasingly away from agriculture and industry towards tertiary activities, Lyon's planners saw the urgent need to continue to encourage industry, but also to focus on the development of infrastructures that would stand the city in good stead in the new economy. Hosting the Olympics in 1968 was seen as an obvious and powerful catalyst for this process of economic modernisation. Concretely (and Mayor Pradel had earned the nickname 'Mr Concrete' for his enthusiasm for redeveloping his city), Lyon looked to the Games as a means of improving transport links, with upgrades to major road, rail and especially airport facilities planned during the mid-1960s in order to open the city to the rest of France, Europe and world. Within the city, the Gerland Stadium dating from 1919 needed some renovation and extension – as Herriot had been known to complain, although it was a key infrastructure it was so under-used that it might as well have served to graze sheep – improvement of some other sporting facilities was required, the renovation of entire 'quartiers' such as that of Gerland around the main stadium was seen as an important contribution to new urban planning, and upgrades to local road systems and parking were deemed important to Lyon's overall attractiveness as a city for business and industry. In particular, the construction of new hotel accommodation and the Olympic village was welcomed as a way of boosting Lyon's tertiary activities in tourism, conference hosting and other non-traditional economic sectors.[7]

Above and beyond the issue of Lyon's relationship to Paris and that of the city's strategic centrality (or otherwise) to developing European spatial dynamics, which, as will be argued in forthcoming studies, were inflected significantly by the process and after-effects of bidding for the Olympics (Benneworth and Dauncey, forthcoming), the question of Lyon's 'place in the world' was an issue that seemed directly relevant to Pradel's team in Baden-Baden as they learned of the IOC's decision: 30 votes for Mexico City; fourteen votes for Detroit; twelve votes for Lyon. The 'Old World', France's ancient Roman 'capital of Gaul', had lost out to the New World.

Conclusion

Rather as in Singapore in 2005, when Paris was beaten by London's bid for the 2012 Games, one French view of why Lyon lost out so heavily in Baden-Baden was that its 'honest' bid had been cheated of success by the dubious campaigning tactics of other cities involving free trips, lavish hospitality and gifts, and general unfair competition (Michela, 1963). Added to this, there was an understanding that the political desire to see the Games organised in a developing country away from Old Europe had also penalised Lyon in its attempt to present itself as both old and new, European and open to the world. Explaining why Lyon failed to win the '68 Summer Games also requires insight into the latent competition between Paris and Lyon that to an extent contributed to undermine the Lyon application even after the French Olympic Committee had rejected that of Paris: seen from outside France by anyone who understood the urban and political primacy of Paris in France, the candidacy of Lyon seemed anomalous, but the fact that only a year later the IOC awarded the '68 Winter Games to Grenoble and the same region of Rhône-Alpes that was home to Lyon, whose bid finally defeated that of Calgary by 27 votes to 24, suggested that it had not simply been doubts over the France's logistical ability to organise a mega-event that had swayed the decision against Mayor Pradel.

---

7   Lyon has been very successful in modernising its economic base since the 1970s, developing into the capital of French videogame production for example, and expanding its tourism potential through exploitation of the city centre World Heritage site of 'Old Lyon'.

Despite the vivid resentment in Lyon at the rejection of the bid and Pradel's subsequent refusal to consider applying for the Games of 1972 or beyond, the city was proud to claim that in the following years it completed the sports infrastructure developments that had been promised for the Games that never were. In addition, the bid-coalition had identified a set of non-sporting strategic projects that were necessary to revitalise and reinvigorate Lyon, and reposition itself as the capital of the Eastern Mediterranean zone of the new European space. These projects included improved road links through an Alpine tunnel (the Fourvière *massif*), reconstruction and modernisation of the city centre (including pedestrianisation, development of the Lyon city centre World Heritage Site and the construction of the Perrache commercial centre) and ensuring that Lyon was well-connected to the newly developed high-speed rail (TGV) system and benefited from enhanced air transport services. All these projects were subsequently realised in the following fifteen years, and helped contribute to Lyon's clear emergence as the second city of France. In part, at least, these achievements were a consequence of the stimulus to Lyon's urban governance provided by planning for the Olympics of 1968.

Perhaps surprisingly, but also drawing on the infrastructural improvements made in all areas during the 1970s and 1980s in Lyon and the region, during the early and mid-1990s, a project was mooted in the Rhône-Alpes region to apply to host the 2004 Summer Games, and Lyon once again produced a bid for consideration by the French Olympic Committee (Rhône-Alpes, 1995). Although the Lyon bid was again sound, the city lost out to the northern conurbation of Lille, whose candidacy fared poorly in the final round of bids, and the Games were awarded to Athens. Conspiracy theorising suggested that Lille was preferred to Lyon as France's national candidate for 2004 because Paris was planning to apply for 2008, and pressure was applied on the French Olympic Committee to choose a bid for 2004 which would *fail*. Parisian ambitions to stage the Games were indeed translated into ultimately narrowly unsuccessful bids for 2008 and 2012, which nevertheless demonstrated France's enduring attachment to the use of sporting mega-events in national self-promotion. Interest in the 2018 Winter Olympics will be shattered or confirmed in July 2011, and there is a chance that France may yet reapply to host the 2024 Summer Games, as a centenary celebration of the Paris Games of 1924, although it has also been suggested that Lyon or Marseille might be possible venues. If France does wish to celebrate its own 'Olympic centenary' in 2024, the problematic politics of sport and of centre – periphery relations that vitiated Lyon's ambitions in 1968 will have to have been resolved.

5

'Nasty Demonstrations by Negroes': The Place of the Smith–Carlos Podium Salute in the Civil Rights Movement

SIMON HENDERSON

Newcastle University, UK

When Tommie Smith and John Carlos bowed their heads and raised a fist as the *Star-Spangled Banner* began to play, they changed the Olympic landscape forever. Their actions became a touchstone for all future political protests at the Games. Indeed in the lead-up to the recent Beijing Olympics, as protestors focused their attention on the human rights record of the host nation, talking heads and Olympic officials made reference to the salute by Smith and Carlos 40 years ago. Much scholarly attention has focused on the impact of their effort on the relationship between race and sport and the construction of the identity of the black athlete in America. What is particularly fascinating, though, is the location of the Smith and Carlos salute within the wider civil rights movement of the 1960s. Dissecting their protest in this context reveals a symbolic reflection of the state of that movement in 1968. The podium salute was both non-violent and threatening, it was simultaneously moderate and radical, and it displayed Black Nationalism and inter-racial cooperation. Indeed, it drew together in one symbolic moment the diverging threads of a movement that had slowly unravelled as the 1960s progressed.

What was unique was the fact that this statement was made in the sporting arena, a place that had consistently resisted the civil rights agenda. Brundage's description of a 'nasty demonstration' was reflective of an ideology dominated by a desire to keep politics separate from sport unless it served the interests of the sporting hierarchy. What Smith and Carlos did on the victory podium was to dramatise the place of black Americans in the United States with profundity. Their protest was not just about the place of blacks in sport but fundamentally about the place of blacks in society as a whole. This is what makes their actions so enduring and what so infuriated sporting administrators who wanted to keep the racial struggle out of sports. This chapter seeks to dissect the myriad ways in which the podium salute provided a unique encapsulation of the state of the civil rights movement in 1968. In this sense, the protest by Smith and Carlos was a reflection of a wider societal reality; it communicated many messages that had been heard throughout the 1960s. The message was not new; it had been rehearsed by many different voices in varying forums. Crucially, however, the podium salute communicated the diverging threads of a civil rights narrative through an iconic gesture on a stage so resistant to hearing that narrative. We must recognise the different ways it did this so the protest is not simply reduced to an individual heroic stand with the consequent loss of its greater significance.

The Podium Moment

On 16 October 1968, the Olympic 200 m final took place. Both Tommie Smith and John Carlos almost failed to make it to the starting blocks. Smith had strained an adductor muscle in his semi-final and required ice treatment while preparing for the final. Carlos had stepped out of his designated lane in his heat and only avoided disqualification because officials failed to spot the error. In the event, they both ran in a race that became the prelude to an act that defined their lives thereafter. Smith won in a world record 19.83 seconds – no sprinter would again run the distance in under 20 seconds until Carl Lewis in 1984. Carlos, who slowed and turned to look at his team-mate in the last few strides, came in third after being passed on the line by Peter Norman.

Earlier in the Olympic track and field competition Tommie Smith and Lee Evans had sat in the stands and discussed what they would do if Avery Brundage tried to shake their hands during a medal ceremony. Evans suggested that they should wear a black glove and hide their hands under their sweatshirts revealing the black gloves at the last moment and therefore frightening Brundage. The athletes' wives purchased the gloves which were then added to their kit bags (Matthews, 1974: 196). The exact mechanics of the events that unfolded in the holding area before the 200 m victory ceremony are a little unclear, with each actor in the events remembering a slightly different picture of the past. Nevertheless, it would seem that Smith was the driving-force behind the protest that followed. Lee Evans explains that 'Carlos never even came to a meeting' of the Olympic Project for Human Rights (OPHR) and that it was he and Smith who were the principal athletes involved in the movement (Evans, 2004). Carlos has claimed subsequently that the suggestion of making a gesture on the victory podium was his and that he slowed up at the end of the race, letting Smith win, because he wanted to make a non-violent protest (Hartmann, 2003: 23). It was, however, Smith who produced the gloves that the two athletes were to wear and who told Carlos, 'the national anthem is sacred to me, and this can't be sloppy. It has to be clean and abrupt' (Moore, 1991a: 73). Peter Norman stated that Carlos did not have any gloves with him and it was Smith who took the lead in the discussions that were held under the stadium before the medal ceremony (Norman, 2004). Sportswriter, Neil Amdur, describes Smith as an 'indomitable' competitor and saw Carlos's gesture as 'a part of what Tommie [Smith] was in total' (Amdur,

2005). Certainly the bend in Carlos's raised arm on the podium compared with Smith's straight, strong gesture and comprehensive explanation of the protest after the event seem to suggest a greater sense of purpose on the part of the gold medallist (Hartmann, 2003: 23).

Smith and Carlos outlined to Norman what they were going to do on the podium. The Australian silver medallist explained that he supported what they were doing and would show his solidarity by wearing the OPHR badge if they could find him one. As the three men walked out to receive their medals, Smith and Carlos wore their gloves, black scarves and black socks with no shoes. Paul Hoffman leaned over the barrier at the side of the track to wish the men all the best and Carlos asked for the OPHR badge he was wearing. Norman pinned the badge on his sweatshirt (Hoffman, 2004; Norman, 2004). As the national anthem rang out, the two black sprinters bowed their heads. Smith raised his right fist and Carlos his left in the defining moment of the 1968 Olympic Games.

The various contrasting reactions inside the United States to the podium incident have been well documented, but a brief reminder of the extremes of opinion serves to highlight the search for meaning in Smith's and Carlos's gesture. The file relating to Smith and Carlos in the Avery Brundage archival collection is full of letters to the head of the IOC both praising and criticising the black sprinters. Some wrote of the 'heroism' and 'dignity' of Smith and Carlos, while others spoke of their 'inappropriate' and 'distasteful' behaviour.[1] One correspondent to Brundage pointed out the hypocrisy of Smith and Carlos being suspended by the USOC when that organisation continuously refused to dip its flag in salute to the host country. Both represented acts of 'blatant political manoeuvre' but only one was punished.[2] Others drew attention to the differing responses of the IOC in relation to the actions of Smith and Carlos and Czech athlete Vera Caslavska. She bowed her head during the playing of the Russian national anthem in protest at the treatment of the Czech people by the Soviet regime. It was noted by one correspondent that bowing your head during the anthem of another nation was surely more serious and disrespectful than bowing your head during the anthem of your own country. Caslavska, however, received no punishment.[3]

Opinion in the US press was varied. The *Los Angeles Sentinel*, an African-American publication, argued on its sports page that the protest was out of place and that the Olympics were no arena for such acts. Columnists elsewhere in the paper praised the heroic effort of Smith and Carlos. The *Los*

---

1   ABC: Smith–Carlos dismissal file. Box 179.
2   ABC: Smith–Carlos dismissal file. Box 179. R. N. Kline to Brundage, 19 October 1968.
3   ABC: Smith–Carlos dismissal file. Box 179. A. G. Belles to Brundage, 28 October 1968.

Angeles Times referred to the podium gesture as a 'Hitler-type salute'. *Time* magazine changed the Olympic motto of 'faster, higher, stronger', to 'angrier, nastier, uglier', when describing the 'public display of petulance' by Smith and Carlos (Bass, 2002: 274–278). The *Pittsburgh Courier* provided coverage from an African-American perspective which praised the black sprinters and criticised the racism of the IOC. The *Courier* ran a cartoon of a giant black gloved fist rising above the Olympic stadium with the caption 'pride prevails' (*Pittsburgh Courier*, 1968). In a balanced piece, *Newsweek* noted that, 'judged against some of the alternatives that black militants had considered, the silent tableau seemed fairly mild' (*Newsweek*, 28 October 1968: 36). This is just a very brief example of the many differing responses the podium salute elicited.

Athletes on the US team held widely varying attitudes towards the actions of their team-mates both at the time and on reflection some 40 years later. Water polo player, Bruce Bradley, asserted at the time that it was an honour to receive a medal and that having seen Smith and Carlos behave as they did the US Olympic Committee was 'well within it rights [to send them home]. It must maintain some sort of order' (*New York Times*, 1968). Speaking to me in 2004, Bradley softened his stance a little, suggesting that the decision to send Smith and Carlos home was somewhat harsh. His criticism of the podium salute itself remained, however. 'I don't think they should have used the forum' they did to make that protest (Bradley, 2004). Again in an interview with me, swimmer Jane Swagerty reflected that she saw a little cowardice in the actions of Smith and Carlos. She described herself and her swim team-mates as being shocked and 'rather embarrassed' (Swagerty, 2004). Track star George Young contended that the sprinters' actions in winning medals showed Black Power, but their stand on the podium was unimpressive (Young, 2004). High jumper Dick Fosbury commented that making a protest during the victory ceremony was misguided, however, veteran discus thrower Al Oerter described Smith's and Carlos's actions as relatively 'moderate' (Oerter, 2004; Fosbury, 2004). Cleve Livingston, a member of the Harvard rowing crew, described the podium salute as a 'very forceful, but affirmative message of both protest and hope' (Livingston, 2004).

Much of the differing opinions both then and now stem from the enigmatic nature of the podium salute. As a symbolic gesture it encapsulated so many facets of the racial struggle in the United States in the late 1960s that it was open to a myriad of interpretations. Many of these interpretations in fact mixed competing or contradictory messages of the civil rights agenda. For example, a piece reporting the podium salute in the *Pittsburgh Courier* focused on the black pride inherent in the raised fist, a potent symbol of 'Black Power'. The same article, however, asserted that 'Smith and Carlos's stand was a visual expression of the theme song "we shall overcome"' (*Pittsburgh Courier*, 1968). In a single article found in an African-American publication, therefore, the podium protest was linked to the mainstream civil rights anthem and the movement for Black Power; two different strands of the racial struggle of the 1960s. Indeed, the ideological father of the Black Power Movement, Malcolm X, had famously mocked the singing of that anthem as contradictory to a black revolution.

The podium protest can be connected to the many tangled threads of the civil rights struggle in the late 1960s in a variety of ways. This reality was deepened by the words of Smith and Carlos in the aftermath of their stand. Smith explained in a TV interview,

> I wore a black right-hand glove and Carlos wore the left-hand glove of the same pair. My raised right hand stood for the power in black America. Carlos's raised left hand stood for the unity of black America. Together they formed an arch of unity and power. The black scarf around my neck stood for black pride. The black socks with no shoes stood for black poverty in racist America. The totality of our effort was the regaining of black dignity (Edwards, 1969: 104).

Smith articulated a message that conveyed the protest as solemn and digni-fied. Choosing to make the stand during the anthem provided an expression of the duality that many black Americans felt, a double consciousness of being both American and black. The racism of American society imposed an iden-tity problem on black citizens. The response to this has had an affect on how African-Americans express patriotism. Some like Frederick Douglass during the Civil War, W. E. B. DuBois before World War One, and Al Sharpton after 9/11 have subscribed to the belief that loyalty and devotion to American culture and ideals would eventually be rewarded with racial equality. This is referred to as 'invested patriotism'. At other moments in history black lead-ers, such as Paul Robeson in the early twentieth century and Martin Luther King during his opposition to the Vietnam War, have rejected traditional patriotism and instead fundamentally challenged American racism. This is called 'iconoclastic patriotism'. What the two sprinters' gesture embodied was an iconoclastic patriotism. They showed devotion to the United States by fundamentally challenging American racism (Shaw, 2006: 33). The expression of black pride and strong group identity simultaneous with the playing of the *Star-Spangled Banner* powerfully expressed a double-consciousness.

While Smith stressed the solemn and essentially non-violent or non-aggressive nature of the protest, in the post-ceremony press conference Carlos infused the podium salute with greater anger and confrontation. Carlos fumed, 'If we do the job well, we get a pat on the back or some peanuts. And someone says, "Good boy". I've heard boy, boy, boy all through the Olympics. I'd like to tell white people in America and all over the world that if they don't care for the things black people do, then they shouldn't sit in the stands and watch them perform' (Bass, 2002: 245). Carlos articulated a powerful race consciousness that provided a more aggressive expression of Black Power than the statement by Smith. What we have not mentioned is that there were three people on the winner's rostrum. Peter Norman, the white Australian silver medallist, wore an OPHR badge. He added an inter-racial element to the protest that contrasted with the message of strident racial pride that is emphasised by viewing the protest through a distorted Black Power lens.

Reactions to a Revolt

Let us now dissect the important ways in which the protest on the podium and the words of Smith and Carlos uniquely encapsulated the landscape of the civil rights movement in the late 1960s. The podium salute is remembered as a 'Black Power' protest. A recent BBC documentary focusing on the incident was simply titled *Black Power Salute* (*Black Power Salute*, 2008). The reporting of the incident at the time and since has placed great emphasis on the raised gloved fist and the Black Power symbolism to which this is connected. Certainly the raising of a black fist was the most recognised symbol of the Black Power movement and various items of merchandise could be purchased that displayed this symbol. Afro-American publications also used the raised fist in cartoons with great regularity. This is not to say that Smith and Carlos were not consciously adopting the symbols and meanings of the Black Power movement in their stand; they undoubtedly were. What is important, however, is to recognise the way their protest was misinterpreted, as was the Black Power movement as a whole. Furthermore, the presence of white protestors in support of the two black sprinters reveals something of the tensions at the heart of racial protest in the late 1960s.

The stand by Smith and Carlos and the gold-medallist's explanation of the podium salute was deeply infused with racial consciousness. Smith talks of black pride, black unity and black dignity. The beads around Carlos's neck were a clear symbol of Black Nationalism. The reaction of the IOC and the USOC saw an attempt to isolate the sprinters as representatives of a minority opinion, a small group of angry young black men who represented a threat to the sanctity of the Olympic movement and society as a whole. The racial prejudice of the US Olympic organisation was barely veiled. The press secretary Bob Paul commented to the sports correspondent for *Newsweek*, Pete Axthelm, that he better have something better to write about than 'niggers'. He also lambasted a journalist from *Ramparts* for being on the side of those 'niggers'. The thoughtlessness of the USOC to the cultural and racial sensitivities was revealed further when one of their representatives spoke

to Smith and Carlos after the podium salute. After it had been explained
to the sprinters that they were to be expelled from the village, the USOC
administrator dealing with the matter asked 'you boys know why you did it?'
Smith snapped back that they were not boys.[4] The US Olympic authorities
were not only insensitive to the cultural significance and racial messages of
what Smith and Carlos did, they were openly hostile to any encroachment
by racial politics on the Olympics. Before the Games, the USOC had sought
to diffuse any possibility of protest at the Games. Roby wrote to Brundage in
the summer of 1968 informing him that a board of consultants had been set
up to meet with athletes and counsel them against any undesirable action.
Jesse Owens was made chairman of this board which included three other
African-Americans. Roby also felt it necessary to mention that one of the track
and field coaches, Stan Wright, and one of the medical staff, Dr. Plummer,
were also black.[5] The Head of the USOC seemed to be suggesting that this
fact alone was likely to have an influence on politically minded black athletes.

After the podium salute, the USOC sent Jesse Owens to speak to the rest of
the black athletes suspected of having the inclination to make further protests.
Owens asked the white athletes in the meeting to leave and wanted to speak
only to his 'black brothers' to counsel them against any further actions of
protest. There was a conscious effort to portray the podium salute as the
product of a radical and dangerous black militant agenda. Owens was chosen
to speak to the dissenting athletes because he represented a more moderate
black voice and believed sport should be kept separate from politics. There
was a distinct sense that Owens was out of touch with black athletes and was
simply a mouthpiece for the Olympic authorities. Vincent Matthews wrote
of Owens: 'he was a messenger sent by the USOC to determine the mood
of the black athletes. The fact that Jesse was black gave him a calling card'
(Matthews, 1974: 191). Lee Evans commented, 'Jesse, I don't know what he
was thinking, he was connected to the Olympic committee' (Evans, 2004).

The 25 or so athletes that Owens was sent to address included some
notable white athletes. Owens represented the traditional image of the 'good
black man' who was lauded by liberal white America as a credit to his race.
Owens preached the liberal white ideals of integration and gradual racial
progress; however, when confronting this inter-racial group of Smith and
Carlos supporters, he responded by asking the white athletes to leave. Owens
said, 'it's nothing against you other men personally, but these are my black

---

4   USOC Archives, A. Lentz papers, Mexico City incident 1968–1969: Proceedings of
    the Meeting of the Executive Committee of the United States Olympic Committee, 1
    December, 1968.
5   ABC: Roby, M, Douglas, F. Box 2. Folder 1968 correspondence. Roby to Brundage, 8
    August 1968, RS 26/20/37.

brothers, and I want to talk to them. I think you can understand' (Matthews, 1974: 191). Owens asked why white hammer throwers Hal Connolly and Ed Burke were present. Connolly remarked, 'he was upset at seeing white athletes there, especially me' (Connolly, 2004). Owens obviously felt that it would be easier to persuade black athletes of his point of view without a white audience. Again, we see a conscious effort to construct a one-dimensional reading of the podium salute and its symbolism.

The badge that was worn by Peter Norman and other white athletes during the Games – indeed Norman was given his by Harvard rowing crew coxswain, Paul Hoffman – represented the Olympic Project for Human Rights, not the Olympic Project of Black Power, nor the Black Militant Olympic Movement. The OPHR badge had a wreath as the focal point and was designed by white students at the University of San José. That Smith and Carlos were making a stand for black people and for justice in racist America is undeniable, but there was an inter-racial message to the symbolism and meaning of that podium salute that has often been overlooked. The USOC's desire to paint the protest as an episode of black militancy was threatened by the vocal support offered for Smith and Carlos by white athletes such as Tom Waddell, Hal Connolly and the Harvard rowing crew. Hoffman was very nearly suspended from the rowing final for simply giving Peter Norman the badge that he wore on the winner's rostrum. The US Olympic authorities were adamant that politics should not enter the sporting arena but they were also worried that an inter-racial protest would be much harder to neutralise. It was one thing to have two angry young black men throw a Black Power salute during the national anthem, quite another to have white team-mates offering support and threatening to pull out of the rest of the Games. Under a heading 'white ones too', the *New York Times* reported that athletes may go home in protest at the treatment of Smith and Carlos (*New York Times*, 1968).

The USOC was extremely concerned about the actions of white athletes such as Hoffman and the Harvard crew who supported the actions of Smith and Carlos. In a letter sent to the Harvard rowing coach, Harry Parker, by the USOC President Douglas Roby, it was argued that the crew had 'embarked on a rather strenuous program of civil rights and social justice with other members of our Olympic delegation to Mexico City'. Roby continued, 'civil rights and the promotion of social justice may have their place in various facets of society, but certainly this sort of promotion has no place in the Olympic Games, and particularly when they are held in a foreign country, which country is not particularly involved in these internal problems of ours'.[6] Furthermore, decathlete, Tom Waddell, one of the white athletes who

---

6 Douglas Roby to Harry Parker, 5 November 1968, copy of letter in author's possession.

had voiced support for the OPHR, was asked by a reporter if he thought Smith and Carlos had discredited the American flag. Waddell replied that he felt that Smith and Carlos as African-Americans had been discredited by the flag more often than they had disgraced it. When questioned about whether the US image had been tarnished, he argued that the nation's image was so bad already it could not get any worse (Waddell and Schapp, 1996: 107). Waddell, a medical doctor serving with the army, saw his comments widely reported in the press. He received a cable from his commanding officer ordering him to retract his remarks or face a court-martial.

Sport, Race and Civil Rights

In the salute by Smith and Carlos and the reaction to it we see a clear reflection of the tensions in the civil rights movement by 1968. Since the mid 1960s the inter-racial coalition focused around the Southern Christian Leadership Conference and the person of Martin Luther King had been increasingly challenged by a more militant generation of civil rights leaders and a burgeoning Black Power movement. Men such as H. Rapp Brown and Stokely Carmichael advocated a black liberation struggle that used 'any means necessary' to affect change. Indeed, Carmichael increasingly argued that black people should not work with whites, that integration was not a desirable goal because it would rob black people of their cultural integrity. The Student Non-Violent Co-ordinating Committee, which Carmichael headed, increasingly advocated armed self-defence and broke its alliance with the Black Panthers because of the latter's acceptance of coalition with white leftist groups (Carmichael and Hamilton, 1968). There was a clear split in the civil rights struggle over the extent to which black activists should engage and cooperate with white liberals. It is worth noting that violent and non-violent forms of protest had long co-existed in the racial struggle and Carmichael, King and Brown were all among those black leaders who went on record to support the initial OPHR initiative of boycotting the Olympics. This initiative, then, drew support from those who advocated militant non-violence and those such as Carmichael who embraced a more aggressive Black Power ideology.

The leader of the OPHR, Harry Edwards, himself struggled to straddle the divide between white liberals and a growing black militancy. Edwards dedicated his account of the OPHR to the white athletes who supported the cause and commended the Harvard crew for their commitment to understanding the problems in black America. Nevertheless, the brash and abrasive character of Edwards and the contentious hyperbole that flowed from him did much to promote a misunderstanding of, and hostility towards, the ideals of the OPHR. Even those sympathetic to the movement were not entirely comfortable with his role. Furthermore, some time after the events of 1968, Edwards explained that he was sceptical about the extent to which whites could help the cause he was seeking to promote, 'I don't care how liberal whites were; there was a container of racism and white superiority that they could not escape' (Edwards, 2004).

The extent to which the protest by Smith and Carlos and the reaction to it represented the tensions of the wider civil rights movement has often been overlooked. Certainly it suited the agenda of the Olympic authorities and the US government – the 1968 Olympic team was not invited to the White House for the customary reception with the president – to portray the podium salute as part of the militant Black Power agenda. The wider message of inter-racial support for the advancement of civil rights was ignored. Images of Smith and Carlos were placed in the same symbolic context as race riots in cities across the United States in the spring and summer of 1968. Historical accounts of the 1960s, or specifically of 1968, often include the image of the podium salute alongside pictures of the slain Dr Martin Luther King, Black Panther rallies or scenes of racial violence; often with a generic caption about Black Power or racial turmoil. What needs to be acknowledged is that the Smith and Carlos protest reflected the very complex state of the civil rights movement in the late 1960s. It is crucial that this is recognised in full and the subsequent meaning of the protest on the victory podium is not reduced.

It would be fascinating to learn what Martin Luther King would have said about the podium salute had he not been assassinated six months before the Games. His support of the original boycott idea can be interpreted as part of his increasingly radical agenda as his career progressed. Nevertheless, he had strongly objected to the use of the slogan 'Black Power' as part of the civil rights movement. He would have admired the courage and dignity of Smith and Carlos but how would he have responded to the raised black fists? The National Association for the Advancement of Colored People (NAACP), the main moderate civil rights organisation, possesses nothing in its sports files or archives relating to the Smith and Carlos salute. Indeed its leader, Roy Wilkins, doubted the feasibility of the proposed Olympic boycott and there is no evidence that the organisation encouraged civil rights protests by athletes.[7] It is difficult not to conclude, however, that what Smith and Carlos did was in many respects 'moderate' and not connected to the black radicalism of the late 1960s in the way it was simplistically portrayed to be. It was in fact very much in the spirit of non-violent and dignified protest that both the NAACP

---

7 NAACP Collection: Group 3. Box A3, Sports. Hand-written Wilkins reply to letter of 15 April 1964.

and King had long endorsed. *New York Times* sports correspondent, Robert Lipsyte, later reflected that in the context of things that they could have done and the build up to the Olympics and the threatened boycott, the sprinters' gesture hardly seems very extraordinary (Lipsyte, 2005). A letter written to the editor of the *New York Times* stated that Tommie Smith 'did not riot, or loot or burn ... His gesture was restrained, even dignified. What more can America conceivably ask from people who have been second-class citizens for so long?' (Bass, 2002: 289).

The black civil rights activist who stood motionless as a policeman beat him for attempting to register to vote received sympathy from many in white America. His contemporary who fought the police in response to discriminatory treatment was looked upon with more suspicion; an angry black man, and a possible danger to society. The black football player who pummelled white opponents and sacked the opposing quarterback was lauded as a fine sportsman and a credit to his race. Yet, if he stepped off the field and complained of the racial injustices he faced, wearing a black armband or black glove to register his non-violent protest, he was criticised for ingratitude and for perverting the sporting ideal. The sports world, therefore, provided a unique landscape for the tactics of protest in the civil rights struggle. This distinctive protest dynamic helps to explain the complexity of the response to the black athletic revolt and the defining moment of that revolt on the winners' podium in Mexico City.

The fact that sport had so long resisted the civil rights agenda intensified the negative reaction to the podium salute, but also important was a fundamental misinterpretation of the message of Black Power. Here again the Smith and Carlos protest encapsulates a key component of the wider civil rights struggle in the late 1960s. The sprinters were cast as ghetto militants; men who shared the same ideology as those rioting and raging against the forces of law and order. Their defiance of Olympic protocol was extended as a metaphor for the black underclass' defiance of white authority. Here were two black men in US uniforms betraying their country by disrespecting the flag. Smith and Carlos, however, bowed their heads on the podium. They did so to remember the fallen heroes of the civil rights movement. Theirs was a solemn and non-threatening defiance of injustice. Indeed, almost in contradiction of his fiery words in the post-ceremony press conference, Carlos's arm is bent, his salute less forceful and strident than Smith's.

The negative reaction to their gesture and its association with racial disorder was, and remains, based on a fundamental misinterpretation of the Black Power movement. As Van DeBurg asserts, 'Black Power was not a one-dimensional social movement sponsored by a small but vocal minority of Afro-Americans whose passion was racism and violence' (Van Deburg, 1992: 28). It was in fact an effort to raise black consciousness and facilitate their gaining of influence on the national stage. This is precisely what Smith and Carlos were aiming to do. The fact that their stand was so anathema to the sporting authorities contributed to the portrayal of the protest as a manifestation of the negative interpretation of Black Power. One correspondent to Brundage in the aftermath of the decision to send Smith and Carlos home interpreted that decision as misguided precisely because it would promote the sprinters as black militants. Rather than being seen as silent and peaceful protest, the podium salute would be viewed as a stand by 'Black Power' heroes because of the expulsion of the two men from the Olympic village. This would in turn widen the mistrust and anger of black America against their white countrymen.[8] The fact that the sprinters made their stand on an international stage, not only intensified the negative reaction as the United States' dirty linen was aired in public; it also highlighted the increasing engagement between the civil rights agenda at home and abroad. This was part of a wider process that saw first the Kennedy and then the Johnson administrations focus increasingly on the legitimacy threatening potential of civil rights abuses at home in the Cold War struggle abroad. Reaction from the Mexican hosts quickly adopted a similar perspective.

As Keith Brewster and Claire Brewster (2010) note, Mexican officials, the press, and public opinion swiftly moved from bemusement to a large measure of sympathy and understanding for Smith and Carlos. An article in the Mexico daily, *Excélsior*, argued that the Smith and Carlos represented just one manifestation against the global injustice that had been done to an enslaved people. Furthermore, Brewster and Brewster observe that other Mexicans drew direct links between their own struggle for human rights and those of Carlos and Smith: 'In the words of one Mexican student: "For me, the only thing that made sense in the Olympics was the behaviour of ... Tommie Smith [and] John Carlos. The black champions were using sport as a political arm and made a deep impression on the Mexican spectators; in this way they indirectly helped our Movement"' (K. Brewster and C. Brewster, 2010). Smith and Carlos also received support from athletes competing for Third World and Latin American nations. Their demonstration for racial justice in an international sporting arena reflected a Black Nationalist agenda that sought to make links between the plight of the black man in America and oppressed peoples in Africa and other parts of the Third World. Some civil rights activists advocated redress for the racial injustice in America through the United Nations. Harry Edwards includes a number of letters of support from Third World countries in his account of the black athletic revolt. Following the actions of Smith and Carlos and their suspension from

---

8   ABC: Smith–Carlos dismissal file. Box 179. M. A. Rutter to Brundage, 18 October 1968.

the US team, the Cuban men's 400 m relay team gave its medals to Stokely Carmichael as a representative of black America (Edwards, 1969: 106).

While the Smith and Carlos salute is connected to these different strands of the civil rights struggle in many clear ways, there is a sense in which the symbolism and explanation of their salute revealed a more nuanced development in this struggle. In wearing no shoes on the victory rostrum the two men were highlighting the poverty of black America, while their arms formed an arch of unity for black America. This unity was increasingly illusory, however, as the poverty of some in black America contrasted with the economic progress of a growing middle class. The violence, destruction and looting that was linked to Black Power by the media had poverty as its root cause. Before his death, King was organising a poor people's campaign that called for a fundamental redistribution of American wealth. The civil rights legislation of the 1960s had not solved the problems of the ghetto but it had helped start the growth of an affluent black middle class. By making their stand, Smith and Carlos sacrificed any hope of a lucrative professional sports career; they restricted their opportunity to climb out of the poverty about which they were protesting.

In the aftermath of the Olympics, Smith was denied a chance to pursue a career with the Los Angeles Rams, who had negotiated a possible contract with him before the Games. He played on the Cincinatti Bengals taxi squad before being cut and playing some football in Canada. Carlos too played football in Canada having been unable to make it in the United States. Smith's marriage broke down; he received death threats and was unable to make ends meet before taking a coaching job for which he was over-qualified in Santa Monica. Carlos never completed his college degree and so had no qualifications to fall back on. He had to do odd jobs including working as a bouncer in a bar. His wife committed suicide and Carlos admitted this had a lot to do with the legacy of 1968 (Moore, 1991b: 65–70).

Tarnished by the dominant negative interpretation of their stand in Mexico City, the two men were victims of the endemic racial prejudice of American society. The podium salute reflected a cry on behalf of an impoverished black underclass that was largely untouched by the legislative advances of the civil rights movement. In the decades that have followed, an affluent black middle class has benefited from that legislation, while an underclass has remained. The radical messages of the civil rights struggle have been ignored as a conservative agenda has sought to proclaim the successful emergence of a colour-blind society in which individuals of any race or creed have equality before the law. Since the 1980s, Smith and Carlos have been championed as civil rights heroes, and their stand offered as a touchstone for racial pride. The broader and more complex meanings of their protest have been ignored and they have instead been cited as courageous men who made a stand for equality in sport and wider society. This popular cultural message overlooks the deeper significance of the podium salute. It is worth repeating that Smith and Carlos wore no shoes to highlight black poverty. They stood as symbolic representatives of a diverging civil rights movement that was increasingly focusing on the economic deprivation of African-Americans and demanded true social justice. This aspect of their podium salute has not been acknowledged by popular culture representations. In the time since the Games, the gap between those African-Americans who 'have' and those who 'have not' has grown and widespread poverty remains.

Conclusion

In popular memory this important message and the other ways in which the protest of Smith and Carlos reflected the tangled threads of the civil rights narrative of the late 1960s has been ignored or forgotten. Their stand has been sanitised as a courageous gesture for civil rights that shocked the sports world. It is celebrated and memorialised with a superficial gloss. Robert Lipsyte describes Smith and Carlos on that podium as 'statues in history' (Lipsyte, 2005). In many respects, what they stood for and what their protest symbolised has been set in stone. The podium salute is there to be admired; it changed the Olympic landscape and provides a context for African-American athletes. The image of Smith and Carlos is, therefore, used in much the same way as King's 'I have a dream' speech. King has been placed in the safe category of civil rights hero and great orator. In the process of commemorating his achievements, the more radical elements of his message have been forgotten. King has been portrayed as a 'non-abrasive hero' who can be used as a resource for 'rocking our memories to sleep' (Harding, 1987: 476).

Similarly the symbolism of the salute by Smith and Carlos has been diluted in an attempt to create a usable past. It provides a cultural reference within a popular narrative of the civil rights movement that highlights a number of heroic moments that changed the racial landscape. This simplifies the reality of race relations and narrows the scope of the civil rights struggle (Hartmann, 2003: 267–69). In the short and medium term aftermath of the 1968 Olympics, the sprinters were represented as angry young black men who disrespected the nation that had given them the opportunity to compete and succeed on the world stage. Within twenty years of their stand they were transformed into American heroes whose personal courage drew attention to the struggle for human rights and racial equality. These two extremes ignore a much more nuanced reality.

There is a tendency to see the symbol of the podium salute without exploring the crucial messages inherent in it. It is important to look closely at what Smith's and Carlos's action said about the state of the racial struggle in America in the late 1960s and what this now says about the situation

40 years later. The image of Smith and Carlos was rehabilitated in the lead up to the 1984 Olympics in Los Angeles and in the years thereafter. Both Smith and Carlos were enlisted as consultants by the Los Angeles Organising Committee. In popular culture their stand has increasingly been seen as heroic. Douglas Hartmann states that 'the actual experiences and grievances and radical intent that prompted their demonstration have been neglected or ignored in favour of their individual courage and an abstracted commitment to equality, dignity, and justice' (Hartmann, 2003: 269). This is certainly the case, but what has also been overlooked is how closely their gesture displayed the different elements of the civil rights struggle. Their intent was 'radical' but the nature of this radicalism and its place in the racial struggle have been misinterpreted because of a simplistic, and in some cases fundamentally racially prejudiced, portrayal of Black Power. To unsophisticatedly categorise the podium gesture as a Black Power salute misses a far more nuanced reality. Simple classification of the civil rights movement into non-violent and violent, moderate and radical phases, integrationist and Black Nationalist impulses perverts the complexity of the racial struggle. Smith's and Carlos's podium salute encapsulated that complexity in many different ways.

Amy Bass argues that the stand made by the two sprinters 'had a lasting effect on the negotiations between the athlete and the nation that were still to come' and that the OPHR as a whole 'created what *Life* magazine had eloquently predicted to be "a lasting racial consciousness"' (Bass, 2002: 303). The podium salute did have a crucial impact on the future relationship between athletes and sports administrators. The extent to which their gesture had a lasting impact on racial consciousness is compromised by a one-dimensional portrayal of the meanings inherent in that gesture. If the iconic image of those bowed heads and raised fists is accompanied by the simple title 'Black Power Salute' then the nuanced ways in which the podium protest reflected the civil rights landscape in 1968 will be lost; as will some important racial challenges for the future. Forty years hence it is important that this is not lost. If it is, if the search for meaning is diluted, then the significance of Smith's and Carlos's effort is compromised.

6

Mexico 1968 and South Africa 2010: Sombreros and *Vuvuzelas* and the Legitimisation of Global Sporting Events

CHRIS BOLSMANN

Aston University, UK

I aim to demonstrate in this chapter the utility of comparing Mexico's experience in 1968 with that of South Africa's hosting of the 2010 Fédération Internationale de Football Association (FIFA) World Cup and its precursor, the FIFA Confederations Cup staged in 2009. In large measure, South Africa's preparations for hosting the 2010 World Cup presented similar hurdles to those confronted by Mexico 40 years earlier. What I believe this comparative approach reveals is that the two countries not only shared common experiences as a result of having to stage mega-sports-events, but that their experiences show similarities explicitly because they were viewed as somehow falling short of expectations set by the 'Western world'. Additionally, as we shall see, the rare opportunity afforded the two states in hosting these events fostered a fundamental debate within each country concerning projection of itself and its role in the world.

By analysing the parallels between Mexico and South Africa on a range of issues, both countries are revealed to have experienced similar challenges in legitimising the hosting of a global sporting event for domestic and foreign audiences. This chapter analyses the contexts that lay behind unprecedented decisions by the relevant international governing bodies. The decision by the IOC to award the Olympic Games to Mexico City in 1968 and by FIFA to award the World Cup venue to South Africa in 2010 represented a step into the 'unknown' for their respective governing bodies. Prior to these decisions, hosting the events had followed practices established over time. In 1963, the mainly white, aristocratic individuals who comprised the IOC had never awarded the Games to a 'developing' country. A mixture of altruism and paternalism surrounded its determination to foster popular participation in sport within the Third World, but this had never extended to entrusting the Games to a host from within such regions. The foundation and early development of football established a different, but equally rigid, model. The popularity of football in Western Europe and its early adoption by Latin American states meant that the FIFA World Cup quickly established a pattern of alternating hosts between the two continents. Set within this context, it is easier to understand why, when Mexico City was awarded the 1968 Olympic Games, it caused much more of an international stir than the decision to host the FIFA World Cup in Mexico two years later. Where the South African bid to host the World Cup becomes relevant, however, is that just as the IOC had to create precedent by heading to Mexico, so too, FIFA would have to break a similarly established pattern to award the World Cup to a country on the African continent. In both cases, the awarding of the events inspired a multi-layered discourse in which the host states tried to redefine themselves and their people. In the following analysis I compare the rhetoric surrounding the events. Despite the fact that the IOC and FIFA are different sports organisations and the events are marked by a 40-year difference during which, since the 1980s, the commercialisation of sport has predominated, the comparison is useful.

What becomes apparent from a comparison of the events is the discourse that developed around the need to overcome international and local hurdles. In this respect, common themes across the cases of Mexico and South Africa emerge. First, is an emphasis on the modern characteristics of the respective countries and the developmental benefits that hosting the events would bring. Second, both countries projected themselves as young and stable democracies and leaders of their continents. Third, the respective populations were prepared for the tournaments in terms of potential benefits. Finally, in the case of Mexico 1968 and South Africa 2010, an important emphasis is placed on the legacies that both events would leave.

One might interpret the decisions to host major sports events in Mexico in 1968 and South Africa in 2010 as reflections of modernising processes within the IOC and FIFA respectively that made them more likely to recognise global trends towards greater inclusion. Yet the degree of international concern and criticism that accompanied both decisions suggests something more fundamental; influences that provoked normally conservative bodies into pushing the boundaries of international expectations. An important argument of this chapter picks up on arguments made in Claire Brewster's chapter in this volume: that a range of factors that had little to do with the strength of Mexico City's bid determined that it should host the Games. These factors, she maintains, account for the depth of scepticism about Mexico's preparations and the consequent actions taken by the Mexican Organising Committee to allay such concerns. Much of the rhetoric emanating from the South African organisers bears a remarkable similarity to that offered 40 years earlier by their Mexican counterparts.

Mexico 1968

In order fully to appreciate how Mexico's experience can inform present developments in South Africa, it is useful to summarise conclusions made in Claire Brewster's chapter and identify other areas that bear comparison. The decision to award the 1968 Olympic Games to Mexico City was taken at the IOC meeting at Baden-Baden in 1963. As Brewster explains, the personal and professional connections between Mexican sports officials and the IOC president, Avery Brundage, played a part in swaying votes towards Mexico. Yet such connections had already been established when Mexico City lost bids for the 1956 and 1960 Games, and hence other factors must have been at play. Brewster's reflection on contemporary global events reveals both the strong influence of Cold War politics in the decision and the need not to ignore the rising voice of the Third World. So rather than a ringing endorsement of the winning city's portrayal as a modern, developed metropolis, the vote to give Mexico City the Games can be seen as a necessary expedient. Within such a context, it is little wonder that when the announcement was made, the news provoked an avalanche of dissenting voices.

As Brewster testifies, the international concerns about the decision to award Mexico City the Games were as vociferous as they were diverse. The ways in which the Mexican Organising Committee reacted to such anxieties are revealing: they suggest that members of an elite sector of Mexican society were simultaneously affronted by the slur on their national character and yet deeply worried about the veracity of derogatory stereotypes emanating from the 'developed' world that they aspired to join.

What is clear is that the Mexican Organising Committee wanted to move the agenda onto those topics that might dispel negative national stereotypes and convince international opinion that Mexico City was not only high in altitude, but also in development and culture. The chairman of the Organising Committee, Pedro Ramírez Vázquez, suggested that his team's task was to reconcile 'sovereignty with non intervention', 'nationalism with universality', 'international coexistence with peace', 'economic development with social justice', 'material well-being with education and culture' and 'modernity with tradition' (cited in Rodríguez Kuri, 1998). If it could achieve this task, surely the world would have to reappraise its perceptions of Mexico and its people.

Addressing Latin America's reputation for political instability, the Organising Committee issued press releases emphasising a US-style political constitution that had guaranteed uninterrupted civilian government in Mexico for over three decades. With such stability came economic prosperity and the Organising Committee was keen to link its successful bid to international recognition of the fact that Mexico had enjoyed dynamic economic growth for over two decades. Gross domestic product was growing at an annual rate of 6–7 per cent, and the expansion of social and welfare programmes contributed towards convincing ordinary Mexicans that they were indeed living through what was often referred to as the 'Miracle Years'. In Mexico City itself, citizens could reflect on the recent completion of the national university campus, new housing complexes and the beginnings of a new underground railway network as signs of such investment.

Despite such aspirations, as international doubts over Mexico's rhetoric of modernity and development continued, it appeared to alter the ways in which the nation used the forthcoming Olympics to position itself on the world stage. As Claire Brewster's chapter shows, while still sustaining its rhetoric of suitability for First World admittance, Mexico perceptibly moved onto the safer ground of defender of the weak. To a large extent, its portrayal as a channel for world peace was an easy hit: it fed directly into the apolitical rhetoric of the Olympic charter, but also spoke to Mexico's developing reputation as an honest broker in regional conflicts. With Cold War confrontation affecting all corners of the world, the so-called 'Peaceful Games' were portrayed as an oasis of fraternity and joy. Far from the Latin American stereotype of impulsiveness and irrational violence, the white dove of Peace that adorned all official Olympic literature was a constant reminder of the calm, conciliatory nature of the host's diplomatic stance.

As Brewster also reveals, a measure of protection from the barrage of foreign doubters came from the Organising Committee's emphasis on Mexico's regional importance. As one of Latin America's more significant economic and political powers, the Olympic Games offered a chance for the country to reconfirm its traditional role as a regional leader and voice of Latin America to the outside world. Simultaneously and, for the purpose of this chapter, ironically, its staunch defiance of IOC pressure to allow South Africa's participation in the Games was completely in accord with the nation's broader diplomatic agenda to uphold the interest of the developing world. Allegedly, the Organising Committee's stand in this matter was backed (even provoked) by President Gustavo Díaz Ordaz who, in typically forthright fashion, had made it clear to the Organising Committee 'that those South Africa bastards should not come to the Games' (quoted in K. Brewster and C. Brewster, 2010).

Set within the context of the ongoing racial and social turmoil tormenting its northern neighbour, the organisers of Mexico '68 sought to underline the cultural and ethnic integration within Mexican society that had long been a central theme of government rhetoric. The problem the Organising Committee faced, however, was how best to portray this sense of inclusion and mutual appreciation. As had happened in previous decades of the twentieth century, the image of the indigenous in Mexico was idealised and civilised. A fundamental aspect of Mexico's portrayal of their indigenous past was the resurrected myth of a 'Golden Age'. For a Mexican elite, long brought up on a diet of the Classics, the rather tenuous link between the Ancient Greeks and the Aztecs was too good an opportunity to miss. Poems, odes and newspaper articles made knowing references to how the Hellenic spirits of the past would be rekindled among the temples of the Aztec gods (see examples in newspapers: *Excélsior*, 1966, 1968). As Claire Brewster's chapter illustrates, the concentric lines of the Mexico '68 logo spoke directly to indigenous designs on pre-Hispanic ceramics displayed in the newly opened National Anthropology Museum: the indigenous past was being used to offer a cultured, acceptable visual image of the country. The Olympic Games gave an opportunity to develop a form of tourism that would appreciate Mexican cultural values and lend legitimacy to the elites' aspirations for their country to be seen in terms of modernity and sophistication. This was in great contrast to the image used two years later to celebrate Mexico's hosting of the FIFA World Cup. The diminutive figure with a drooping moustache, cheesy grin, and wide sombrero played into a stereotype that Ramírez Vázquez scorned as being a crude commercial decision made 'by entirely different people for an entirely different audience' (K. Brewster and C. Brewster, 2010).

One of the most interesting aspects of Mexico's preparations were the campaigns of beautification and public education that preceded the arrival of competitors and visitors. Part of the criticism against renovating areas of the capital city and constructing new sporting facilities fed into the more general concern regarding the redirecting of scarce funds away from social and welfare schemes. As one politician stated, '[these actions] are concerned less for the poor conditions in which people live and more by what such a sight says about Mexico to foreign visitors'.[1] Yet a significant alternative strand of criticism, voiced both at the time and afterwards, claimed that the whole nature of the campaign was in danger of removing the essential elements of the Mexican character from the Games and converting Mexico City into the cultural mode of the sophisticated West (K. Brewster and C. Brewster, 2010).

Criticisms of this sort directly addressed the question of national image that was being created by the Organising Committee. The tenor of the debate suggests that there were many in Mexico City who believed that the city authorities and the Organising Committee were being more than a little disingenuous. They were trying to mould their countrymen and their country to suit their own aspirations, rather than having the confidence to reveal Mexicans for what they were. Perhaps the most tangible example of this campaign was, as discussed in Keith Brewster's chapter in this volume,

---

1   Archivo del Congreso Nacional, *Diario de los Debates*, 8 October 1965, pp. 5–6.

the use of humour in the form of Cantinflas to rectify perceived deficiencies in the Mexican character.

Taken together, then, we have a multiple, often contradictory, self-portrayal of Mexico on the world stage. Eager to counter erroneous stereotypes of its country and people, the Organising Committee wanted to emphasise a modern, forward-looking country; a country of the developed world, but also one that sought to retain its leadership role within the region and the developing world; a country that in the midst of global conflict, could offer an oasis of peace.

South Africa 2010

After being expelled from the IOC in 1970 and FIFA in 1976, South Africa was readmitted into the international fold in the early 1990s and South African sporting bodies regained access to international organisations and competitions. South Africa's 2006 World Cup bid was launched at the Confédération Africaine de Football (CAF) congress in Ouagadougou, Burkina Faso in February 1998 (competing bids were launched by Brazil, England, Germany and Morocco). The vote held in July 2000 was controversial, as South Africa narrowly lost the final count by twelve to eleven after Charles Dempsey (president of the Oceania Football Confederation) abstained from voting in the final round. He had been instructed by the Oceania Football Confederation to vote for South Africa if England were eliminated from earlier voting rounds. Had he followed this order, his vote may have meant that FIFA president, Sepp Blatter, would have had to cast the deciding vote and the 2006 tournament could have been awarded to South Africa instead of Germany.

In 2000, FIFA announced the rotation principle for future World Cup tournaments and as a result, an African nation would host the 2010 competition, followed by a South American country in 2014. Egypt, Libya, Morocco, South Africa and Tunisia all put forward bids for the 2010 tournament. FIFA's Inspection Group team ranked South Africa ahead of the other candidates reporting that a South African World Cup would 'generate significant unity amongst ethnic groups [and] the legacy compared to the investment needed will be a great contribution to the country' (FIFA, 2004). In the vote in May 2004, South Africa beat Morocco by fourteen votes to ten. Despite the South African organisers' reference to an African event and the perceived continental benefits, it is alleged that the four CAF members from Botswana, Cameroon, Mali and Tunisia voted for the Moroccan bid (*Sowetan*, 2004).

As a precursor to the 2010 tournament, the FIFA Confederations Cup was staged in South Africa in 2009. FIFA's Confederation Cup had first been contested in 1992 in Saudi Arabia. The tournament, the brainchild of the late Prince Faisal bin Fahd, was named the Intercontinental Championship during the 1992 and 1995 events. The tournament pitted continental champions against each other. In the 1992 competition, four sides competed for honours. FIFA took control of the tournament in 1997 and announced that the competition would be held every two years. South Africa first participated in the 1997 competition. Early winners of the trophy reflected the European and South American dominance of the sport: between 1997 and 2003 the trophy was lifted by Mexico, Brazil and France (twice). In 2005, FIFA effectively tied the competition to the World Cup, announcing that it would be held every four years in the preceding year and in the same location as the forthcoming World Cup finals. The tournament would thus provide the host country with an opportunity to trial run a FIFA competition on a smaller scale over a two-week period. In 2001, the competition was staged in Japan and South Korea and the 2005 competition was in Germany. As South Africa therefore staged the Confederations Cup in 2009, the event is also included in this analysis.

In the 2006 and 2010 bid books, the organising committees of both of South Africa's campaigns emphasised the following broad themes: a Pan-Africanist rhetoric and imagery; a discourse of development and modernity; the country as a young and stable democracy; possessing infrastructural and human capacities; low risk in terms of insurance due to having hosted previous tournaments and a financially secure option; and, finally, as a country with 'world-class' stadiums, with 'excellent' transport, 'advanced accommodation structure', information technology and a 'mature' media (Bolsmann and Brewster, 2009). In Mexico City 40 years earlier, the local organisers had emphasised similar attributes in their justification for hosting the Olympics in their city.

A pan-Africanist appeal is clear in both South Africa's 2006 and 2010 bids in terms of imagery and text. The theme of 'Africa's Call' runs throughout the 2006 submission. In Nelson Mandela's letter in the 2006 bid book, he states 'Africa's time has come'. The 2010 bid book used a fluttering South African flag to box the four parts of the bid. Rather than employing the African motifs of wild animals as was the case in 2006, the 2010 bid book employed images of young attractive people from a cross-section of ethnic groups. Each of the separate bid documents were graced with an attractive young black woman dressed in a football-related motif with a header strap that referred to 'Africa's Stage'. In the 2010 bid book, a letter from Mandela stated that 'this confidence was borne out by the historic decision ... [that] the 2010 World Cup finals would be staged in Africa. By this one gesture, by this unequivocal recognition that Africa has waited long enough to stage the showpiece of football' (SAFA, 2010). The official emblem and poster of the

2010 tournament are distinctly pan-Africanist. The emblem depicts a figure resembling a rock art painting against a brightly coloured African continent and the poster shows a man's head at the top of the African continent heading a ball. Moreover, the catch phrase for the 2010 World Cup is 'ke nako ['it's time' in the Sotho language]. Celebrate Africa's humanity'. In the case of Mexico City, a highly selective and class-ridden portrayal of Mexico's indigenous past was used in the imagery for the Olympics. The reference was to an acceptable form of 'civilisation' while simultaneously projecting an outward appearance of modernity. In the case of South Africa, the organisers have emphasised African heritage and characteristics.

Despite domestic and international criticism of South Africa's ability to host the 2010 event, in the build up to the Confederations Cup, a general mood of optimism and excitement was evident in the press. South African journalist Max du Preez wrote in his newspaper column that the 2010 spectacle:

> could become South Africa's *annus magnificus* [and] I'm excited because of what the event can do to us and for us and our continent. A successful World Cup can give us the one factor we don't nearly have enough of: confidence in our own abilities ... If the 2010 tournament were to go that well, it could go a long way in changing the way the world views Africa ... we will be the colourful, warm, interesting fun place to go. And people will start respecting Africa a little bit more (du Preez, 2009).

In an editorial two days before the opening ceremony of the Confederations Cup, the *Cape Argus* shared this optimism and wrote:

> When South Africa was awarded the rights to host the FIFA World Cup on African soil, many predicted we would not pull it off ... the Confed [*sic*] Cup will offer a taste of what is to come ... it will also test our infrastructure and South Africa's overall readiness to host the world. There is growing reason to believe this will be a well-run, successful and smooth World Cup and that the Afro-pessimists will be silenced. Let's go for it (*Cape Argus*, 2009a).

Similar sentiments were expressed in a rival Cape Town newspaper, the *Cape Times*. It reported that 'the biggest achievement might be a shift in all our minds. Is it too much to hope that a successful hosting of this great event will finally inspire in us a self-belief as South Africans and a common commitment to this country? Stadiums cost money, but this would be priceless' (*Cape Times*, 2009a). The above quotations illustrate the attempts by the local press to hype up the perceived psychological benefits of hosting the tournament in the minds of South Africans. In addition, the portrayal of the event as an African one, in which South African successes will be continental, occurs. Claire

Brewster's chapter in this volume provides evidence of similar rhetoric in the case of Mexico City, where Latin America more broadly would benefit from a successful Olympic Games. Interestingly, though, when making its bid to host the Olympics, the Mexican team had not greatly featured their role as Latin American leaders. This only emerged after the bid was successful.

The opening Confederations Cup match between South Africa and Iraq was staged at the renovated Ellis Park stadium in Johannesburg. In his address to the opening ceremony, Sepp Blatter stated 'we are convinced ... we are committed, FIFA's committed to Africa ... the world of football trusts you and the confidence is in you, is in Africa, in South Africa today'. South African president Jacob Zuma remarked in his speech to the crowd of approximately 50,000 people that 'this is a great day for Africa, for South Africa ... the time has come, today is a day, ke nako'.

As the tournament progressed, a range of issues emerged that were dealt with by the local organisers and FIFA. An immediate concern for the tournament organisers was the significant numbers of empty seats at many of the group matches. The game played in Rustenburg between Spain, the European champions and number-1-ranked side in the world, and New Zealand was poorly attended (21,649 spectators, the lowest of the tournament) with an estimated half of the seats in the Royal Bafokeng Stadium empty. None of the first four matches played were sold out. Stadium attendances averaged 33,170 during these matches as compared to 37,694 in Germany in 2005 (*Mail and Guardian*, 2009). Danny Jordaan, chief executive of the local organising committee had remarked six months earlier that this would be a challenge, especially in games not involving high-profile teams (Gleeson, 2009). Blatter stated: 'we are not happy with the crowd at the opening match ... the local organising committee should have done more to sell tickets and bring people to the stadium' (*Cape Argus*, 2009b). In addition, he remarked: 'there must be action. The African organisers must do it, and they have the ability to do it. They must find people who are young or poor and cannot afford a ticket and bring them' (*Cape Times*, 2009b). The Congress of South African Trade Unions (COSATU) remarked that the low turnouts were 'a serious embarrassment to the country' (*Mail and Guardian*, 2009). Yet significant numbers of corporate seats and boxes were empty at games played at the three rugby stadiums. These would usually be filled with white supporters during rugby matches. FIFA responded by handing out free tickets to a number of group stage matches rather than reducing the price of tickets. This suggests that such a strategy would not have been successful either.

Despite empty seats at the four stadiums used during the tournament, South Africans made up for the relative lack of fans by generating much noise from their *vuvuzelas*: plastic trumpets, a metre in length and used at local football matches, which are inspired by *kudu* horns used to summon villagers to community gatherings. FIFA initially attempted to ban the instruments from stadiums as they were seen as potential weapons and could have been used in ambush marketing where non-official paraphernalia could be visible in the venues. The South African football authorities argued that the *vuvuzela* was part of the South African football experience and FIFA agreed in July 2008 to permit their use in stadiums during the Confederations Cup and World Cup. *Guardian* journalist, David Smith said the *vuvuzela* has 'been likened to a swarm of bees or herds of flatulent elephants' (Wilson, 2009; *News 24*, 2008). Xabi Alonso, the Spanish midfielder remarked, 'those trumpets? That noise I don't like ... FIFA must ban those things ... it is not nice to have a noise like that' (*Cape Argus*, 2009c). Blatter responded that 'that is what African and South African football is all about – noise, excitement, dancing, shouting and enjoyment. This is celebration' (*Cape Argus*, 2009c). In addition, he remarked 'it's a local sound and I don't know how it is possible to stop it. I always said that when we go to South Africa, it's Africa, not Western Europe' (Nail, 2009). Interestingly, these words contain the same mix of self-defence and frustration as those shown by the head of the IOC in 1967 when he defended holding the Games at altitude by arguing that 'the Olympic Games belong to the world – North and South, East and West, hot and cold, dry and humid, high and low' (see Claire Brewster's chapter in this volume). The mass-circulation South African *Daily Sun* retorted 'South Africa is a noisy country' (quoted in Smith, 2009). Jordaan jokingly remarked 'our fans blow their *vuvuzelas* before the match. Maybe because they know that they might not be celebrating afterwards' (quoted in Smith, 2009). Despite the criticisms, the organisers did not ban *vuvuzelas* from the Confederations Cup and World Cup. This instrument has consequently become a poignant symbol of the South African event.

Despite a few highly publicised incidents that included alleged theft from the Brazilian and Egyptian team hotels and transportation problems, FIFA hailed the two week long tournament a success. Jerome Valcke, FIFA's general secretary remarked: 'the world has seen South Africa is able to host a tournament [and] on a scale of one to ten, you are more than a five, and closer to eight' (*Sunday Times*, 2009a). Blatter stated: 'what the world will see in 2010 is a truly successful African World Cup with excitement and tons of energy' (Evans and Mazola, 2009). Jordaan said: 'seeing the incredible progress that has been made is a relief. It gives us a sense of accomplishment, joy, pride and achievement ... it's been easy for people to cast doubt because the event hasn't happened yet. But we as South Africans and Africans are undoubtedly in the process of delivering ... when people questioned us ... and said we would fail, they also questioned Nelson Mandela's legacy' (quoted in Mkhize, Evans, Bradlow and Kamaldien, 2009). The *Cape Times* editorial reported that the 'final was played in Johannesburg, bringing to an end the competition that has confounded the doomsayers and delighted the rest of us ... today South Africans can look forward with optimism to the World Cup ... and the benefits that it will undoubtedly bring. The beneficiaries will be all South Africans – even those who insist that this cup is half empty' (*Cape Times*, 2009c). The BBC's Gabby Logan concluded:

> as usual we have approached the 2010 World Cup with arrogance and ignorance we carry for most sporting events outside Western Europe or the US ... South Africa has to rebut everything from apathy, violence and a potential lack of power ... let's embrace the horns, the sandy pitches, the crowds mingling and occasional power cuts because it's Africa [*sic*], and staging a World Cup there is actually a brilliant idea (Logan, 2009).

South Africa successfully staged the 2009 Confederations Cup as a precursor to the 2010 tournament. What was evident, despite certain organisational problems, is that South Africans brought a distinct flavour and atmosphere to the stadiums as was witnessed in the stands and on the pitch. The South African and foreign press generally reacted positively to the tournament and acknowledged the problems and challenges that face the 2010 event.

Conclusion

The comparison with the 1968 Mexico City Olympic Games offers unique insight into South Africa's preparations for the FIFA 2010 World Cup. Rather than relying on conjecture or speculation, the ways in which the Organising Committee responded to the changing discourse regarding Mexico '68 offers a firm basis for analysing the ongoing process in South Africa. Through comparative analysis the evidence clearly points towards salient themes that link both countries' experiences.

The most common characteristic of preparations is the developmental rhetoric. While all bidding candidates tend to be bullish regarding their own attributes, more than with many other hosts of mega-sports-events Mexico and South Africa needed constantly to provide reassurances of their financial stability and organisational ability in the face of unrelenting foreign criticism. In this respect, the hosts were viewing their winning of the bid from different perspectives. Mexico saw the awarding of the 1968 Games as international recognition for two decades of unprecedented political and economic stability that had allowed them a point of entry into First World status. The Games were confirmation of Mexico's economic and political development. In the case of South Africa, the bid made great play of the competitive edge that its economic and political stability gave it over other bidders, yet greater emphasis was placed upon how the World Cup would act as a catalyst for future growth and development. The one country reflected back at its achievements; the other towards its bright future: both viewed their relatively advanced stages of development as right of passage towards hosting mega-sports-events.

The second salient feature of the hosts' international rhetoric was the extent to which they pushed their position as continental leaders. That a successful bid would mean bringing these mega-sports-events to a new continent played heavily within the bids of Mexico City and South Africa. Particularly in the case of South Africa, the notion that it was 'Africa's turn', and 'Africa's stage' to host the FIFA World Cup converged with a broader message of South Africa being the gateway to the African continent. No doubt in both Mexico in the 1960s and South Africa in the 2000s, this portrayal as a continental leader gained considerable legitimacy because of their economic and political strengths when compared to their neighbours. Yet as the preparations unfolded, the symbolism that wove through the rhetoric took on greater poignancy. In the case of Mexico, its self-adopted role as defender of the Third World saw its increasing portrayal as the conduit through which Latin Americans might disprove all the negative stereotypes that had been drawn against them: prejudices that were maligning its own efforts to convince the world of its ability to put on a great spectacle. So behind the bullish rhetoric of development and regional importance, Mexico's stance may have represented a degree of retreat from attempting to hold its own with countries of the developed world. South Africa, on the other hand, appears to be sustaining this rhetoric from a position of self-confidence and through the successful staging of the Confederations Cup. The 'why not?' attitude that sustained the bid and subsequent preparation may well have sprung from the fact that, given that FIFA had committed 2010 to the African continent, it was indeed the strongest, perhaps the only, viable option. The degree, then, to which South Africa emphasises its continental leadership role, may reveal a greater degree of magnanimity towards its neighbours than Mexico, where similar rhetoric obscured a search for reassurance about its place on the international stage.

A third feature, particularly in the case of Mexico and possibly in South Africa, is the need to focus more than usual on the preparation of the respective populations for the influx of visitors. Improvements to the physical landscape are not unique to Third World hosts, although the extent to which this needs to be done would understandably be more in such countries. It is true that, at certain times, the organisers of both events displayed a degree of confidence in suggesting that their preparations would be limited to those that their limited economic circumstances could reasonably expect to achieve. At the same time, however, the Mexican programme of public education showed a distinct class tension: that 'ordinary' Mexicans might shatter the veneer of sophistication and development and become an embarrassing confirmation of the country's Third World status. Most significantly, in the context of South Africa's hosting of the World Cup, this process in Mexico only really began to reveal itself in the final stages, when the generic rhetoric of communal responsibility began to focus more sharply on those social ills perceived as being associated with the Third World. The distinctly South African atmosphere evident in the stadiums during the Confederations Cup is a precursor to how the World Cup will be supported and celebrated in 2010. If one is searching for indications of how public discourse might develop in South Africa in the months leading up to the World Cup, Mexico's experiences of public instruction might point the way. The vital difference between the two processes might be the degree to which race combines with class to fuel such fears.

Finally, an important corollary to the developmental rhetoric of each country's bid was the absolute imperative to guarantee a demonstrable legacy. Regarding the material legacy, the suspicion that scarce resources were being moved away from welfare towards sports construction meant that neither country could pay mere lip service to this aspect of their bid. Mexico '68 may well have proved to be one of the most successful in terms of legacy, long before the term became common currency. Although many of the Olympic sites across the city now appear dilapidated, this is a result of overuse rather than being abandoned. Generations of the capital's youths have benefited from the decision to locate the sports facilities within existing densely populated areas. In the South African case, local organisers are faced with escalating costs and growing speculation on the capacity of the country to stage the finals. Ten stadiums will play host to the tournament. Five world-class stadiums are being built and three rugby and two football stadiums are being upgraded. These stadiums and training facilities will leave a material legacy as in the case of Mexico. A range of infrastructural developments, from transportation to accommodation, are also being undertaken.

The aspect of legacy concerning whether the mega-events achieved the objectives of the organisers in projecting a positive image of their country is less certain and more arbitrary. In the case of Mexico, the relative success of the Olympic Games did do much to confirm the nation's capacity to stage mega-sports-events. Indeed, the success of Mexico '68 provided the Mexican nation with more confidence that it could stage a successful World Cup only two years later, and again, at very short notice, in 1986. Yet the lasting reputation of Mexico '68 will be marred by something beyond the control of those organising the Games: the massacre of protesting students days before the Opening Ceremony. This one event managed to undo much of the good work that Mexico had achieved in convincing the world that it did not conform to the Latin American stereotype of military repression and human rights abuses. South Africa has a tradition of successfully hosting mega-events including the FIFA Confederations Cup, and the World Cup in 2010 has the potential to add to this legacy. The psychological benefits of the successful Confederations Cup are evident as reported in the press and from the assessments of the local organisers and FIFA. However, the finals will be the largest mega-event ever undertaken in South Africa, and the material and in particular intangible legacies are uncertain.

The parallels between Mexico 1968 and South Africa 2010 are striking particularly in the manner in which the local organisers have had to legitimate the hosting of the events in their respective countries. The social and political contexts and timeframes are different, but the underlying assumptions and prejudices that question the ability of the host nation to successfully stage a mega-sports-event are the same. 'Mexico '68' offers a chance to observe a nation that not only wanted to project a specific image to an international audience, but that conducted very real debates concerning what such an image should show, how it should be presented and who had the right to decide such matters. Some of these debates concern South Africans as they prepare for the 2010 World Cup.

7

Luis González de Alba's *Los días y los años* (1971) and Elena Poniatowska's *La noche de Tlatelolco* (1971): Foundational Representations of Mexico '68[1]

CHRIS HARRIS

University of Liverpool, UK

In Memory of John Corf (21 July 1958 to 21 January 2008)[2]

> The official version of events was crystal clear and beyond question: the entire conflict was caused by the Communists and other professional agitators who had initiated yet another campaign to tarnish Mexico's image. (González de Alba, 1997a: 29)

> A society is democratic to the extent that its citizens play a meaningful role in managing public affairs. If their thought is controlled, or their options are narrowly restricted, then evidently they are not playing a meaningful role: only their controllers, and those they serve, are

1   The author would like to record his sincere gratitude to Claire and Keith Brewster for organising such a successful conference at Newcastle University on the fortieth anniversary of 'Mexico 1968' and for the invitation as a speaker. The author would also like to thank Professor Rosenhaft (University of Liverpool) for reading a final draft of this article and for suggesting a number of significant changes. In addition, thanks go to Professor Charles Forsdick and Dr Kate Marsh, colleagues at Liverpool, for their comments on the sources, uses and limits of Saidian counterpoint.
2   John Corf's connection with this article is in one sense purely coincidental. He and I discussed aspects of 'my work' during a holiday together in Fuerteventura in January 2008. The topic of Mexico '68 engaged him. Nobody knew then that he was so close to being tragically taken away by an unsuspected thrombosis in the mesenteric artery. In another sense his connection is fundamental; if the life-affirming values he lived by consistently were all the more prevalent globally, the need to research the cultural memory of trauma would be all the more diminished. I dedicate this work to John: husband, father, son, brother, grandfather, uncle, friend – and in every capacity loving and generous.

doing so. The rest is sham, formal motions without meaning. (Chomsky, 1992: 6)[3]

Relax, don't cry, said a comrade in a hushed tone, this a not a time for crying; it's a time for capturing every detail so all can be recalled when those who will have to pay are called to account. (González de Alba, 1997a: 191)

Introduction

The principal and rather modest aim of this chapter is simply to re-read *contrapuntally*, and comparatively, two key representations of the 1968 state – student conflict in Mexico that appeared in print during the presidency of Luis Echeverría (1970–1976): Luis González de Alba's *Los días y los años* and Elena Poniatowska's *La noche de Tlatelolco*. Both of these narrative accounts were first published in 1971.[4] Poniatowska's (1975) text was translated as *Massacre in Mexico* and is, of course, known by all who have ever taken an interest, academic or otherwise, in this episode of Mexican political history. It combines photographic images, authorial essay, and excerpts from state and student documentation as well as editorialised testimonies collected and recorded by Poniatowska herself in the wake of the massacre at Tlatelolco – including testimony from González de Alba. In terms of readership and circulation, *La noche de Tlatelolco* is arguably perceived as *the* defining account of the Mexican student experience in 1968. By contrast, González de Alba's hybrid text, part prison memoir and part documentary novel, has not yet been translated into English. The title literally means 'The Days and the Years' and carries with it a sense of 'As Time Goes By'.[5] It articulates the author's experience of the conflict from his first involvement in July through to the time it was written whilst he was being held as a

---

3   Despite Mexico's perceived differences from other countries in Latin America during the 1960s, that is, despite the country's alleged democratic status in relation to the authoritarianism of countries such as Brazil and Argentina, the events of Tlatelolco revealed that the semblance of democracy in Díaz Ordaz's Mexico was exactly that: a 'sham'.

4   All quotations and references provided are to subsequent editions of these texts. Full details for the editions cited (González de Alba, 1997a; Poniatowska, 1998) are provided in the 'References' section at the end of the volume. Given the arguments advanced, there is a self-consciously elaborated emphasis on González de Alba's text and so a deliberate imbalance in citation. In addition, but beyond the limits of the present article, Monsiváis (1970) requires a similar elevation of status as a foundational representation of Mexico '68.

5   All translations into English used in this article, from this and other texts produced in Spanish, are the author's own.

political prisoner at Lecumberri. In comparison with Poniatowska's work, *Los días y los años* has rarely gained anything like the same level of popular and intellectual recognition.

Contrapuntal analysis is the chosen methodological approach in this article (drawing on one of Edward Said's contributions to postcolonial theory and practice, which in turn draws on the work of Cuban anthropologist Fernando Ortiz) because it is beyond doubt that both of the primary texts were consciously designed to function *contrapuntally*.[6] Overall, the contrapuntal function of these texts ensures that as readers we experience the constant dismantling or deconstruction of the official version of history just as swiftly as it appears in our minds through the contextualised citations of military officers, government officials, state documents and extracts from the work of partisan, or co-opted, journalists. In other words, both texts display a 'simultaneous awareness' of the official version of history and of those 'other histories against which (and together with which) the dominant discourse acts' (Said, 1994: 59). They combine, in brief, the perspectives not of coloniser and colonised, but certainly of the authoritarian state and dissident groups within Mexican civil society. In this sense, a contrapuntal reading is a logical choice to make. Even though the objects of analysis are not representations of colonial relations of domination and subordination, the texts do engage with a situation of conflict born of analogous inequalities of power with an entirely relevant emphasis on contrasting subjectivities and identities, as well as vastly differing interpretations of historical events in a context of tense social relations.[7] On the question of a comparative reading as a supplementary

---

6   There is no fully elaborated model of this methodology in Said's writing, and it is significant to note that Charles Forsdick (1999) was already considering the limits of counterpoint ten years ago. This debate should be renewed. For the purposes of the present study, while there is potentially an over-simplification in any deconstructive or comparative analysis that rests unquestioningly on a series of obvious binaries, especially without considering their interaction and the inevitable contradictions and aporia that arise, this methodology still works exceptionally well for these texts. Both of them were published before the rise of theory in the 1970s and 1980s, and both are indisputably shaped and structured by the authoritarian politics of the time and so by the marked division between state and dissident perspectives. However, González de Alba's and Poniatowska's texts do not generate aporia, strictly speaking; they generate contradictions that were designed in 1971 to promote the reader's sense of mistrust, even disbelief, in the face of pronouncements by the country's leaders on the events at Tlatelolco.

7   Bart Moore-Gilbert's assertion that 'postcolonial criticism' can be understood 'as preoccupied principally with the analysis of cultural forms which mediate, challenge or reflect upon relations of domination and subordination' is entirely apt (Moore-Gilbert, 1997: 12). Equally relevant is the influence of Gramsci on colonial discourse analysis and the potentiality here for identifying not the students, but Mexico's workers as subaltern subjects whose voices on the subject of 1968 have often been

methodological move, the choice of primary texts deliberately re-opens a debate about their relative value as sources for understanding the rise and fall of the Mexican Student Movement from the perspective of the students themselves; a debate that once brought the authors into a bitter dispute that was made public through the pages of *Nexos* in 1997.[8]

One broad aim of this contrapuntal and comparative re-reading is to identify and explicate the principal ways in which the student experience of conflict in Mexico in 1968 is characterised by González de Alba and Poniatowska, highlighting both similarity and difference, and granting *Los días y los años* an equal status as a key representation that it is rarely afforded. In pursuit of that aim, the more specific objectives are to argue: (i) that *both* of these texts articulate foundational representations of the particularities of the Mexican student experience in the sense that they evidently prefigure, and in different ways directly influence, the now dominant narrative of Mexico '68 that is circulating in Mexican society as well as in academia in this first decade of the twenty-first century (i.e. they have both had a profound impact on cultural memory); (ii) that González de Alba's text is an equally valuable source for understanding the Mexican student experience because, despite the striking similarities with Poniatowska's account in the refusal to represent the students as revolutionaries, it also provides a markedly different form of representation by concentrating far more on what it was that inspired the students to protest in the first place, and on the factionalism that emerged, rather than on what it was they wanted to achieve and what happened to them in the pursuit of their six demands; (iii) that in both texts the distance, rather than synergies, between students and workers is obscured far more than it is explicated even though it was a distinctive feature of the Mexican state – student conflict.

Forty Years Later: The Dominant Narrative of Mexico '68

In order to facilitate the argument that both *La noche de Tlatelolco* and *Los días y los años* are foundational representations that have shaped today's dominant narrative of the Mexican student experience in 1968, this first section serves to sketch the broadest contours of that narrative as a reference point for what follows. The starting point is the now standard characterisation of the Mexican Student Movement as politically moderate, *reformist* in its ambitions.

---

marginalised or silenced, even in these two 'popular' accounts by González de Alba and Poniatowska.

8   In particular, see: González de Alba (1997b). He accused Poniatowska of producing a text that contained factual errors. As a response, Poniatowska published a 'corrected' version of her text in 1998.

In 1968, according to those historians who have shaped today's dominant narrative, Mexico's students were only indirectly struggling to transform conditions of poverty and exploitation; only indirectly concerned with regime change; at no point did they constitute a unified movement self-consciously aspiring to revolutionise the country's socio-economic structure or to oust the president and the Partido Revolucionario Institucional (PRI) from their positions of dominance. In *Refried Elvis: The Rise of the Mexican Counterculture*, for instance, Eric Zolov writes:

> Formalized in the CNH [Comite Nacional de Huelga/Student Strike Committee], the student movement actually pushed for limited, *reformist* goals. Unlike student movements in the United States or France, for instance, the Mexican movement did not advocate a distinctively radical social or political agenda. Rather, student demands and discourse were carefully structured in terms of respect for the 1917 Constitution, which contained guarantees of free speech, democratic process and economic redistribution. (Zolov, 1999: 120–21; my emphasis)

With a similar emphasis on reformism, in *Mexico under Siege: Popular Resistance to Presidential Despotism*, Hodges and Gandy make the following claim:

> The student movement focused not on the antithesis of bourgeois and proletarians, exploiters and exploited, but *on the opposition of power and powerlessness, authority and freedom.* Although a minority of student revolutionaries made common cause with organized labour against the veiled exploitation in nationalized enterprises besides that in the private sector, the two struggles should not be confused – nor the two modes of popular resistance. (Hodges and Gandy, 2002: 103; my emphasis)

And with eloquent concision, Brian Hamnett has also expressed a very similar view. He claims that although subversive dissidence (supported by non-Mexican Communists) was indeed the singular political identity the Díaz Ordaz regime attempted to create for the students, the state's arguments were never and have never been convincing:

> The government saw this growing movement as a revolutionary conspiracy designed to bring down the existing political order. Naïve appeal by student protestors to far-left heroes of the late 1960s such as Che Guevara, inadvertently gave credence to such a view. Given the Mexican context, and above all the social composition of the movement, demand for civil liberties rather than attempted revolution provided the explanation for the scale of protest. (Hamnett, 1999: 270)

Stated succinctly, then, those writers and academics who have constructed the twenty-first-century's dominant narrative collectively maintain that the Mexican Student Movement was primarily aimed at tempering the political power of the PRI – it was an attempt to persuade Díaz Ordaz to grant specific concessions and thereby to demonstrate the efficacy of popular protest in securing civil liberties.

In relation to this particular understanding of the Student Movement's *reformist* politics in 1968, it follows logically that the Tlatelolco massacre marked an immediate defeat for the students and their sympathisers because none of their six demands had been met. However, over the last decade, as a second feature of today's dominant narrative, the students' immediate defeat has consistently been reframed as a longer-term victory on the grounds that Tlatelolco and its aftermath marked the beginning of the end for the PRI's dominance in an era of presidential despotism. For example, with a characteristic use of wordplay, Carlos Fuentes has suggested that the events of Summer '68 in Mexico City can and should in retrospect be seen as a 'pyrrhic defeat' (Fuentes, 2005: 11). And to emphasise his point, Fuentes proceeds to ask a revealing rhetorical question of the Mexican experience in the year 2000: 'Could Mexico have undergone a transition from an authoritarian, single-party political system to a pluralist democratic system without the terrible sacrifice of Tlatelolco?' (Fuentes, 2005: 20). In this respect, Fuentes echoes Hamnett, who states that: 'The moral and political catastrophe of 1968 began the long and painful decline of the PRI' – a decline that ended with Vicente Fox's victory in presidential elections on behalf the Partido de Acción Nacional (PAN) in 2000 (Hamnett, 1999: 272). This positive vision of the Mexican Student Movement and its role in the longer-term transformations of the Mexican national political system is also where the brief but insightful analysis from Hodges and Gandy leads. In their words:

> The student insurgency was bound to end in utopia. But the heroes and martyrs of the 1968 struggle wrote another chapter in the history of the popular resistance that was *not* utopian. The students ripped away the revolutionary mask of the PRI government and revealed the truth to the nation. The truth would feed and strengthen the popular resistance in years to come ... The limited amnesty and the political opening for the left-wing parties during the 1970s owed much to the popular student movement of 1968. The democratic opening of the year 2000 owes even more. (Hodges and Gandy, 2002: 105)

By implication, then, the forever shocking act of mass murder in the Plaza de las Tres Culturas at Tlatelolco was not symptomatic of a crisis *already* affecting the PRI and the ruling classes; rather, the massacre produced *for the first time* a substantial crack in the foundations of the *priista* edifice that brought the party and the social order into crisis in the first place.[9]

It follows from this last point that the Tlatelolco massacre is invariably perceived as an event that represents a watershed in Mexican political history. As Scherer García and Monsiváis claimed when they placed General García Barragán's documents in the public domain, the violence at Tlatelolco made Mexico a different country:

> From that day forth Mexico was an 'other' country. Other, because the roads to freedom were closed; other, because a political system that still asphyxiates us was perpetuated; other, because society was wounded, lacerated, by the assassination of its youth; other, because we could never know the truth, the origin of the government's decisions, and we had to be satisfied with vain declarations which, while we were crying for our dead, spoke of safeguarding national institutions. (Scherer García and Monsiváis, 1999: 13)

Yet these slightly negative words were written ten years ago, before the fall of the PRI, and therefore in a context that was still too close to the events themselves for *Los días y los años* and *La noche de Tlatelolco* to be seen as foundational representations. From the perspective of the present, their status in the textualised history and cultural memory of Mexico '68 must be seen in this way.

Foundational Representations of Mexico '68

In *Los días y los años* and *La noche de Tlatelolco* both González de Alba and Poniatowska map out certain broader social and historical dimensions of the state – student conflict. González de Alba's account, for example – in line with insightful and subsequent historical narratives such as Raúl Álvarez Garín's (1998) study and Sergio Aguayo's analysis published in the same year – sets the history of the Mexican Student Movement in a context of popular resistance, referring to a range of precedents including not just strike action by railway workers, but also by doctors and earlier generations of students, as well as the assassination of peasant leaders such as Rubén Jaramillo and the revolutionary legacy of Zapata and Villa (González de Alba, 1997a: 59–60). There is also discussion of the student movement in France (González de

---

9   The term 'genocide' can legitimately be applied to the killings following a 2007 court ruling in Mexico on the grounds that: 'government authorities at the time jointly conducted a prearranged and coordinated action aimed at exterminating a national group of students from various universities'. See *Los Angeles Times* (2007).

Alba, 1997a: 37). Poniatowska's text also alludes to this context of popular resistance and extends it by adding a gender dimension for consideration and analysis. Essentially, her deliberate insistence on highlighting the experience of women and especially the experience of mothers serves to *gender* overtly the historical narrative produced by her eclectic montage of materials.

In these broad contexts of class and gender, *Los días y los años* and *La noche de Tlatelolco* both provide ample testimony of the resilient commitment of Mexico's student protestors not to revolutionary radicalism but to specific forms of legal and institutional *reform*, to 'exigencias puramente reformistas', 'entirely reformist demands' (González de Alba, 1997a: 37). Throughout both texts there are repeated references to the Student Strike Committee's persistent calls for the Díaz Ordaz regime to meet six demands as a potential contribution to transforming conditions of political marginalisation in Mexico. Significantly, subsequent historical accounts have retained that same emphasis on the reformist orientation of the Mexican Student Movement and on the 'pliego petitorio' or list of six demands: (i) freedom for political prisoners; (ii) dismissal of the police chiefs (Generals Luis Cueto Ramírez and Raul Mendiolea Cerecero, Chief and Assistant Chief of Mexico City's police force respectively, plus Lieutenant Colonel Armando Frías, Commander of the *granaderos*/riot police); (iii) abolition of the *granaderos*; (iv) abrogation of the crime of social dissolution[10] (v) compensation for the families of the dead and wounded; (vi) determination of responsibility for the repression (See: Hodges and Gandy, 2002: 96). In tandem with this overt emphasis on reformism, Poniatowska and González de Alba also emphasise the fact that only a small minority of (Communist) student protestors were motivated by a desire to see Díaz Ordaz and the PRI forced out of power, and that even they were conscious that a prolonged campaign of non-violent resistance could not envisage regime change as anything other than a utopian dream. Echoing this, Zolov remarks that the Student Movement attempted to distance itself from those who were inspired by the Cuban Revolution and cohered as a 'radical wing of student activism advocating a guerrilla strategy of revolutionary insurrection' (Zolov, 1999: 119). Simply put, and in complete accord with today's dominant narrative of the Mexican Student Movement, the evidence found in the two accounts of Mexico '68 under consideration strongly suggests that a revolutionary desire for regime change, resistance to capitalist exploitation and a passionate commitment to

---

10   Zolov explains that this clause 'dated back to World War II efforts to fight internal subversion instigated by the Axis powers. The article provided harsh penalties against those who "in word, writing, or by whatever other means propagate ideas, programs, or conduct that tend to produce rebellion sedition, riots, disorders, and the obstruction of the functioning of legal institutions"' (Zolov, 1999: 122).

transforming conditions of poverty in Mexican society were never high on the agenda of the Student Strike Committee.

The Principle of Peaceful Protest

In order to add a degree of detail and illustration to the argument that the two primary texts considered here are both foundational representations, especially of the reformist nature of the Mexican Student Movement, we can usefully ask, according to these accounts, how the protestors attempted to challenge state authoritarianism and contribute to the democratic transformation of conditions of political marginalisation? As a first response to that question, in both representations the students are shown to have consistently conducted a campaign of non-violent resistance and so defended a constitutional right of all Mexican citizens to protest peacefully against their government. More recent accounts written by survivors are in complete accord. Raúl Álvarez Garín writes: 'All of the events organised by the Student Strike Committee were peaceful, conducted in an atmosphere of exemplary responsibility and order, such was the profound and absolute belief in the justness of the struggle' (Álvarez Garín, 1998: 89). At the same time, and in a perfect illustration of the contrapuntal function of these texts, both representations set images of peaceful protest in opposition to the state's idea of the student protestors as armed agitators trying to overthrow a democratically elected government. The desired impact on cultural memory is in this sense entirely transparent. What both writers manifestly wanted their readers to 'remember' in 1971 was the exceptional success the students had experienced in organising large-scale non-violent protests that contained elements of thoroughly enjoyable spontaneous creativity.

González de Alba and Poniatowska both narrate at length the student experience of participating in protest marches in support of the six demands. They document the fact that attendance at those marches – approximate figures are given as exact figures remain contested – grew and then declined as follows: the initial 1 August march headed by Javier Barros Sierra, the Rector of Universidad Nacional Autónoma de México (UNAM), attracted some 50,000; the first march to the capital's main square or Zócalo on 13 August saw a significant rise to 200,000 with chants of 'sal al balcón hocicón' ('come onto the balcony, pig-nose'), attacking and insulting Díaz Ordaz directly; and the Movement appears to have peaked on 27 August when 400,000 marched to the Zócalo and were greeted by the peal of the cathedral bells and chants of 'el pueblo al poder!' ('power to the people!') (González de Alba, 1997a: 61, 98). González de Alba records not only that according to the Student Strike Committee some 300,000 attended the Silent March on 13 September, but also that the subsequent militarisation of the State's response with the occupation of UNAM campus and the Instituto Politécnico Nacional (IPN) facilities in the Casco de Santo Tomás, as well as the leafleting of parents as a scaremongering tactic, meant that just 10,000 or less attended Tlatelolco on 2 October – some of whom were curious local residents and foreign journalists. They had not been involved in the earlier marches and there was no march planned this time. It had already been cancelled because of the threats of military action (González de Alba, 1997a: 120, 181).

For González de Alba, the cheerful creativity involved in student protests and activism included the staging of the Silent March itself. He recalls that, in part, the highly theatrical Silent March was a deliberate show of self-discipline following ill-disciplined incidents of earlier days: in the Zócalo on 13 August there had been attempts to break into the National Palace; and then, again in the Zócalo on 27 August, at the moment when the Mexican flag was replaced with a black and red strike flag, a soldier on the roof of the National Palace was spotlighted as the crowd chanted 'asesino, asesino' ('murderer, murderer') (González de Alba, 1997a: 99). Yet González de Alba also explains that good-humoured creativity in the context of peaceful protest had preceded the Silent March too: in part during a first meeting at Tlatelolco on 7 September when pro-student slogans were painted on blankets draped over stray dogs; in part through the use of hydrogen-filled balloons to distribute leaflets simply by rising high and eventually bursting or descending (González de Alba, 1997a: 117). In addition, and throughout the conflict, of course, as Poniatowska reveals, small student brigades held lightning meetings to inform the public of their demands and to collect money to pay for printing costs: 'They put me in charge of the "Che Guevara" brigade: a really great brigade with ten men and six women. We painted graffiti, held lightning meetings and collected money on buses, in the streets and in markets' (Antonio Careaga García quoted in Poniatowska, 1998: 31).

In connection with the formation of a dominant narrative, with the process of shaping cultural memory, if González de Alba and Poniatowska both wanted their readers to establish images of peaceful and creative protest, it is possible that they also both consciously wanted certain other features of the student experience to slip into oblivion. In other words, it is important to note that processes of forgetting might also be facilitated by these two foundational representations. González de Alba's account does not reveal, for example, that he went to Tlatelolco armed and tried to rid himself of a pistol as quickly as possible (Aguayo Quezada, 1998: 226). By contrast, Poniatowska's account does recognise that some protestors were armed, and suggests, emphatically, that the number and nature of the arms found and documented was insignificant in the context of an alleged attempt to overthrow the Díaz Ordaz regime (Poniatowska, 1998: 214–215). In other words, Poniatowska's text voices an emphatic claim that a handful of pistols could never have been an armament designed to underpin an attempted *coup d'etat*. Aguayo Quezada's subsequent historical narrative goes further still in this direction by accepting that some students fired at the security services. In addition to declarations made by student survivors, the FBI and foreign journalists, Aguayo Quezada states: 'For my part, as author of this study I identified other students and residents of Tlatelolco who fired shots that evening, though they prefer to remain anonymous. In each instance, they claim to have fired with pistols of a low calibre' (Aguayo Quezada, 1998: 226–227) Nevertheless, what Aguayo Quezada also shows is that there is no longer any doubt about the identity of the snipers who opened fire on soldiers and so initiated the massacre: the snipers were 'a group of paramilitaries organised by the State Department for Mexico City'.[11] The consensus here, in brief, is that the use of weapons by students, albeit in acts of self defence, never served to further their demands and did not characterise their campaign.

The Principle of Public Negotiation

With the right to peaceful protest highlighted, a second challenge to state authoritarianism and a second contribution to the democratic transformation of conditions of political marginalisation that González de Alba and Poniatowska both illustrate in their testimonial accounts concerns political talks. What they show is that Mexico's students insisted without wavering on the principle of high-level talks as a way to proceed and so struggled to lever the principle of democratic negotiation into the national political culture if only as a goal to be achieved (and that in doing so they also inevitably insisted on presidential and government accountability and responsiveness to the public). In relation to this call for political talks González de Alba points out that there was in fact already a tradition of negotiation in Mexico, but adds that political talks tended to be behind closed doors – 'pláticas de recámara' as he calls them – and often with co-opted representatives of popular sectors: the most obvious example being the corrupt trade unionist Fidel Velázquez (González de Alba, 1997a: 60, 85, 89). Consequently, González de Alba describes this established process of negotiation as the tradition of

---

11 Poniatowska reproduces testimonial evidence to the same effect, such as the statement made by anthropologist Mercedes Olivera de Vázquez: 'The so-called sharpshooters – and I tell you this because those of us who were there and who saw it can state this without fear of equivocation, the sharpshooters were members of the government security forces' (Poniatowska, 1998: 183).

the 'Mexican monologue', of the State talking to the State (González de Alba, 1997a: 81). He further explains that the students tried to prevent this authoritarian model from being implemented anew by ruling out any possibility of channelling talks through the PRI-controlled student body, the Federación Nacional de Estudiantes Técnicos (FNET), and by ensuring as far as their own democratic principles allowed that none of the co-opted students in the Student Movement possessed sufficient popularity to be elected as a delegate for high level negotiations (González de Alba, 1997a: 22, 26, 81).

In terms of actual events, as *Los días y los años* reveals, the Díaz Ordaz regime, or more precisely the Home Office minister and future president Luis Echeverría, embraced at first the idea of talks as a route to resolving the conflict. González de Alba states that on 22 August, Echeverría made this public statement:

> The Mexican Government is well disposed to receive representatives of teachers and students from the UNAM, the IPN and other educational centres concerned with the present problem in order to exchange views with them and learn at first hand of the demands they are making and the proposals they are putting forward, with a view to bringing to a definitive end the conflict that our capital city has witnessed in recent weeks and that has affected, in truth, and to a greater or lesser extent, all of its inhabitants. (Quoted by González de Alba, 1997a: 82)

In fact, González de Alba maintains that the initial signs were so positive that there was reason to hope that concessions and a victory of sorts were distinct possibilities. The Mexican Student Movement was, he claims, 'never any closer to winning a victory than during those five days from 22 to 27 August' (González de Alba, 1997a: 90). In support of this claim, he explains that the students were given a phone number to enable them to establish contact with government representatives and that the next day, 23 August, the Student Movement elected four representatives, two from the UNAM (Gilberto Guevara and Marcelino Perelló) and two from the IPN (Raúl Álvarez Garín and Socrates Amado) as delegates for talks (González de Alba, 1997a: 87–88).

According to *Los días y los años*, this brief period of hope rapidly disappeared. By 26 August there had been no official response to a call for the regime to say where and when talks would take place. The fact that the students had added a precondition, that political talks would have to be conducted *in public*, had apparently created a permanent stumbling block: 'the government expected us to compromise on an issue that for us was essential: the talks had to be public' (González de Alba, 1997a: 90). González de Alba's account records that in the absence of an agreement with Díaz Ordaz's regime on talks, on 27 August, following the march to the Zócalo, Socrates Amado called from the microphone to the students to ask them where they wanted public talks with the government to take place and they chanted 'Zócalo, Zócalo' (González de Alba, 1997a: 99). Consequently, an impromptu decision was made, without consultation through the usual democratic channels of the Student Strike Committee, to the effect that public talks would be with the President in person in the main square on 1 September after his State of the Nation address. González de Alba notes at this juncture in the narrative, that 5,000 students remained in wait in the central plaza. He asserts that this was undoubtedly a strategic error, citing as incontestable evidence the fact that overnight tanks emerged from the National Palace and the waiting students were forcibly removed (González de Alba, 1997a: 99–100).

Nevertheless, the students did not give up on the possibility of a negotiated settlement involving compromise on both sides and González de Alba describes the 'talks' that did occur on the morning of the Tlatelolco massacre. Three students, of whom he was one together with Gilberto Guevara and another student named only as Múñoz, met with two representatives of the Díaz Ordaz regime: Jorge de la Vega and Andrés Caso. The meeting took place at the home Barros Sierra, but did not last long. De la Vega insisted that the students would have to give up their hopes for public talks: 'He said that the government was in total disagreement and would never go to a "Roman circus" like the students were requesting' (González de Alba, 1997a: 176).[12] Unable to agree, the group decided they would meet again the next day. Tragically, however, the next day brought the blood-red dawn of Tlatelolco, and the proposed talks were no longer relevant.

In spite of González de Alba's ephemeral optimism about the outcomes of political talks, the representations of 1968 articulated in *Los días y los años* and *La noche de Tlatelolco* strongly suggest that the idea of specific presidential concessions in response to the six demands was almost always an unlikely outcome because the mechanisms of state power were far too effective. To cite one specific example, any approach to understanding 1968 through the accounts provided by these two texts makes it evident that even at a relatively low level of social control, the PRI could easily influence the media, or at least the nature of dominant media representations. Consequently, the Mexican state was always in a position to disseminate its misleading vision of the students as subversives, and thereby to justify repressive and militarised

---

12 Ironically, one of the popular sayings that was often voiced by the Secretary of Public Education Agustín Yáñez during his campaign for the governorship of Jalisco in the 1950s was 'hablando se entienden las gentes' – 'by talking with each other people reach understanding' (Yáñez, 1958: 233). Yet *Los días y los años* suggests that it was not politicians but Mexican students who established that principle and defended it, in non-violent protests, and ultimately at the cost of their own lives.

actions in its own terms. Zolov has since reinforced this perception, referring to the influential role of 'PRI-dominated mass media' in the course of the conflict (Zolov, 1999: 119). And beyond media misrepresentation, as González de Alba and Poniatowska both document, the state also had available a repertoire of alternative options for exercising social control including intimidation and force if deemed necessary. In this regard, both writers document in detail the fact that, ultimately, the state did have recourse to threats such as those expressed in Díaz Ordaz's annual address to the people of Mexico, and also violence, from the aggressive occupation of the UNAM and IPN student campuses to the massacre at Tlatelolco.

Significantly, later accounts of Mexico's state – student conflict echo the earlier foundational representations by González de Alba and Poniatowska in their discussion of the state's repressive potentialities and actions. As Jorge Volpi notes, referring to the state's tactics of 'last resort', 'las últimas consecuencias', the most infamous threat came in Díaz Ordaz's State of the Nation speech on 1 September when he warned the students and their parents: 'We don't wish to take undesirable measures, but we will take them if it is necessary: whatever it is our duty to do, we will do: however far we are forced to go, we will go that far' (cited by Volpi, 1998: 282).[13]

This was just hours after tanks had emerged from the National Palace to clear the Zócalo of the 5,000 or so students who had remained there naively awaiting a public dialogue with the president following the demonstration on 27 August. Citing various journalistic sources as evidence, Volpi also illustrates the state's orchestrated use of military force with reference to the occupation of the UNAM campus on 18 September and then of the IPN campus in the Casco de Santo Tomás five days later (Volpi, 1998: 299–309). Finally, at the extreme, the PRI was eventually ready and willing to enact repression of the most shockingly violent kind – an act of mass murder against its people. In the words of Hodges and Gandy: 'The 5000 soldiers with hundreds of tanks completely surrounded the plaza: there was no way out or around or through. A helicopter tossed out flares, and the army began shooting to kill' (Hodges and Gandy, 2002: 100). The massacre at Tlatelolco prompted intellectuals publicly to distance themselves from the state. Octavio Paz resigned his position as ambassador to India in horror and disgust at

---

13   Díaz Ordaz's attitude was consistently and insistently focused upon his duty to the nation as the guarantor of public order. Volpi comments, astutely:

It is curious that, faced with a need for first person singular, so beloved of the president, at the very moment when he was announcing his most difficult decision he did so with a royal we. Again it seems like the students are those who are forcing him to act; that, underneath it all, he is not the agent of his acts, just the person responsible, to his regret, for the security of the nation.

what he later described as the re-animation of pre-Columbian sacrificial rituals destined to perpetuate the power of the elite. Claire Brewster notes that Paz's resignation was 'widely felt' and covered by the *London Times Literary Supplement*. She also comments on the protest poem that Paz penned at that time and that was published in *La Cultura en México*: 'Writing the poem was a brave, antigovernment stance; publishing it in Mexico was a yet more courageous move' (C. Brewster, 2005: 57). Mass murder in Mexico also brought condemnation from Carlos Fuentes and Carlos Monsiváis. Poniatowska's critical response to 1968 came in various textual forms, the most famous being *La noche de Tlatelolco*. The only mystery that remains concerning the stance of Mexico's prominent intellectuals of the day is why Agustín Yáñez remained in post as Secretary of Public Education.

The Principle of Popular Resistance

As a third challenge to state authoritarianism and a third contribution to the transformation of conditions of political marginalisation in Mexico, González de Alba and Poniatowska both insist that the students and their sympathisers stood firm in the face of escalating repression and thus allowed the authoritarian excesses of the Mexican state to be exposed by the non-partisan national press, such as those working for the investigative news journal *¿Por qué?*, and also by the gathering numbers of international reporters whose anticipated role in Mexico was to cover the Olympic Games. In this latter group we find the British correspondent John Rodda, who has made a lasting intervention and contribution to contemporary understandings of Mexico '68. As Claire Brewster comments:

> British sports correspondent, John Rodda, described how he was trapped inside a building at Tlatelolco on the night of 2 October. Rodda, who spoke no Spanish, quoted a Mexican journalist who told him 500 people had been killed. The man 'wrote the figure down in case we misunderstood'. Rodda could not confirm this, 'because I had my face pressed hard to the floor most of the time'. After his return from Mexico, Rodda stated, 'an accurate figure of the deaths will never be known but the 500 I reported on the following day is not likely to be far off the mark'. (C. Brewster, 2002: 176, note 13)

Rodda's estimate, of course, bears no relation to the 49 deaths eventually admitted by the state (Zolov, 1999: 130). There is still no accepted figure and it is possible that an accurate death toll may never be reliably calculated because the bodies of some who went missing were never found. Paco Ignacio Taibo

II claims that these were dumped in the Gulf of Mexico by military aircraft on the night of the massacre (Taibo, 1991: 103).

Los días y los años and *La noche de Tlatelolco* both propose, with the inauguration of the Olympic Games looming ever closer, that September 1968 was the month when the Díaz Ordaz regime started to escalate the levels of repression in a concerted attempt to bring the conflict to an end. These foundational representations show that prior to the Silent March on 13 September, parents were leafleted warning them not to let their children attend demonstrations as there was a serious risk of confrontation with the military (González de Alba, 1997a: 118). González de Alba tells us that in this period Barros Sierra made an unexpected call for students to return to normality in their university life. He was evidently under some form of pressure and a high-ranking administrator in UNAM said to González de Alba: 'Some day I'll tell you the secret history of that appeal' (González de Alba, 1997a: 114). Whatever the real cause of Barros Sierra's call for normality, as González de Alba explains with reference to the Silent March: 'The possibility that the demonstration would be met with violent repression was foremost in everyone's mind' (González de Alba, 1997a: 117). *Los días y los años* reveals that over the days following the Silent March, street conflicts left a number of students dead, some of them killed in Tlatelolco, and the military also occupied the National Polytechnic campus in the Casco de Santo Tomás. The scenes of flying truncheons and Molotov cocktails, street fighting, burning buses and injured victims that had been visible at the start of the conflict in July are shown to have reappeared with greater frequency and with an alarming additional element – the use of armed force and the deaths of student protestors. As González de Alba's text movingly reveals, in September everything was gearing up for the massacre at Tlatelolco, which he represents as a calculated and orchestrated act of mass murder that began with the agreed signal of two flares being thrown from a low-circling helicopter (González de Alba, 1997a: 183–84). In relation to the foundational status of such a representation, from the vantage point of 1999, General García Barragán's bequeathed military plans have subsequently corroborated this claim. And with even greater prescience, the outcomes of Mexico's judicial enquiry in 2007 were predicted by Poniatowska's categorisation in 1971 of Tlatelolco as an act of genocide through an intertextual link with an essay by Leonardo Femat published in *Siempre!* (Poniatowska, 1998: 177–178).

In this context of escalating state pressure, González de Alba and Poniatowska both bring the students' continual and admirable determination to resist repression into sharp relief. For example, González de Alba points out that of the 300,000 who turned out for the Silent March, despite the atmosphere of increased fear that the state had deliberately generated, many walked with a hand in the air displaying a V for Victory sign (González de

Alba, 1997a: 119–120). He also notes that when the military occupied the UNAM campus this did not generate a sense of defeat. Quite the contrary; it galvanised spirits and made the students determined to continue with their struggle:

> The scale of the error made by the government was manifest that night; while a detachment of paratroopers were unceremoniously raising the flag that the rector had put at half mast on the morning of 30 July, the students who had been arrested, face down on the concrete, were lifting up their arms and making V for victory signs between the soldiers' boots. That was the attitude that would predominate over the coming days; no defeatism, just indignation. (González de Alba, 1997a: 127)

Turning to the massacre at Tlatelolco on 2 October, this is powerfully described and documented by González de Alba and all the more evocatively in Poniatowska's extensive collection of survivors' testimonies (1999: 161–274). Tellingly, what both writers insist upon is that even mass murder, the ultimate form of military repression, did not effectively bring to an end the students' resistance to state terror. Both texts record the fact that the Student Movement was formally dissolved on 6 December, two days after its leaders issued a call for a return to classes (González de Alba, 1997a: 172). Nevertheless, from his prison cell at Lecumberri, González de Alba organised a project to produce a collectively authored history: 'we considered the possibility of writing a jointly authored account that would capture the experience of 1968 from within [the Student Movement]' (González de Alba, 1997a: 24). The sole-authored *Los días y los años* is a direct product of that initiative. Poniatowska greatly enhanced this contribution to the formation of Mexican cultural memory in *La noche de Tlatelolco*, emblematically with her emphasis on the memorial poem by Rosario Castellanos and on annual commemoration, and her text remains as another foundational publication.[14] Since then, other revealing accounts have followed, and have built on the cornerstones laid down by González de Alba and Poniatowska, including a 1993 Truth Commission Report,[15] and the two (1998) accounts referenced just above by Raúl Álvarez Garín and Sergio Aguayo. Curiously, though, and in spite of a clear presence of Mexico '68 in *trans*cultural memory, none of these texts are translated into English and – excepting Brewster's excellent study of

---

14 Every year on 2 October there is a commemorative march. In 1993, a memorial stone was erected at Tlatelolco with the names of some of the dead inscribed upon it together with a poem by Rosario Castellanos. (See Poniatowska, 1998: 163–164.)

15 Lorenzo Meyer at the Colegio de México kindly provided me with a copy of this report. I am not aware of it existing as a publication that can be referenced.

intellectual responses to Mexico '68 (and other political developments) – there is currently just one book-length historical account of Mexico '68 available in English.[16]

Underlining the point, in 1971, *Los días y los años* and *La noche de Tlatelolco* were themselves signs of a continuing intellectual resistance to state authoritarianism in the sense that they challenged the official version of events and so damaged the state's ability to use misinformation as a strategy for maintaining power. In the aftermath of Tlatelolco, the state had made claims that González de Alba and Poniatowska convincingly contested. One of the most significant of those claims was the state's denial of operations carried out in the Chihuahua Building by Batallón Olimpia, a military body ostensibly created for enforcing public order during the Olympics. Yet this claim was contradicted outright by González de Alba's detailed eye-witness experiences:

> As I was in the middle I could see out of the corner of my eye. All of the individuals who had occupied the floor were wearing a white glove on their left hand or a handkerchief of the same colour tied on their wrist. 'Olympia Battalion' they shouted from one staircase. 'Olympia Battalion' they answered from another . . . others were shouting 'Olympic Battalion' and there was even one who shouted 'Batallón de Limpia' (Cleansing Battalion). (González de Alba, 1997a: 185–86)

González de Alba also documents an ill-fated attempt to escape by one student who pretended to be a member of this battalion using a white washing-up glove. This attempt ended with a sharp pistol whipping and bloodshed (González de Alba, 1997a: 195). Citing Gilberto Guevara Niebla, Poniatowska similarly documents the role played by 'Batallón Olimpia' in the Chihuahua Building: 'The balcony was seized by the 'Olympia Battalion' and, with our arms up and faces pressed into the wall, we were forbidden to turn and look at the square, the slightest movement would prompt a blow on the head or a dig in the ribs. The trap was sprung and the mass murder began' (Poniatowska, 1998: 175–76). With the benefit of hindsight, we now know that by resisting what Hodges and Gandy have termed 'presidential despotism'

---

16 See Carey (2005). There is scope for other analytical frameworks, especially those of subaltern studies to examine the role and representation of Mexican workers and (trans)cultural memory and to examine the continuing contemporary resonance of 1968. As 'The Mexico Project' – run by Kate Doyle at George Washington University in the USA (Doyle, 2006) – makes clear on its webpages, it is still not possible to identify all of those who died by name. Unless and until the names of those who died are known, as Sergio Aguayo stated ten years ago, 'it will be difficult to draw a line under Tlatelolco' (Aguayo, 1998: 250).

the students were significantly reducing the opportunities for repressive action of this nature to be used in future conflicts in Mexico and certainly making it virtually impossible for any attempt at a cover-up on a similar scale. The students' resilience continues to inspire other forms of popular protest and has contributed to a remarkable process of re-democratisation. More importantly in relation to the arguments set out here, our contemporary understanding of the Mexican Student Movement rests, to a considerable extent, on the foundational representations produced by González de Alba and Poniatowska.

Conclusions

The first main conclusion to be drawn from this study is that *Los días y los años* and *La noche de Tlatelolco* are foundational representations of the state – student conflict in Mexico in 1968, both of which emphasise the reformist nature of the Mexican Student Movement's campaign. In this respect, possibly the most concise way of reaffirming answers to the central question posed in this article – concerning the representation of the students' contributions to challenging state authoritarianism and to transforming conditions of political marginalisation – is to think in terms of a lasting legacy of democratic principles that informed the Student Movement throughout its campaign. One simple way to summarise these is to note that González de Alba and Poniatowska both draw attention to a series of expectations of the Mexican state (though such expectations do inevitably appear utterly innocuous and self-evident taken out of the context of political activism in Díaz Ordaz's Mexico). Essentially, the Mexican Student Movement expected, and demanded, that in conditions of non-violent political conflict in Mexico the state should: (i) permit citizens to protest peacefully without fear of reprisals of any kind; (ii) be willing to engage in negotiations with protestors; (iii) never deliberately misrepresent protestors and/or their activities through any medium (especially through manipulation of the media and/or censorship); (iv) use reason not force to assert its position; (v) ultimately be willing to make concessions and so modify policy and procedure in response to public protest. On this last point, the student protests did, only a few years after Tlatelolco, bring about change and so institute in Mexican political life, in whatever weakened form, a principle of accountability and responsiveness to social protest. As Hodges and Gandy explain, 'within the next three years, some of the demands of the movement were granted' (Hodges and Gandy, 2002: 101). More specifically, Hodges and Gandy note that Díaz Ordaz revoked the law against the crime of social dissolution, that Demetrio Vallejo and Valentín Campa were freed (although other political prisoners took their place), and that Luis Echeverría dismissed the chiefs of police.

The second conclusion that has emerged from this study, and that requires further illustration and analysis, is that there are not simply significant similarities between the two foundational representations of Mexico '68 considered here but also important differences. Of these, the most notable is that González de Alba records the factionalism that divided the Mexican Student Movement internally and that was based, in large part, on an adherence to rival political ideologies and to disputes about strategy. For example, he describes the situation at Lecumberri as follows: 'the population of "C" wing, although it is very diverse, can be divided into three clearly differentiated sectors' (González de Alba, 1997a: 66). By this he means: (i) the Communists; (ii) the non-Communist members of the Student Strike Committee; and (iii) the bystanders who were arrested at Tlatelolco by the *granaderos* just because they were there. He records the fact that ideological disputes amongst the survivors who were imprisoned at Lecumberri were bitter, and that the most divisive issue was whether or not to dissolve the Student Movement and call for a return to classes as normal. The Communists wanted to pursue this path, others did not. However, by December 1968 the Communists held sway in the Student Movement and they were the ones whose decisions were carried forward into action (González de Alba, 1997a: 165–168).

The third main conclusion that emerges from this study is that Mexican workers' viewpoints remain persistently at the margins in these foundational representations, and that the workers' apparently inconsequential relations with students therefore constitute an enigma that requires greater research. This is all the more intriguing when we consider the fact that *Los días y los años* makes it clear that one of the starting points for protest in 1968 must necessarily be the call the students made for the release of political prisoners and the deletion of Article 145 of the Penal Code on the crime of social dissolution. What González de Alba highlights is that even before the initial skirmishes between students and *granaderos* in the Ciudadela Park in July, Demetrio Vallejo was on hunger strike to demand his release from Lecumberri prison. He also refers to the fact that a number of political science students at the UNAM had begun hunger strikes as an expression of solidarity and that those student protestors were calling for a strike by the university as a whole. Moreover, as Hodges and Gandy state, their slogan was 'Freedom for the Political Prisoners!' (Hodges and Gandy, 2002: 93). From the start and throughout, then, according to González de Alba, there was a necessary link between student protest and working-class protest and, in particular, a link with the legacy and collective memory of repression against railway workers during the López Mateos presidency (1958–1964). Yet, curiously, the students are shown not to have engaged with the revolutionary potential of a student – worker alliance in any sustained manner. In both *Los días y los años* and *La noche de Tlatelolco*, historical consciousness and potential bonds of solidarity are not shown to have prompted radical collective action. In particular, there are no passages that detail concerted and *sustained* efforts by students to join forces with workers. In fact, González de Alba is left to lament the fact that working-class mobilisation was desperately needed after the smaller turn-out for the Silent March but was no longer a distinctly feasible option: 'Some of us saw a way out of the situation through the mobilisation of working-class support, which at that stage was probably out of reach though, because if such mobilisation had not been achieved when the Movement was at its height and near to success, now, in evident decline, it would be all the more difficult' (González de Alba, 1997a: 116).

Finally, *Los días y los años* and *La noche de Tlatelolco* retain a contemporary relevance because there are key issues that remain open to this day. Three key demands from 1968 remain as unfinished business. Even if we accept that the disbanding of the *granaderos* was a utopian demand, there are still two others. One of those amounts to a call for the state to attribute blame for crimes against humanity and to prosecute those found guilty; another is a related call for the state to compensate the families of the victims. In this regard there have been developments, but no resolutions. Despite the fact that Díaz Ordaz assumed responsibility to clear the way for Echeverría to become president, responsibilities have never entirely been assumed by the politicians involved. Under the Fox administration (2000–2006), an investigation into 1968 was established and, in 2006, Echeverría was placed under house arrest and became the first Mexican president ever to face criminal charges. However, he was eventually cleared of having organised the killings of students in 1968 and also in 1971 during the so-called 'halconazo' – an organised attack on student protesters that left some forty-five dead – as well as having masterminded certain 'disappearances' during his presidential term (see *MSNBC*, 2006 and Kraul, 2004). Without attribution of responsibilities there can be no prosecution. As for compensation, when there is sufficient political will to meet such a demand, the names of all those who died at Tlatelolco will be known and the past will acquire different meanings once more.

8

Traumatic Time in Roberto Bolaño's *Amuleto* and the Archive of 1968

RYAN LONG

University of Oklahoma, USA

Roberto Bolaño's posthumous fame coincides uncannily with the thematics of his novels, which often depict writers at the mercy of the circumstances that shape their lives and legacies. The translations into English of his two most ambitious works – *Los detectives salvajes* (1998) [*The Savage Detectives* (2007)] and *2666* (2004) [*2666* (2008)] – garnered extraordinary critical acclaim; and he would now, in the words of Janet Maslin, 'be enjoying literary superstar status if fate had been kinder' (Maslin, 2008: 1). Bolaño's work earned him relatively late but significant renown in Spain and Latin America before he died at the age of 50 in 2003.[1] But the irony of his more recent global success would probably not be lost on him. For instance, the Chilean writer Carlos Franz recalls asking Bolaño how it felt to triumph among critics after decades of writing in relative obscurity. According to Franz, Bolaño replied bitterly: 'It came too late' (Franz, 2007: 41).[2] This statement contains an additional irony since Bolaño's novels tend to reject the teleology it implies. On the contrary, they tell stories in which hardly anything happens 'on time', in which lives unfold and events reverberate out of step with linear notions of biography and chronology.

Amuleto (1999) [*Amulet* (2006)] is no exception. Expanding a brief episode that originally appeared in *Detectives* into a novel of over 150 pages, *Amuleto* is the first-person account of Auxilio Lacouture, a Uruguayan woman living in Mexico who spent a miserable two weeks hiding in a bathroom of the Department of Philosophy and Literature during the Mexican army's occupation of the National Autonomous University (UNAM) between 18 September and 30 September 1968. Lacouture's traumatic experience returns incessantly, long after its physical duration has ended. Further chronological distortion occurs in the text when Lacouture's trauma shapes her perception of experiences that preceded it; and, remarkably, when her confinement

---

1 For example, *Los detectives salvajes* won the 1998 Herralde Prize and the 1999 Rómulo Gallegos Prize.
2 All translations from the Spanish and French are mine unless otherwise noted.

provides her space to reflect upon events that could not yet have happened. The experiences from before and after 1968 that serve as focal points for Lacouture's narrative include her arrival in Mexico at an undetermined point in the 1960s, the nomadic nature of her existence, and her relationships with a number of writers and artists, both actual and fictional, including Pedro Garfias, León Felipe, Remedios Varo and the young poet Arturo Belano, Bolaño's autobiographically based alter ego.

Amuleto's basis in history is a fascinating story in its own right, which, like Bolaño's legacy, bears on questions of posthumous fame and how the dead circulate among the living. Like Belano, Lacouture corresponds to an actual person, in her case the Uruguayan poet and educator Alcira Soust. Soust arrived in Mexico in 1952, and was in fact trapped in the Philosophy and Literature bathroom in 1968. She met Bolaño in 1970 and saw him for the last time in 1976.[3] After decades working odd jobs in and out of the university, and suffering from mental illness, she returned to Uruguay in 1988, where she died in 1997. This deceptively neat timeline of Soust's adult life owes itself in part to Bolaño's recent fame, because Lacouture's story in *Amuleto* and *Detectives* has inspired renewed interest in Soust. In spring 2008, a Mexico City theatre company performed a play based on the episode in *Detectives* titled 'Alcira o la poesía en armas' (Alcira or Poetry Armed). And in January 2009, a journalistic investigation into Soust's life appeared in the Uruguayan weekly *Brecha*,[4] including the first published account of her death, the circumstances of which were unclear until 2008 (see Yacobazzo, 2009).

The final section of one of the *Brecha* stories – 'Tras las huellas de Alcira Soust' (On the Trail of Alcira Soust) by Ignacio Bajter – is tellingly titled 'En intemperie' (Bajter, 2009: II), a word that in this context approximates the English term 'adrift'. This section of Bajter's article focuses on Soust's final years, about which very little is known. Its title is relevant because it recalls a guiding theme of *Amuleto*, an almost overwhelming experience of abandonment and isolation, a threatening sense of exposure, or *intemperie*.[5] Notably, however, *Amuleto* portrays *intemperie* as a necessary counterpart to shelter. Furthermore, Bolaño's novel deliberately acknowledges and develops this dialectical relation. The fact that the text actively rejects linear chronology

---

3   Notably, 1976 is the pivotal year of Belano's story in *Detectives*, which, among other things, describes the search for a female poet who has been missing for years.

4   I thank Giovanni Rodríguez for sending me a copy of this article, which I first read about on his blog, 'mimalapalabra'. Earlier published accounts of Soust's story include notable, though passing, references in Poniatowska (1971: 71) and Revueltas (1978: 76–78). Revueltas's longer account includes a poem Soust had given him ten months earlier, titled 'L'amor che move il/sole e l'astre stelle'.

5   For reasons related to the particular density of this term, which I discuss below, I think it is more precise to keep it in Spanish throughout.

and the abstract concept of time it relies upon adds an important temporal dimension to its depiction of *intemperie*, resulting in, I conclude, a strong critique of the ideologically motivated insistence upon teleology and progress that often informs discussions of 1968 in Mexico and its legacy.

In their recent, and separate, analyses of how the present shapes our understanding of the past, Néstor García Canclini and Fredric Jameson offer helpful points of departure for my analysis of how time functions in *Amuleto*. In reference to the work of John Berger, García Canclini identifies as critical the task of 'grasping hold of the quality and density of the present' (García Canclini, 2004: 21). Jameson contributes additional meaning to the phrase 'density of the present' when he reminds his readers 'to alert [them]selves to the deformation of space when observed from the standpoint of time, of time when observed from the standpoint of space' (Jameson, 2003: 698). A similar dual process of distortion structures *Amuleto*, whose narrative returns relentlessly to the traumatic chronotope of Lacouture's confinement in September 1968.

Teleologies of 1968

A spectral tale in a work by an author who is currently enjoying a spectral sort of fame, Lacouture's story (and Soust's, though in a different way) demonstrates the 'density of the present' by acknowledging and drawing upon the coexistence of different moments, a coexistence more often than not uncomfortable and maladjusted. The events of 1968 in Mexico and their legacy are likewise characterised by unsettling and unsettled juxtapositions. To take a particularly dramatic example, the violence the Mexican government unleashed upon its own citizens contrasted sharply with the official welcome given the world's athletes, journalists and tourists who were visiting Mexico for the Olympic Games, which began only ten days after the massacre of Tlatelolco. More broadly, the Games were touted by Mexico's leaders as evidence of their nation's entrance into modernity.[6] But the repression of the Mexican Student Movement not only exposed the limitations of that claim, but also of the teleological thinking underpinning the very notion of an entrance into modernity.[7] The radically uneven development that characterises Mexican society and culture raises important questions about the validity of progress and modernisation as concepts, let alone about

---

6 See Aguayo Quezada [1998]; see also Claire Brewster and Keith Brewster in this volume.

7 I have argued this point more extensively elsewhere. See *Fictions of Totality* (Long, 2008) for an analysis of how Mexican novels register the contradictions inherent to the modernising discourse of national-popular ideology.

the programmes and often fetishised events, such as the Olympic Games, intended to achieve or demonstrate the attainment of these chimerical goals.[8]

The legacy of 1968 and its literary archive are also subject to troubling juxtapositions and ideologically motivated attempts to smooth over them in the name of teleology. *Amuleto* is notable in this regard for being a critical analogue of that archive. Time in the novel is distorted to such an extent – and particularly from the vantage point of the space in which Lacouture finds herself trapped – that conventional distinctions between past, present and future hardly function. The text's acknowledgment of unsettled time enables a critique of the archive as cultural institution by rejecting appeals to origins and chronology. *Amuleto* demonstrates why, ultimately, the archive cannot reliably perform its intended function, which is, as Jacques Derrida notes in reference to the etymology of the term 'archive' and its Greek root 'arkhe', to establish 'at once the *commencement* and the *commandment*' (Derrida, 1996: 1; emphasis in original); in other words, to originate and to order.

Samuel Steinberg elucidates the dangerous implications of fixing an origin to and ordering the legacy of Mexico 1968 by focusing on how the events of that year are often overly defined by the massacre: 'the cultural narrative of Mexico 1968 has reduced this year to a single moment: 2 October 1968 ... This moment organizes the archive of 1968; it is ... the 'cutting' of this moment from all other moments that establishes the principle of the historical, cultural memory of 1968' (Steinberg, 2009: 3). Steinberg's analysis demonstrates how cultural production negotiates, contributes to, or resists the overwhelming dominance the Tlatelolco massacre has exercised over other events and possibilities of 1968.[9] For Steinberg, the sacrificial narrative of 1968 helps insert the events of that year into the dominant narrative of democratic transition, a consequence and desire of which is the suppression or subordination of other moments, tendencies and potential accomplishments. As Steinberg notes, 'many of the most technocratic thinkers in Mexican politics today ascribe to 1968 the status of origin vis-à-vis the contemporary "democratic" transition, and more ominously, the neoliberal transition to which it has been conceptually allied' (Steinberg, 2009: 19). Triumphantly

---

8   See Zermeño (1978). Zermeño's sociological and economic analysis of the student-popular movement, its origins, and the government's responses to it is a particularly well-developed study, demonstrating, for example, the complex relationships between economic 'modernisation', foreign debt, authoritarianism and widespread exclusion from the political process for many social actors.

9   For example, Octavio Paz's *Posdata* (1969) is a founding text in the narrative of sacrifice, in which Paz compares the Tlatelolco massacre to Aztec ritual sacrifice. By contrast, for Steinberg, Carlos Monsiváis's *Días de guardar* (1970) presents a more productive narrative of 1968 by not allowing the massacre to overshadow the student-popular movement's successes, and by resisting teleology in its form and structure.

positing 1968 as the origin of the present order risks obscuring the past, Steinberg concludes. Citing Barry Carr, he explains that 'the alignment of 1968 with the contemporary order is not a form of remembering the past, of affirming the student-popular movement's posthumous incidence, but rather, extend[ing] "the drastic closure of political space that Tlatelolco seemed to announce"' (Steinberg, 2009: 20). Steinberg warns against the desire for closure implicit in the dominant archive of 1968, which seeks to construct that year as the origin of the new order.

His project sets itself in opposition to the archive by tracing its remainders, that which is excluded upon its foundation. But Steinberg also acknowledges the force of Tlatelolco, an event whose 'memory ... burns into the cultural surface, is etched onto film with gunpowder residue [forming] a haunted surface that extends the memorial incidence (and thus political potential) of the gunfire on the square' (Steinberg, 2009: iii). *Amuleto* is in its own way a haunted surface, and it contains depictions of and meditations upon other haunted surfaces and beings. And while Bolaño's novel indeed expresses a desire to calm these unsettled and unsettling places and people, it also acknowledges the impossibility of realising that desire. The space of that acknowledgment is where the text's critical force lies, and it can be found in a particularly dense Spanish word, *intemperie*.

Exposure Time

Amuleto adds a linguistic dimension to its critique of the archive and its acknowledgment of the density of the present through its use of the term *intemperie* in a centrally important passage, which I analyse below. But before I turn to the text, the history of this word and its relevance in relation to thinking about time are worth mentioning briefly. *Intemperie* shares a Latin root with the Spanish word for time, *tiempo*, but it does not have a temporal connotation in modern Spanish. The *Spanish Royal Academy's Diccionario de la lengua española* (Real Academia Española, 1992) offers the following definition: 'Unevenness or inconsistency of weather' ('Destemplanza o desigualdad del tiempo') (Vol. IV, 831). The adverbial phrase 'a la intemperie' connotes exposure and lack of shelter in its definition: 'Exposed to the sky, without roof or any other recourse' ('A cielo descubierto, sin techo ni otro reparo alguno') (1992: Vol. IV, 831). According to Joan Corominas's etymological dictionary, *intemperie* comes from the Latin *temperare*, a verb defined as: to 'combine adequately' ('combinar adecuadamente') or to 'moderate, temper' ('moderar, templar') (Corominas, 1991: Vol. III, 457). *Tiempo*, alternatively, comes from *tempus*, which Ernout and Meillet define as 'time, considered above all as in terms of a specific duration' ('temps, considéré surtout en tant que fraction de la durée') (Ernout and Meillet, 2001: 681). The fact that *tiempo* means both time and weather in Spanish hints at the actual etymological connection between *intemperie* and *tiempo*. In his etymology of *tiempo*, Corominas notes that many Romance and other languages use one word for both 'time' and 'weather'. But he also clearly identifies different Latin and Greek roots for both separate terms (Corominas, 1991: Vol. V, 486–487). Notably, however, Ernout and Meillet identify an etymological connection between *temperare* and *tempus*, wherein the former derives from the latter (Ernout and Meillet, 2001: 682).[10]

This shared history provides support for the idea that *intemperie* can have temporal connotations. Referring to a maladjustment both in terms of time and space, *intemperie* suggests a more complete exposure, an at once historical and geographical condition of being unsettled. Furthermore, as *tempus* refers specifically to a portion of time, *intemperie* suggests a portion of time that finds itself out of place. *Amuleto*, with its reflections upon trauma and its critique of chronology, presents time as always being out of place. The novel also demonstrates that to posit anything other than a condition of *intemperie* is to insist upon a dangerous illusion.[11]

In his critique of post-Soviet teleological thinking at the service of global capital, *Specters of Marx*, Derrida urges his readers to recognise that, in the present age, *'The time is out of joint'* (Derrida, 1994: 77; emphasis in original). Writing only a few years after the fall of the Berlin Wall, Derrida's emphasis on out-of-joint time – on what in standard Spanish would be called *lo intempestivo* and not *intemperie* – stands as a corrective against the exuberance that provided the context for some, most famously Francis Fukuyama, to claim that history had ended and that free-market capitalism had won the Cold War. Instead of relegating allegedly outmoded ways of thinking, that is Marxism, to the 'dustbin of history', Derrida suggests negotiating openly with 'untimely spectres that one must not chase away but sort out, critique, keep close by, and allow to come back' (Derrida, 1994: 87). The act of recognising the untimeliness embodied in such spectres also acknowledges the injustices concealed by triumphant narratives of neoliberal progress or

---

10 Ernout's and Meillet's dictionary explains the connection between *tempus* and *tempero* (the root of *temperare*) by pointing out the association between *tempus* as 'circumstances' and *tempero* as 'mixture of the air' ('melange de l'air'), an association wherein the relation between a specific time and weather conditions is evident (Ernout and Meillet, 2001: 682). I owe thanks to Calvin Byre for helping me with the etymologies of Latin terms.

11 In one of the few existing critical analyses of *Amuleto*, Celina Manzoni refers briefly to *intemperie*, relating it to 'estrangement', 'defeat' and 'desperation' (2003: 31). While it indeed connotes these conditions, I argue that *intemperie* can also serve as a productive condition, an unease that must be acknowledged in order to provide a careful consideration of the relationship between the present and the past.

democratic transition. Derrida expands upon this observation in terms that share a strong affinity with Bolaño's writing, *Amuleto* included:

> A deconstructive thinking ... cannot operate without justifying the principle of a radical and interminable, infinite (both theoretical and practical, as one used to say) critique. This critique belongs to the movement of an experience open to the absolute future of what is coming, that is to say, a necessarily indeterminate, abstract, desert-like experience that is confided, exposed, given up to its waiting for the other and the event. (Derrida, 1994: 90)

Even though *lo intempestivo* is a better modern translation into Spanish of 'untimeliness', it does not carry the connotation of exposure that *intemperie* does. Notably, the place of the deconstructionist critique, in Derrida's terms, is in fact a place of exposure, containing and making possible a 'desert-like experience' that also enables a special relationship to time, one that is radically open, both to the future and to the spectral return of the past, no matter how unsettling either may be.[12]

Traumatic Time

The crucial passage about *intemperie* in Bolaño's novel occurs within the context of the following reflections Lacouture makes on her life story, which appear at the beginning of the fifth chapter. And as I will show in the conclusion, the themes developed in this passage return at the novel's end. Lacouture begins the fifth chapter, 'If I didn't go crazy it's because I always kept my sense of humour' (Bolaño, 1999: 42). Then she lists a number of things she has laughed about, including her Prince Valiant haircut, the runs in her stockings, the gossip, infighting, and brown-nosing among students and faculty, and many other details, events and people; all of whom exist under 'the trembling sky of Mexico City, that sky I knew so well, that stirred-up and out-of-reach sky like an Aztec jar, underneath which I moved around carefree, with all of Mexico's poets and with little Arturo Belano who was seventeen, eighteen years old, and who grew up while I watched' (Bolaño, 1999: 42). This totalising enumeration of Lacouture's and other's experiences becomes explicitly a desire for shelter in the following sentence: 'All of them were growing up, sheltered by my gaze! [¡'Todos iban creciendo amparados por mi mirada!]' (Bolaño, 1999: 42). Typical of the ambiguity that structures

---

12 Though it is certainly not in the scope of this analysis, it could be productive to relate this observation to the importance of the desert as a space of critical experience in Bolaño's longer novels, *Detectives* and *2666*.

her narrative, Lacouture acknowledges, immediately afterwards, that her sheltering gaze cannot be separated from its antagonist, *intemperie*:

> That is, they were all growing up in the Mexican *intemperie*, in the Latin American *intemperie*, which is the biggest *intemperie* because it is the most divided and the most desperate. And my gaze shimmered like the moon over that *intemperie* and it stopped on the statues, on the surprised, intimidated figures, on the murmuring cliques in the shadows, on the silhouettes that had nothing but the utopia of the word, a pretty miserable word, for that matter ... And I was there with them because I didn't have anything either, except my memory. (Bolaño, 1999: 42–43)

This passage conveys a profoundly unsettled perspective through its contrast of shelter to *intemperie*, an unstable vantage point that corresponds also to Lacouture's position as witness.

In an interview from 2000, Bolaño describes Lacouture as 'the amnesiac witness to a crime who tries to recover her memory', and he continues by noting: 'so in that sense she operates like a metaphor: Latin Americans have been witness to crimes that we have later forgotten' (Pron, 2008: n.p.).[13] The phrase 'amnesiac witness' (testigo amnésica) is a succinct characterisation of the contradictory position Lacouture occupies in the passage cited above. Her gaze shelters all she sees, but all she sees is *intemperie*, the absence of shelter. In fact, the passage directly associates her gaze with *intemperie*. Furthermore, at one point in the passage Lacouture describes herself as watching everyone else; but at the end she includes herself as part of the community of those who have nothing, nothing except her memory. But that memory is actually something quite useful, because it is Lacouture's traumatised perspective on the past that produces her particularly productive vantage point.

Like the gaze that shelters homelessness, this perspective offers up a puzzle, a puzzle whose recognition as such, in Cathy Caruth's terms, is the starting point of a way of associating trauma and understanding that resists the seduction of a transparent comprehension of the past and an orderly understanding of its relation to the present. Caruth writes:

> in the equally widespread and bewildering encounter with trauma – both in its occurrence and the attempt to understand it – ... we can begin to recognize the possibility of a history that is no longer straightforwardly referential ... Through the notion of trauma ... we can understand that a rethinking of reference is aimed not at eliminating history but at resituating it in our understanding, that is, at precisely permitting

---

13   I thank Ignacio Bajter for directing me to Pron's interview.

> *history* to arise where *immediate understanding* may not. (Caruth, 1996: 11; emphasis in original)

For Caruth, history is not the simple recounting and organising – or tempering, as in *temperare* – of facts, but instead an operation that requires a serious consideration of subjective factors, not least of which is the relationship between the present moment of perception and the past event being perceived.

In *Amuleto*, Lacouture's trauma influences her perception of every event in her life. Referring to an encounter with Arturo Belano, she writes:

> I don't know why I remember that afternoon. That afternoon in 1971 or 1972. And the most curious thing is that I remember it from my watchtower of 1968. ... From the women's restroom on the fourth floor of the Department of Philosophy and Letters, my time-machine from which I can observe all the moments in which Auxilio Lacouture breathes, that aren't many, but that are. (Bolaño, 1999: 52)

Throughout the novel, Lacouture's narration returns to the fourth-floor bathroom as a space from which she observes her life. Trauma in Lacouture's case produces an understanding of an entire life through the lens of one two-week period, an anachronistic comprehension of history that rejects immediate understanding in favour of an insistent recognition of mediation because of, and through, the traumatic experience.

Often calling herself, and often ironically, the mother of Mexican poetry, Lacouture struggles with the sense of responsibility she feels for the young people, suffering in *intemperie*, whom she would like to shelter with her gaze. At one point this internal dialogue overlaps with a particularly evocative description of her bathroom prison and its function as memory device. Narrating initially from a moment years after her confinement, Lacouture returns to the past and recounts a particularly surreal episode:

> At night a voice, of the guardian angel of dreams, said to me: *che*, Auxilio, you've discovered where the youth of our continent ended up. Shut up, I answered. Shut up. I don't know anything ... And then the voice murmured something, it said mmm, something like that, as if it weren't very convinced by my response, and I said: I'm still in the women's restroom of the Department of Philosophy and Letters and the moon melts, one by one, all of the tiles on the wall until it opens a niche in the wall through which pass images, films about us and what we read and about the future as fast as light and which we will not see. (Bolaño, 1999: 132–133)

In despair, Lacouture returns to what she knows, her imprisonment in a suffocating space whose wall becomes a haunted surface upon which are projected films about her, the youth of Latin America and their future. The persistence of her traumatic memory enables Lacouture's fractured but more accurate perspective on the past, as well as its relation to the present and the future.

The operation of her gaze, similar to that described in the image of the projector, is defined earlier in the text as a combined function of perception, memory and narrative: 'life is loaded with enigmatic things, small events that are just waiting for epidermic contact, our gaze, in order to unfold in a series of causal connections that later, seen through the prism of time, cannot but produce shock or fear within us' (Bolaño, 1999: 28). Lacouture explains that subjects construct stories about discrete experiences in a way that is both deferred and not entirely under their control. The way this observation appears in the text is typical of Bolaño's style, whose density is often surprising alongside its equal degree of clarity. Included within this description of Lacouture's coming to terms with her experience is a general observation about narrative, particularly its unexpected provenance and impact, even in the context of telling one's own story. Here Lacouture describes an intimately subjective way of understanding experience. It is as if the subject's passage through daily experience were akin to moving among electrically charged objects and events that either cling to her skin or not. This 'epidermic contact' shifts in Bolaño's prose to a metaphorical identification with the gaze, which orders objects and events into a narrative visible only through hindsight.

In his short text titled 'A Note upon the "Mystic Writing-Pad"' (1925) Sigmund Freud describes how new experiences are integrated into a subject's perception and influenced by memories, be they traumatic, conscious, or unconscious. Freud relates the way the different parts of a *Wunderblock*, or Magic Slate, function as analogues of conscious perception and unconscious comprehension of external stimuli: 'The layer which receives the stimuli . . . forms no permanent traces; the foundations of memory come about in other, adjoining, systems' (Freud, 1961b: 230). It is important to note that for Freud perception is at the crossroads between external stimuli and the unconscious. In fact, perception, consciousness, and the unconscious exist within a dynamic relation, which Freud summarises as follows:

> cathectic innervations are sent out and withdrawn in rapid periodic impulses from within into the completely pervious system *Pcpt.-Cs.* [Perception-Consciousness]. So long as that system is cathected in this manner, it receives perceptions (which are accompanied by consciousness) and passes the excitation on to the unconscious mnemic systems; but as soon as the cathexis is withdrawn, consciousness is extinguished and the functioning of the system comes to a standstill. It is

as though the unconscious stretches out feelers, through the medium of the system *Pcpt.-Cs.*, towards the external world and hastily withdraws them as soon as they have sampled the excitations coming from it. (Freud, 1961b: 231)

There is a useful similarity between the 'feelers' of Freud's unconscious and the 'epidermic contact' described by Lacouture. The Magic Slate, basically a piece of cellophane over a soft surface allowing one to write words and remove them at will, helps Freud explain how immediate perceptions become part of a system of perception that has developed over the life of the subject. The soft surface underneath the cellophane, made of wax in Freud's day, maintains traces of previously written words no longer visible on the cellophane. New experiences are integrated into the subject's comprehension only and always in relation to past experiences.

When Lacouture mentions how narratives are formed in hindsight, her thinking corresponds to another idea in Freud's thought, specifically that the subject's conception of time emerges from the need to protect itself from excessive external stimuli. We tell stories in order to avoid being overwhelmed by experience. Trauma is, by definition, an overwhelming experience, so the stories it produces reveal the limits of a subject's capacity to narrate her life. Near his conclusion to 'The "Mystic Writing-Pad"', Freud alludes to time by contrasting it with perception, which does not function in a linear fashion but instead relies upon interruptions of the reception of new experience and intermittent returns of past perceptions. Notably, he suggests that 'this discontinuous method of functioning of the system *Pcpt.-Cs.* lies at the bottom of the origin of the concept of time' (Freud, 1961b: 231). In Freud's discussion of perception, then, discontinuity, *lo intempestivo*, stands at the origin of continuity, or abstract time.

A more developed distinction between perception and time appears in *Beyond the Pleasure Principle*, where Freud compares conscious perception to a shield, protecting the subject from an excess of external stimulation (Freud, 1961a[1920]). The analogy between consciousness and the cellophane of the *Wunderblock* is again useful: consciousness resists permanent traces from external stimuli, enabling the subject to perceive and sort through dozens if not hundreds of experiences every day. Time, Freud suggests, becomes part of this shield and filter: 'our abstract idea of time seems to be wholly derived from the method of working of the system *Pcpt.-Cs.* and to correspond to a perception on its own part of that method of working. This mode of functioning may perhaps constitute another way of providing a shield against stimuli' (Freud, 1961a[1920]: 22).

Freud's discussion of time, perception and the unconscious helps combine a rather basic idea – that we rely on the concept of time in order to make sense of our lives – with considerations about the effects of trauma, which he defines as 'excitations from outside which are powerful enough to break through the protective shield ... bound to provoke a disturbance on a large scale in the functioning of the organism's energy and to set in motion every possible defensive measure' (Freud, 1961a[1920]: 23). A secondary problem that appears as a consequence of trauma is of particular interest to a discussion of narrative time. Freud continues: 'There is no longer any possibility of preventing the mental apparatus from being flooded with large amounts of stimulus, and another problem arises instead – the problem of mastering the amounts of stimulus which have broken in and binding them, in the psychical sense, so that they can be disposed of' (Freud, 1961a[1920]: 23–24). Mastering her trauma is Lacouture's primary task. She binds experiences from throughout her entire life to her memory of being trapped in the bathroom, sometimes even speaking from the spatial and temporal vantage point of her entrapment, even though she is recording her thoughts years later.

The well-known and unsettling conclusion Freud makes in *Beyond the Pleasure Principle* is that traumatic experiences compel the subject to repeat them. The repetition of trauma, which is at face value illogical, represents the subject's effort to bind the overwhelming experience of trauma to something the subject can comprehend. 'Binding' is a dense term in Freud's thought, but perhaps it can be understood by making an analogy between, on one hand, unbound and bound, and, on the other hand, experience and narrative. Supporting this analogy, Freud writes: 'there seems to be no doubt whatever that the unbound or primary processes give rise to far more intense feelings in both directions [pleasure and displeasure] than the bound or secondary ones' (Freud, 1961a: 57). Binding is a taming operation, an effort at the mastery over trauma, and it corresponds to the 'death instincts', or the *'need to restore an earlier state of things'* (Freud, 1961a: 51; emphasis in original). The paradox at the heart of Freud's theory of the compulsion to repeat a traumatic experience is that binding is at once necessary for the preservation of the subject and inextricably associated with a desire for order that is ultimately a desire for stasis, or death. The overall relationship between trauma, perception and time thus suggests that the practice of constructing narratives is a manifestation of the paradoxically simultaneous desire for both life and death. Crucially, *Amuleto* refuses to pretend otherwise.

Bolaño's novel resists narrative order by obscuring the origins of the story it tells (a gesture repeated throughout when Lacouture demonstrates how her traumatic episode infects every moment of her life). For example, the date of Lacouture's arrival in Mexico is uncertain: 'I arrived in Mexico City in 1967 or maybe 1965 or 1962. I don't remember anything anymore about dates or pilgrimages, the only thing I know is that I arrived in Mexico and I didn't leave again' (Bolaño, 1999: 12). Immediately following this claim is a disturbing comment on memory that contributes surprisingly to the validity of insisting upon the possible temporal connotations of *intemperie*: 'Let's see, let's try the memory a bit. Let's stretch time as if it were the skin of an unconscious woman in the operating room of a plastic surgeon' (Bolaño, 1999: 12). This grotesque imagery establishes a relationship between trauma and creation wherein the subject of trauma is passive in the face of imminent violence, an analogy of Lacouture's entrapment. Lacouture's narrative about her entrapment, on the other hand, is a more active allusion to the cut that begins representation, which occurs again in the image of the bathroom-wall projector, and which also relies upon a rupture, 'a niche in the wall through which pass images' (Bolaño, 1999: 133).

The idea of stretching time before surgically dividing it coincides remarkably with Michiel de Vaan's etymology of the Latin word '*tempus*', defined as 'time, moment', and which he attributes to a re-constructed term of Proto Indo European: 'temp-os', which means 'to stretch' (de Vaan, 2008: 611). Regarding the relationship between this reconstructed term, *tempus* and *temperare* (the Latin root of *intemperie*), de Vaan writes, 'The meaning "to restrain, modify" of [*temperare*] shows [a] semantic shift from "stretching" to "measuring"' (de Vaan, 2008: 611). Measuring, balancing and ordering are operations necessary for transforming experience into narrative. In Lacouture's narrative, the shift from stretching to measuring implies a cut, an originary disturbance that enables representation. In other words, a prior moment of *intemperie* is necessary for the shelter of narrative, the story that tempers time.

In a way that resonates significantly with de Vaan's etymology of *tempus*, Derrida urges a clear acknowledgment of the origin as cut in the following terms:

> So make some incision, some violent arbitrary cut ... It is of course a beginning that is forever fictional, and the scission, far from being an inaugural act, is dictated by the absence – unless there exists some illusion to discount – of any de-cisive beginning, any pure event that would not divide and repeat itself and already refer back to some other 'beginning,' some other 'event'. (Derrida, 1981: 300)

A paradoxically oft-repeated 'beginning', Lacouture's trauma cuts into every other moment of her life. It will remain an intrusion as powerful as the one described in a particularly terrifying moment in her story, which occurs just after the army takes over the university. Trapped in the cubicle of the bathroom, she hears a soldier shouting to his commander in the hallway. Then he opens the door of the bathroom, intrudes upon what has become her sanctuary, and begins looking around. Lacouture writes:

while I waited for the soldier to search the cubicles one by one and I braced myself morally and physically, if necessary, to refuse to open the door, to defend the last autonomous territory of the UNAM [el último reducto de autonomía de la UNAM] . . . there came about a special silence [se produjo un silencio especial], a silence that does not even appear in musical dictionaries or philosophical dictionaries, as if time cracked [como si el tiempo se fracturara] and scattered in many directions at once [y corriera en varias direcciones a la vez], a pure time, composed neither of gestures nor actions, and then I saw myself and I saw the soldier who was looking at himself trapped in the mirror [arrobado en el espejo], . . . and I shuddered . . . because I knew that momentarily the laws of mathematics protected me, because I knew that the tyrannical laws of the cosmos, which are opposed to the laws of poetry, protected me and that the soldier would see himself trapped in the mirror and I would hear him and imagine him, trapped also, in the singularity of my cubicle [en la singularidad de mi water], and that both singularities constituted from that second onward [constituían a partir de ese Segundo] the two sides of a coin as atrocious as death [las dos caras de una moneda atroz como la muerte]. (Bolaño, 1999: 33–34)

This description densely juxtaposes poetry and mathematics, freedom and order, life and death, pure time and the arbitrary origin, protection and entrapment, silence and words. The unbound and the bound appear in this passage as two necessary but counteracting functions of the same machine, the binding machine whose always fundamentally unbound state – of *intemperie* – allows the transformation of experience into narrative. The moment of this transformation is a moment of potential exposure, to the soldier, and a moment of actual exposure, to the fracturing of time and the vertigo it produces. Laws that bind – the laws of mathematics – save Lacouture from discovery and enable her to continue working with the originally unbound – poetry and creation.

In the passage describing the soldier in the bathroom, silence fractures time. In the passage discussing the projected images, the moon melts the tiled walls. Both cuts take place within the space and time of trauma, the comprehension of which can never be pinned down to a specific origin. In fact, in Derrida's terms, Lacouture's trauma is an event that always repeats itself and always refers to something else. Hence its terrible, and terrific, power.

Conclusion: Poetry and Creation

The traumatic moment that intrudes upon every moment of Lacouture's life is, in its pervasiveness, unbound. But, it is also a binding machine, a narrating machine that, when compared to a projector, produces images of numerous possible futures. Just after describing the images that appear on the wall, Lacouture explains, 'I took a deep breath, hesitated doubtfully, cleared my mind and finally said, these are my prophecies' (Bolaño, 1999: 134). This is her deliberate moment of cutting, her unbound process of binding emerging from – the play on words is demonstrative, I hope – the bind she finds herself in. Lacouture's prophecies concern many poets and their readers, and verge on the surreal. For instance, she predicts that Vladimir Mayakovsky will find new fame in 2150 and that Alejandra Pizarnik's last reader will die in 2100 (Bolaño, 1999: 134–135). One prediction stands out for its generality: 'Metempsychosis. Poetry will not disappear. Its non-power will make itself visible in another way' (Bolaño, 1999: 134). Thus poetry's future is undetermined, as yet unbound.

The novel's insistence upon poetry's potential corresponds to the story of Alcira Soust, who reportedly recited poetry over the university's loudspeakers during the occupation. José Revueltas claims: 'the troops were received by the voice of León Felipe. It was Alcira who, in this way, received the invaders' (1978: 77). The metempsychosis to which Lacouture refers can be read as the basis of a community of poets – a constant theme in Bolaño's work – and in this case a community of young people Lacouture describes as having witnessed in a dream, whose desert-like landscape recalls Derrida's description of deconstruction, cited earlier. Describing her vantage point from within her dream, Lacouture narrates:

> So I kept moving, and at the same time, from an eagle's viewpoint, even though there were no eagles there, I saw my body moving through snowy ravines, over enormous drifts [terraplenes de nieve], over interminable white esplanades like Moby Dick's fossilised back. But I kept walking. I walked and walked. And from time to time I stopped and I said to myself: wake up, Auxilio. Nobody can stand up to this [Esto no hay quien lo aguante]. Nevertheless I knew I could stand up to it. And so I baptised my right leg with the name of will [voluntad] and my left leg with the name of necessity [necesidad]. And I stood up to it. (Bolaño, 1999: 149)

Her destination unclear, Lacouture literally puts one foot in front of the other as she negotiates the cold desert of her dream. Between will and necessity she finds shelter in the *intemperie* of her unconscious, which is in turn bound into the conscious perception of her narrative. She describes seeing in her dream 'a multitude of young people, an unending legion of young people that were heading somewhere'; and continues, 'I saw them. I was too far away to distinguish their faces. But I saw them. I don't know if they were actual, flesh-and-blood young people or ghosts. But I saw them. They were probably ghosts' (Bolaño, 1999: 151). Lacouture listens to them sing as they 'Walked toward the abyss' [Caminaban hacia el abismo] (Bolaño, 1999: 152). The song fades as they fall away, but it remains, 'A barely audible song' (Bolaño, 1999: 154). Lacouture's final words in the novel, which do not contain the end of her story – who knows when her last reader will die – represent the unbinding bind, the endless struggle between love and death that the novel alludes to in its conclusion: 'And even though the song I heard spoke of war, of the heroic feats of an entire generation of sacrificed Latin American youth, I knew that above everything it spoke of valour and of mirrors, of desire and pleasure. And that song is our amulet' (Bolaño, 1999: 154).

The young people of Latin America have been introduced into the logic of sacrifice, like, for Steinberg, the victims of the Tlatelolco massacre. But the logic of sacrifice in *Amuleto* is not the logic that leads to fictional plenitude, such as the story of democratic transition and the criminal complacency of triumphant free-market discourse. It is a sacrifice whose victims remain alive enough to sing, as ghosts who insist on the importance of the past, whose passage through *intemperie* signals the only possibility for hope, the forceful recognition that time is indeed out of joint.

Finally, it must be noted that Bolaño's novel develops this recognition around a character named Auxilio, the connotations of whose name indicate her role as midwife (auxiliary to birth) at the spectral arrival and return of Latin America's 'lost generation', the youth her maternal, narrative-making gaze intermittently shelters. As a noun, *auxilio* has several meanings in Spanish, including 'aid', and, as a performative, a cry for help. Notably, *auxilio* is also a synonym of *amparo*, or shelter. As a word that contains a call for help and the connotation of shelter, Auxilio finds a material manifestation in the object identified by the novel's title, 'amulet', a magical device able to provide a space for contradictory forces, like those within the song Lacouture describes in the novel's final passage. *Amuleto*, like Bolaño's other works, develops the theme of writers, their works and their legacies. The passage describing Lacouture's prophecies is a somewhat humorous reference to how works live beyond their writers' days. The fact that 'amulet' is the final word in Lacouture's story returns to this topic, because it contains yet another contradiction: the novel's ending is also the beginning of its reception and its legacy.

Samuel Steinberg describes Tlatelolco's symbolic power as deriving from 'the "cutting" of this moment from all other moments' (Steinberg, 2009: 3). He also critiques the suturing of Tlatelolco into simplistic narratives of progress, suturing that reveals the desire for an ordered archive of Mexico 1968. *Amuleto* also concerns itself with how narratives are formed by cuts. But the specific moments of time cut out in Lacouture's story are neither reassembled to construct a narrative that ultimately desires closure, nor the deceptive shelter of the archive. In *Amuleto*, interruptions in time instead lead to a paradoxically fertile state of *intemperie*.

9

'Writing Our History in Songs': Judith Reyes, Popular Music and the Student Movement of 1968

HAZEL MARSH

University of East Anglia, UK

Social movements can create arenas in which modes of cultural action are redefined and given new meaning as sources of collective identity (Eyerman and Jamison, 1998: 6). The Mexican Student Movement of 1968 created such an arena; it impacted upon the cultural and social life of the nation as well as the political realm (Zolov, 1999: 1). This chapter discusses Mexican popular music in the late 1960s and early 1970s, and the ways in which its performance and consumption at that time created arenas for practitioners and audiences to express their collective discontent with a hegemonic system of government that stifled political dissent. First, I focus on singer/songwriter Judith Reyes, who has been described as the 'chronicler of the 1968 Student Movement' (Velasco García, 2004: 77).[1] Redefining the late nineteenth century revolutionary corrido tradition, Reyes created songs that functioned as oral 'eye-witness' accounts of grassroots mobilisation and as critiques of political repression about which official sources and media outlets frequently remained silent. Second, I look at the ways in which the Partido Revolucionario Institucional (PRI) government sought to appropriate Mexican and Latin American folk-based protest music (*nueva canción*) as a vehicle for its own hegemonic ideologies while officially censoring rock because of the latter's perceived threat to social and 'family' values. This policy drove rock 'underground', converting it into the preferred medium of political and social dissent for urban middle-class youths and led to the marginalisation of Judith Reyes and her 'folkloric' corridos. I conclude by arguing that Reyes's compositions embody memory and opinion and act as a valuable (though neglected) resource for scholars keen to approach a deeper understanding of the ways in which lower class and politically dissident sectors of Mexican society have interpreted their lived experience of the Student Movement of 1968 and its repression (Reyes, 1974[1968]).

---

1 All translations unless otherwise stated are my own.

Judith Reyes: The Chronicler of 1968

In her *Chronology of the Student Movement*, a collection of twelve songs created during 1968 about the Student Movement and its repression, Judith Reyes (Reyes, 1974[1968]) uses the corrido form to 'relate and diffuse [news of] events in the face of the silence imposed on the mass media by political authorities' (Velasco García, 2004: 77). In these corridos, the events of 1968 are 'recorded passionately rather than with dispassionate objectivity, yet the passion is not so much that of a singer's personal response as that of a collective interpretation of events from a particular "committed" standpoint' (Pring-Mill, 1987: 179). Reyes recounts events from the viewpoint of the lower classes and student activists in 'Tragedia de la Plaza de las Tres Culturas' – 'Tragedy of the Plaza of Three Cultures'.

El dos de octubre llegamos Todos pacíficamente A un mitin en Tlatelolco Quince mil en la corriente Año del sesenta y ocho Que pena me da acordarme, La plaza estaba repleta Como a las seis de la tarde	On the 2 October we went peacefully to a rally in Tlatelolco about 15,000 of us, in the year of '68 It makes me sad to remember it the jam-packed plaza at about 6 pm
Grupos de obreros llegaron Y el magisterio consciente Los estudiantes lograron Un hermoso contingente.	Groups of workers arrived politically aware teachers, and students, together we made a beautiful contingent
De pronto rayan el cielo Cuatro luces de bengala Y aparecen muchos hombres Guante blanco y mala cara	Suddenly, the sky is pierced by four flares, Many men appear, white gloves and bestial faces.
Zumban las balas mortales Rápido el pánico crece Busco refugio y la tropa En todas partes aparece	Bullets zing, panic creeps in, I look for shelter and the troops are everywhere.
Alzo los ojos al cielo Y un helicóptero miro Luego sobre Tlatelolco Llueve el fuego muy tupido	I raise my eyes to heaven and see a helicopter over Tlatelolco It is raining heavy fire.

Figure 9.1. 'Tragedia de la Plaza de las Tres Culturas'/'Tragedy of the Plaza of Three Cultures'[2]

---

2   Translation by Barbara Dane, Reyes (2006 [1973]), sleeve notes.

Que fuerzas tan desiguales	How unequal the forces!
Hartos tanques y fusiles	So many tanks and guns!
Armados los militares	The military armed, the civilians with
Desarmados los civiles	empty hands.
Once años tiene un chiquillo	Next to me, a twelve-year old boy
Que muerto cae a mi lado	fell dead,
Y el vientre de una preñada	and the belly of a pregnant woman
Cómo lo han bayoneteado.	was pierced with bayonets.
Hieren a Oriana Fallaci	Oriana Fallaci, voice of the foreign press,
Voz de la prensa extranjera	is wounded.
Ya conoció la cultura	At last, she met the culture
Del gobierno de esta tierra.	of the government of this land.
Ya vio que vamos unidos	She saw that we are united, students
Estudiantes con el pueblo	and the people,
Contra un sistema corrupto	against a corrupt system
Y la falacia de un gobierno.	and a false government.
Recordará a los muchachos	She will remember the students, face
Contra la pared su cara	to the wall,
Las manos sobre la nuca	hands clasped behind their heads,
Y su derecho entre las balas	with their rights between the bullets.
Jóvenes manos en alto	University students with raised arms
Con la V de la Victoria	making a V for Victory.
V de Vallejo me dicen	High school students making
Los de la preparatoria	a V for Vallejo.[3]
Piras de muertos y heridos	Pyre of dead and wounded,
Solo por una protesta	all because of a rally,
El pueblo llora su angustia	while the people cry in anguish
Y el gobierno tiene fiesta	and the government gives a party!
Que cruenta fue la matanza	How bloody was the slaughter.
Hasta de bellas criaturas	Even our beautiful young women.
Como te escurre la sangre	Oh Plaza of Three Cultures,
Plaza de las Tres Culturas	you are dripping [with] blood.
Y porque en esto murieron	And because of this,
Mujeres y hombres del pueblo	men and women of the people died,
El presidente le aumenta	the president raises the salary
Al ejercito su sueldo	of his army.

Figure 9.1. (*Continued*)

---

3 Demetrio Vallejo was a railway workers union organiser who had been imprisoned since 1958.

Judith Reyes viewed herself as a chronicler of events rather than a protest singer, and chose to create songs which dealt directly with 'what she saw, what she lived through' (Alarcón, 2008). 'I like to write our history in my songs', she asserted, 'I include statistics as well as the words of my people'.[4] Indeed, in corridos such as 'Tragedy of the Plaza of Three Cultures', Reyes records dates, times and numbers, names individuals and describes military attacks on civilian individuals in what appears to be a vivid eyewitness account of the Student Movement and its subsequent repression. Reyes approached the traditional corrido as a vehicle for expressing what she called 'the other, hidden face of the nation' ('la otra cara de la patria'). She redefined the corrido as 'the voice of the people' at a time when 'the idea you had of [corridos] was of those you heard on [commercial] radio ... but with Judith Reyes, you start[ed] to take on another way of understanding the corrido' (Ismael Colmenares quoted by García, 2008b).

The corrido is a ballad form that emerged in mid- to late nineteenth century Mexico. It is usually seen to embody lower-class notions of justice, which often defy the authority of the state, and to act as an archive of popular history that provides insights into the opinions, values, grievances and heroes of common people (Frazer, 2006: 131). It appears that the corrido evolved from the Castilian *romance* and that it retained the latter's emphasis on epic-lyric narrative as an oral form of reporting and commenting on current affairs and issues within a predominantly illiterate population (Frazer, 2006: 136). The corrido developed its modern form between 1875 and 1910 (Nicolopolous, 1997). After the 1930s, with the growth of the Mexican film industry and the commercial recording industry, new corrido compositions contained few narratives about contemporary challenges to the status quo. At the same time, many earlier corridos celebrating the Mexican Revolution (1910–17) were appropriated by the state and became vehicles of hegemonic PRI ideology:

> At the moment of composition, these ballads went beyond expressing alternative values to posit those that were profoundly oppositional. When these historical moments passed, these corridos became integrative in relation to elite domination and hegemony ... these corridos helped to fashion a lower-class historical memory that encouraged the lower classes to accept elite domination. Yet these corridos also contained latent elements of instability, for they implied the legitimacy of rebellion against injustice and bad government. (Frazer, 2006: 139)

Reyes aimed to reclaim the corrido and to restore its function as a form of history 'by and for the people' in an atmosphere where political dissent was

---

4 Quoted in Reyes (2006 [1973]), sleeve notes.

difficult or impossible to articulate via the media or electoral politics. In his memoir of 1968, Paco Ignacio Taibo II writes of a sense that the press at the time:

> was lying ... [but] their lies strengthened our convictions. For our part, we knew the truth; we got our news by word of mouth. Eyewitness accounts were told and retold; everything had been seen by someone, heard by someone, and was recounted by everyone (2004 [1991]: 34).

Reyes's corridos were an important means of circulating such eyewitness accounts. On 2 May 1969, she embarked upon a series of recitals.[5] At the Universidad Nacional Autónoma de México (UNAM), she gave two or three concerts a day, and later performed at the universities of Zacatecas and Oaxaca, and at prisons, markets and town squares in Mexico City and throughout the nation (García, 2008b). As Soldatenko explains, Reyes's compositions were among those embraced by and circulated among urban students and leftist intellectuals as a form of 'oral reporting' with which to counteract the perceived 'lies' of the 'sell-out' press:

> The rupture of official political discourse [caused by events of 1968] paralleled the rise of a new language ... often captured in songs that students sang on buses, on street corners, and at school assemblies. Songs by Judith Reyes, Oscar Chávez, Margarita Bauche and José de Molina became popular, and less well-known songwriters and musicians proliferated (Soldatenko, 2005: 123).

It is significant that song should be referred to as the carrier of a new language. While speech is directly expressive of mental states, it 'cannot allow many people to talk all at once without destroying meaning and coherence' (Cochrane, 2007: 5). Music, however, appears to contain the capacity to allow large groups of people to share emotional and mental states (Cochrane, 2007: 7). Emotional perceptions are significant determiners of human behaviour because they 'inform us about our relationship to the world, they embody our convictions, and they factor intelligibly into our decisions in life' (Jesse Prinz quoted in Cochrane, 2007: 25–26). Empirical evidence suggests that listeners are able accurately to interpret the emotion that a performer of music intends to express with a success rate comparable

---

5   During the latter half of 1968, Reyes was convalescing following surgery to remove a tumour. She had reportedly postponed this surgery in order to participate in the Student Movement. Consequently, the lyrics for her *Chronology* are largely based on information she received at second-hand from witnesses and other participants (García, 2008b).

to the decoding of vocal expressions (Cochrane, 2007: 88).[6] This basic form of emotional recognition is often the foundation of more sophisticated acts of empathy that may lead to the arousal of similar emotional states in the listener to those perceived in the music (Cochrane, 2007: 307). Music may therefore at times alter or intensify the emotional state of listeners. Lyrics add another dimension to this experience. Collective singing can have the power partially to subsume individual experience in shared images, reinforcing bonds of social solidarity (Stewart, 1997: 200–201). Shared musical experiences may at times create a profound sense of reaching beyond the normal boundaries of the self (Cochrane, 2007: 311) and can assert collective identity and distinctiveness from other social groups. It has been suggested that the group cohesion encouraged by shared musical production may even be the evolutionary reason for the development of music (Cochrane, 2007: 5).

Judith Reyes: The Mother of 'Revolutionary' Song

The violent repression of the Student Movement of 1968 exposed the contradictions of the official 'Mexican miracle' of development and led a number of musicians and singers to seek to become 'independent from official influence' (Jimenez, 2008). These young artists sought to work outside the culture industries that were perceived to lie 'in the hands of the hegemonic sectors of society which propelled the industrialisation of the country' (Velasco García, 2004: 28). Judith Reyes was one of many artists who, after 1968, provided the model for 'the beginning of the movement of alternative popular music' in Mexico (Velasco García, 2004: 19). Francisco 'El Mastuerzo' Barrios of Los Nakos, a group founded in 1968 to diffuse the slogans and ideologies of the Student Movement via songs, has said that Reyes is referred to by many leftist artists as one of 'the originators, who started to construct a song that we can call revolutionary' (2008).

By 1968, Judith Reyes was already known as a politically active singer.[7] Born in 1924 in Ciudad Madero, Tamaulipas, she experienced economic hardship in her youth and reportedly witnessed discrimination and oppression of the rural poor in her home state. Reyes saw little of her father until she was nine years old, because he – unable to support his family through farming locally – lived and worked as a labourer in the United States. In her 1974 autobiography, *La otra cara de la patria*, Reyes (Reyes, 1974) recalls the anger and resentment that her father's experiences of racism and

---

6 Currently, the main theories regarding the relationship between music and emotional states differ in *where* they locate the emotion being expressed.
7 Biographical material selected from Garcia (2008a, 2008b), and Reyes and Pérez (1997).

discrimination in the United States caused her to feel, suggesting that this early experience of social injustice was to influence the development of her political consciousness.

Known as *La Tamaulipeca* (she who comes from Tamaulipas), the young Reyes worked in *carpas* (large circus-like tents; common places for popular entertainment for rural and urban lower classes) and appeared on radio shows. She composed several songs that the film star Jorge Negrete recorded and made famous. However, her growing political involvement caused conflicts with radio managers, and after the death of Negrete in 1952, Reyes gave up writing commercial songs and turned instead to journalism in order to be able to report on the struggles of the *campesinos* for land reform. In Chihuahua, Reyes reportedly promised one *campesino*: 'I am going to write about your problems. And not only write . . . I am going to sing! I am going to write songs about the things that happen to you!' (Reyes and Pérez, 1997). As she later recalled in her autobiography: 'I said this in a low voice, but I really wanted to shout it out . . . I would write songs again, this time with a reason and a will, [. . .] from now on, my songs would have the taste of history to be sung at the top of the lungs!' (Reyes and Pérez, 1997).

Reyes travelled throughout Chihuahua and Durango, accompanying herself on guitar as she sang her compositions at meetings and rallies, and participating directly in *tomas de terreno*.[8] In 1962, the governor of Chihuahua ordered her arrest and she spent time in prison because of her 'subversive' songs and activities. After her release, she founded the daily newspaper *Acción: Voz Revolucionaria del Pueblo* (Action: The Revolutionary Voice of the People) and published news sympathetic to the struggles of the *campesinos* of Chihuahua. As a result of these actions, in 1963 she was banned from the state and moved to Mexico City.

In the capital over the next few years, Reyes performed her corridos on university campuses and in schools, and became involved in supporting the *Preparatoria Popular*, an educational project that sought to provide opportunities for students who could not afford to attend state high schools. She composed corridos chronicling events centred on many of the leftist struggles and movements with which she had links at that time, such as those of railway-workers, guerrilla movements in Madera, Chihuahua, teachers, doctors, telegraph operators, as well as students.

As Luis Tomás Cervantes underlines, the social and political movements of the late 1960s had a significant impact on many cultural forms of expression:

---

8   This translates as 'taking of land'; a strategy used by rural/urban peoples to take over unused land for the self-construction of housing or for farming, usually involving a high degree of organisation and the physical, unarmed 'invasion' of unused land at night by large groups.

The 1968 movement was a song to life. We were living through the triumph of the Cuban Revolution ... the protests against the Vietnam War ... the Prague Spring, ... the Beatles and the Rolling Stones ... In Mexico, we liked rock music ... At that moment you had on the one hand los Teen Tops, ... Angélica María, César Costa ... and los Hermanos Carrión. On the other hand, there was Judith Reyes singing for the people's liberation, throughout Latin America there were singers like Atahualpa Yupanqui, Mercedes Sosa or Soledad Bravo. ... It was a renaissance of culture, of life, of poetry. (Cervantes, 1998)

The repression of the Student Movement in 1968 profoundly marked many Mexicans. Reyes confessed at the time that she would 'never be the same again' (García, 2008b). She completed her *Chronology of the Student Movement* that year and, as soon as her health allowed, began to travel and perform directly to audiences throughout the nation. On 21 July 1969, she was again arrested and held incommunicado for three weeks. She was released on condition that she leave the country, and she spent the next four years in exile in Europe and the United States.

Nueva Canción and the Mexican State

Throughout Latin America there were indeed many leftist singers and songwriters who sang for the 'people's liberation' from economic, political and social injustice. The Cuban Revolution and the social and political confrontations of the 1960s had led many urban, educated artists to become more 'conscious of the contradictions and conflicts inherent in their national situations' and begin to recognise them as 'features of a larger phenomenon: underdevelopment and economic and cultural dependency' (Reyes Matta, 1988: 452). *Nueva canción*, a folk-based song movement with vernacular and poetic lyrics that emerged in the Southern Cone in the 1950s, has been described by Carrasco as a 'reaction in national terms' to the dangers perceived to lie in the increasing influence of the recording industry (Carrasco, 1982: 601–602). It was an attempt to redefine popular music as 'made by and for the people' that would 'rescue' the form of cultural expression from the perceived effects of a capitalist system that had turned songs into commercial products. *Nueva canción* practitioners sought to counteract the massive penetration of foreign (mainly Anglo-US) music that, it was argued, threatened to stifle local production and erase popular memory (Carrasco, 1982: 601–602). The arrival of radio and cinema in the region had provided a massive boost to the diffusion and popularity of a first wave of early twentieth-century Latin American music styles such as the Mexican *ranchera*, the Cuban *son* and the Argentine/Uruguayan *tango*. Radio and cinema, however, were also vehicles for the diffusion of foreign music, which by the 1950s 'occupied a central place' in the region and left little space for the diffusion of national forms (Carrasco, 1982: 602). For many *nueva canción* artists, folk music provided a resource with which to resist what they perceived as 'cultural colonialism'. In Mexico, the raising of political consciousness associated with the Student Movement initially privileged the role of Latin American folk and the rediscovery of indigenous roots over foreign rock, which was widely perceived by leftist intellectuals to colonise the mind. In a public statement, the Mexican *nueva canción* group Los Folkloristas proclaimed:

> [We are] pledged to spread the best music of our continent, [we are] dedicated to the youth of our country who have discovered their own music, [we are] opposing it to the colonising assault and alienation of Rock and commercial music. (quoted in Zolov, 1999: 229)

Throughout Latin America in the late 1960s and early 1970s, leftist intellectuals criticised rock for its perceived capacity to distract young people from political action and to reinforce subservience to foreign, capitalist values. The prevalence of Anglo-US mass culture throughout Latin America was perceived by leftist intellectuals such as the Chilean Ariel Dorfman (author of *How to Read Donald Duck: Imperialist Ideology in Disney Comics*, 1971) as a cultural invasion aimed at the promotion of US consumer values and the erasure of indigenous and traditional ways of life. In the hugely influential 1973 volume *The Open Veins of Latin America: Five Centuries of the Pillage of a Continent*, Uruguayan Eduardo Galeano argued that Latin America was not an under-developed region because of a lack of natural resources but rather because those resources were extracted and used to finance the development of wealthy nations. Dependency theorists in the 1960s and 1970s: 'tended to place all of Latin America's economic ills at the door of the rich metropolitan countries of the North, blaming them for having locked the region into an endless cycle of commodity dependence and poverty' (Green, 2003: 70). Musical traditions were compared to raw resources that needed protection from such relations of dependency. As one participant at a meeting of Latin American music held in Cuba in 1972 expressed it:

> As with other deeply rooted popular and nationalist expressions, but with particular emphasis on music for its importance as a link between us, the colonialist cultural penetration seeks to achieve not only the destruction of our own values and the imposition of those from without but also the extraction and distortion of the former in order to return them [now] reprocessed and value-added, for the service of this penetration. (quoted in Zolov, 1999: 226).

These sentiments coincided in many ways with official and right-wing discourses in Mexico at the time that provided support for folk music and *nueva canción*. According to Víctor Guerra, in the early 1970s there was a 'boom' in the popularity of Chilean *nueva canción* in Mexico, with Chilean groups such as Inti Illimani and Quilapayún representing the 'inconformity and rebelliousness' of the peoples of Latin America. Nevertheless, Guerra points out, these groups sang about the governments and problems of their own countries, but did not sing about the Mexican system. In the 1970s, according to Guerra, there were two tendencies in *nueva canción* in Mexico:

> [There was t]he official music associated with President Luis Echeverría, like that of *Los Folkloristas*. This music was about the problems of South America, but not those of Mexico. [On the other hand there were] the Chileans, who gave 'legitimacy' to the democracy and freedom of expression that Echeverría boasted about so much; he gave them official spaces to criticize Pinochet, but not the massacre of 2 October. (Víctor Guerra quoted in Llaven, 2008)

The government neither censored nor withdrew its support from either of these tendencies, indicating that folk music and *nueva canción* were not perceived to pose a threat to the hegemonic order (Zolov, 1999: 227). The state donated space previously occupied by the National Symphony for the founding of Discos Pueblo, the label on which Los Folkloristas recorded, and in addition made concert halls such as the Palacio de Bellas Artes available for performances by Mexican and foreign *nueva canción* artists (Zolov, 1999: 228). However, while *nueva canción* was widely interpreted as a direct challenge to the status quo in other Latin American nations (Fairley, 1984, 2000; Martín, 1998; Morris, 1986; Reyes Matta, 1988; and Scruggs , 2004), in Mexico it served to focus the attention of protest away from the government and towards the more general concept of imperialism, as well as to reinforce a notion of cultural 'authenticity' and to reassert the boundaries of 'respect and discipline' between audience and performers that rock music undermined (Zolov, 1999: 230). Rock musicians received neither official performance spaces nor support. Consumed in semi-underground *cafés cantantes* and *hoyos funquis* (improvised outdoor concerts), the performance of rock music created unmonitored spaces in which (initially only middle- and upper-class, but later also lower-class) youths imitated the styles, sounds and gestures of youth culture from abroad (Zolov, 1999: 100). The Mexican state perceived rock audiences' embracing of sexual liberation, drug experimentation and 'hippy' fashions and their questioning of authority as a direct threat to a hegemonic value system that was 'grounded in patriarchy and heroic nationalism' (Zolov, 1999: 134).

While the Mexican government did not criticise rock for the same reasons as leftist intellectuals, for President Echeverría (1970–1976) the leftist language of cultural and economic imperialism and of Third World struggle became a 'useful polemical tool' (Zolov, 1999: 190). The PRI 'manipulated conflicts over cultural issues as a way of absorbing criticism without directly threatening its hold on power' (Zolov, 1999: 53). In February 1968, the federal Judicial Police began a campaign to 'clean up' Mexico City of 'dangerous' hippies, marijuana smokers and LSD 'addicts' (Zolov, 1999: 110). Such official condemnation contributed, towards the end of the 1960s, to the gradual conversion of rock music into an arena where young people could express their cynicism and disillusionment about the likelihood of political change. The Student Movement's demands and marches had not led to greater democratisation but had been met with state violence, provoking the radicalisation of a minority and a retreat from political action by the vast majority (Zolov, 1999: 110). Underground rock represented for many young people a focal point for the expression of anger, fear and mistrust towards authority. As one participant expressed it: 'We fought against a corrupt society, [one] that was suffocating us, that was deceiving us . . . and rock [music] helped us scream; rock for me is about that scream, a universal scream' (Zolov, 1999: 133).

Rock versus Folk

Like Víctor Guerra, Mexican singer/songwriter Leon Chávez Teixeiro (2008) identifies two musical tendencies in Mexican *nueva canción* and folk music after 1968. However, for Chávez Teixeiro, these tendencies differ from those delineated by Guerra. For him, the first type was characterised by folk music forms from across the continent and lyrics concerned with the general problems of South America. It was diffused via media coverage, record sales, festivals financed by the Communist Party, and by official performances, and it was closely linked to the continental *nueva canción* movement and to political parties financed by and in dialogue with the state. The second type was diffused in urban barrios and rural zones via *Brigadas Populares* (Popular Brigades), groups of artists who used theatre and song to bring attention to and give information about the ideas and demands of the Student Movement and to link this movement with pre-existing social movements such as those of campesinos and railway-workers. In the early 1970s, the Centro Libre de Experimentación Teatral y Artística (CLETA; the Free Centre of Theatrical and Artistic Experimentation) was established in order to continue this work:

> CLETA is an organisation of people working in art, [who are] dedicated to getting to know, digging out, diffusing and generating – together with workers, *campesinos* and the marginalised – our cultural values,

thereby contributing to the development of a class consciousness and to the political organisation of groups whose struggle is directed at the extermination of the system of exploitation of man by man. We are not the cultural arm of any political party, we have an open politics, which we understand as the participation of different tendencies within the left that we adopt with the common and fundamental aim of constructing the socialist revolution. (Velasco García, 2004: 85–6)

Unlike officially-backed *nueva canción* artists, Judith Reyes lived, worked and travelled in urban barrios and rural zones, and maintained a much stronger commitment to ordinary Mexicans than many other artists (Chávez Teixeiro, 2008). She has been described as an artist who 'sang and told of the truth in the country' (Guerra, 2008) and who dared to denounce Mexican authorities at a time when many other folk and *nueva canción* artists preferred to sing about more general problems of poverty and imperialism in other nations. While in the early 1970s the Echeverría government allowed folk groups like Los Folkloristas to perform in official spaces such as the Palacio de Bellas Artes and facilitated recording opportunities for these groups, Reyes was threatened, arrested, imprisoned and exiled. In *Cantares de la memoria*, musician René Villanueva describes how:

after the terrible night of Tlatelolco, to present Judith to the students was like a guerrilla operation of the most rigorous clandestinity . . . being kidnapped [and] the threats against you and your family that came from the highest political level, forced you into exile. (Reyes and Pérez, 1997)

Apparently unconcerned with recording her compositions,[9] Reyes was uncomfortable with what she perceived as the 'opportunism' of some artists within CLETA, and she remained on the outskirts of the organisation (Chávez Teixeiro, 2008). At a meeting of political song held in San Luis Potosí in 1978, during which folk and *nueva canción* artists discussed the development of their music in Mexico, Reyes disagreed with other artists who sought a space in the mass media and official institutions to diffuse their music, arguing that popular movements should not cede any concessions to representatives of the dominant classes (Velasco García, 2004: 90). Out of this meeting the Liga Independiente de Músicos y Artistas Revolucionarios (LIMAR; Independent League of Revolutionary Musicians and Artists) emerged in order to 'struggle for the creation of an art in agreement with the present and historical interests of the proletariat' (Velasco García, 2004: 93). Reyes, who had been sceptical

---

9   The recordings that exist of Reyes were made while the singer was living in exile in France and Italy (García, 2008b).

of such organisations (Velasco García, 2004: 92), did become a member of LIMAR, but according to Chávez Teixeiro (2008) she remained on the margins of the organisation, preferring to 'really throw herself into participating in the movements' of the time.

The events of 1968 deepened Reyes's political commitment. The Tlatelolco massacre had succeeded in dismembering a political and social movement. While one element of the student population became further radicalised and took to organising armed struggle, for the majority the repression produced feelings of 'a terrible sense of frustrated impotence' (Zolov, 1999: 133). Reyes belonged to the minority who were radicalised by the repression of the Student Movement, and in the 1970s she lent her explicit support to the guerrilla movements that had emerged as a result of this radicalisation (Chávez Teixeiro, 2008). Choosing to live in a lower class *barrio* that had been established as the result of a land invasion, Reyes continued to chronicle the everyday concerns of her neighbours:

According to Quiroz Trejo, many urban youths in the late 1960s and early 1970s:

> ... moved without problem between hippie dogmas and the dogmas of the militant new-old left. ... The relationship between rock and folk music was evident in the 1960s. People listened to anything from the militant corridos of Judith Reyes and José de Molina which, at times, could sound like a pamphlet, to the protest music of Margarita Bauche – who later became a hippie - and Oscar Chávez, and also the music of Joan Baez, Bob Dylan, Peter Paul and Mary, Simon and Garfunkel, The Beatles, The Rolling Stones, The Doors, Pink Floyd, The Who, etc. (Quiroz Trejo, 2000)

With the massacre of 2 October 1968, the PRI revealed its commitment to one-party rule. Official cultural policy supported and promoted folk and *nueva canción* as long as these genres addressed general problems of poverty and imperialism, or of political repression in other nations. By the mid 1970s, urban youth had rejected officially sanctioned folk and *nueva canción*, and anything that sounded like it, as channels for the expression of their values and preoccupations. Rock music took centre stage as the vehicle for the expression of a general loss of respect for authority both in the family and for the government (Ponce, 1998: 59). The role of rock music in the Student Movement was reassessed and redefined. As one participant wrote:

> If they ask me what the student movement of 1968 was all about ... I could tell them that it was the history of how a son rebelled against his government because he could not confront his father, while a president

who felt impotent against his own son's rocker lifestyle took revenge against hundreds of students. (quoted by Zolov, 1999: 131)[10]

Folk music and *nueva canción* were no longer perceived to be the only genres capable of articulating popular feelings. For leftist intellectuals such as Carlos Monsiváis, the emergence of the Mexican rock movement was an indication of the depoliticisation of youth and the transference of political action to cultural rebellion. By 1971, political repression, and the widespread incorporation of the lower classes through outdoor performances on the outskirts of Mexico City, had transformed rock into a space for Mexican youth to imagine an alternative community free from state control. Rock music did not so much represent a shift away from political action as 'the rupturing of the state's monopoly over cultural capital' (Zolov, 1999: 177). It was precisely the exclusion of rock from leftist and official spheres that allowed the genre to shift from being perceived as a consumer product imported from the United States to becoming a form of popular urban music that provided space for the symbolic creation and re-creation of cultural and political identity (Velasco García, 2004: 136). Many Mexican former folk and *nueva canción* artists created rock and fusion groups in the late 1970s. Though their lyrics were not directly political, they were concerned with the lives of 'the people'.[11] As the drummer for rock bands La Maldita Vecinidad and los Hijos del Quinto Patio commented:

> Our work is not political, if by political you mean doctrinaire, ideological songs, like the '60s protest songs were and the '70s, with the folkloric Chilean music and *nueva canción*. We don't intend to educate anyone, we don't believe in ideologies or doctrines. It is political in the broader sense of the word since we speak of the street life, of the everyday person. If you write about them, you're going to confront things that could be considered to be political. (quoted in Zolov, 1999: 258)

As rock shifted to central stage as the voice of urban protest, young Mexicans began to look upon the songs of Judith Reyes as 'primitive' and to reject corridos, which they perceived to be written in 'a very *campesino* style in versification and lyrics' (Chávez Teixeiro, 2008). Reyes was never interested in performing for the government or in official spaces; her work remained 'hidden from the media' and other folk and *nueva canción* artists

---

10 Zolov's informant is referring to Alfredo Díaz Ordaz, the president's son who was considered to be a hippy.

11 This rock movement led to the *rupestre* urban rock movement of the 1980s (associated with Rockdrigo Gonzalez) and in the early twenty-first century to *gronch* (a Spanish pronunciation of 'Grunge'), a movement of self-titled 'urban poets'.

held her work in contempt in aesthetic terms because by the 1970s, according to Chavez Teixeiro, 'if you made a song about a problem it was considered to be a pamphlet'. While *nueva canción* was 'sold to the highest bidder' and Los Folkloristas used media and official support to diffuse their work, Reyes showed no interest in compromising her performances and continued to sing directly to the public in informal, outdoor contexts (Chávez Teixeiro, 2008). In 1973, releasing a collection of Reyes's songs in the United States on the Paredon label,[12] Barbara Dane commented in her sleeve notes:

> She's pretty marginalised from the mainstream of the left . . . because she really is a woman of the lower classes . . . she's not an intellectual . . . she doesn't cater to [being sponsored by middle class intellectuals] . . . [her] real fame is among peasants and workers. (Dane, 2006)

Reyes became marginalised by the dogma of the political left, which supported *nueva canción*. It is this very same 'compact culture of iron-fisted militants, who were seeking a single totality into which all ideas, customs and hobbies as exclusively defined by the heads of . . . political parties should fit' (Quiroz Trejo, 2000), which also led urban youth to turn to rock as an expression of their rejection of state authority.

Conclusion: Song as Oral History

In *Footsteps in the Dark: the Hidden Histories of Popular Music*, George Lipsitz argues that in modern societies 'control over electoral politics by the rich and monopoly control over media outlets preclude meaningful public dialogue about political issues . . . yet people continue to long for better and more meaningful lives in the arenas open to them and with the tools they have available' (Lipsitz, 2007: xv). Popular music is one arena open for people to engage in meaningful public dialogue about political issues. While the PRI was able to use folk protest music as a vehicle for its own hegemonic ideologies, rock music was redefined by Mexican youth and made into an arena for the expression of anger and disagreement with the prevailing order. It is in the lyrics of the corridos of Judith Reyes, however, that we find a form of 'oral reporting' that, though excluded from official representations of the events of 1968 and marginalised by subsequent generations, vividly depicts the ways in which Mexicans experienced and thought about 1968 at that time:

---

12   These had originally been recorded in exile in France on the Chants du Monde label.

through [Judith Reyes's] compositions, the history of Mexico can be known, the real history, not the official version, because these corridos carry information about events and people's feelings. The work of Judith Reyes fulfils this function too; it gives the [1968 student] movement its just and popular historical significance. (Grupo Mártires de Tlatelolco, 1968, quoted in Alarcón, 2008)

Paco Ignacio Taibo II ([1991] 2004) refers to the year 1968 as a 'ghost', arguing that the constant interpretation and reinterpretation of the events of that year turns it into a mythology while its lived experience fades into oblivion. More than 40 years later, the songs of Judith Reyes act as direct links to the lived experience of that time.

10

References

Aguayo Quezada, S. (1998) *1968: Los Archivos de la Violencia*. Grijalbo: México, DF.

Alarcón, Y. (2008) Personal communication with Hazel Marsh, 15 September.

Alvárez del Villar, P. (1968) 'El Antisubdesarrollo'. *Excélsior*, 10 July.

Álvarez Garín, R. (1998) *La Estela de Tlatelolco: una Reconstrucción Histórica del Movimiento Estudiantil del 68*. Grijalbo: México, DF.

Arnaud, P. and Terret, T. (1993) *Le Rêve blanc, Olympisme et Sport d'hiver en France: Chamonix 1924, Grenoble 1968*. Presses universitaires de Bordeaux: Bordeaux.

Bajter, I. (2009) 'Tras las huellas de Alcira Soust' *La Lupa*, supplement to *Brecha*, 9 January, I–II.

Barrios, F. (2008) Personal communication with Hazel Marsh, 19 September.

Bass, A. (2002) *Not the Triumph but the Struggle – The 1968 Olympics and the Making of the Black Athlete*. University of Minnesota Press: Minneapolis.

Benneworth, P. and Dauncey, H. (forthcoming) 'International Urban Festivals as a Catalyst for Governance Capacity Building: The Legacy of Lyon's Failed Olympic 1968 Bid'.

Berthet, A. (1963) 'Correspondance à propos des jeux olympiques'. *Résonances* **114**: 4–6.

Bertrand, T. (1994) *Si j'ai bonne mémoire. Imprimerie du bâtiment*. Imprimerie du bâtiment: Villeurbanne.

Bolaño, R. (1999) *Amuleto*. Anagrama: Barcelona.

Bolsmann, C. and Brewster, K. (2009) 'Mexico 1968 and South Africa 2010: Development, Leadership and Legacies'. *Sport in Society* **12**(10): 1284–1298.

Booth, D. (2003) 'Hitting Apartheid for Six? The Politics of the South African Sports Boycott'. *Journal of Contemporary History* **38**(3): 477–493.

Brewster, C. (2002) 'The Student Movement of 1968 and the Mexican Press: The Cases of Excélsior and Siempre!'. *Bulletin of Latin American Research* **21**(2): 171–190.

Brewster, C. (2005) *Responding to Crisis in Contemporary Mexico: The Political Writing of Paz, Fuentes, Monsiváis and Poniatowska*. University of Arizona Press: Tucson.

Brewster, C. and Brewster, K. (2006) 'Mexico 1968: Sombreros and skyscrapers' in A. Tomlinson and C. Young (eds.) *National Identity and Global Events: Culture, Politics and Spectacle in the Olympics and Football World Cup*. State University of New York Press: Albany, 99–116.

Brewster, K. (2004) 'Redeeming the "Indian": Sport and Ethnicity in Post-revolutionary Mexico'. *Patterns of Prejudice* **38**(3): 213–231.

Brewster, K. (2005) 'Patriotic Pastimes: The Role of Sport in Post-revolutionary Mexico'. *International Journal of the History of Sport* **22**(2): 139–157.

Brewster, K. and Brewster, C. (2010) *Representing the Nation: Sport, Control, Contestation, and the Mexican Olympics*. Routledge: Abingdon.

Brohm, J.-M. (1981) *Le Mythe olympique*. Editions Bourgois: Paris.

Brohm, J.-M., Perelman, M. and Vassort, P. (2005) 'Paris 2012: Non à l'imposture olympique!'. *Le Monde diplomatique*, 3 July.

Butler, R. (1968) 'Mexico Awaits Starting Gun'. *Seattle Post Intelligencer*, 7 April.

Callède, J.-P. (2000) *Les Politiques sportives en France. Eléments de sociologie historique*. Editions Economica: Paris.

Campos Bravo, A. (1963) 'Reconocen el Esfuerzo del Pueblo Mexicano'. *El Nacional*, 19 October.

Cape Argus (2009a) 'Ready for Kick-Off'. 12 June.

Cape Argus (2009b) 'Free Cup Tickets to Counter "Serious Embarrassment for SA"'. 18 June.

Cape Argus (2009c) 'Ban the Noisy *Vuvuzela*, Says Spanish Star Xabi Alonso'. 18 June.

Cape Times (2009a) 'A Golden Goal'. 11 June.

Cape Times (2009b) 'FIFA Slams Empty Seats'. 16 June.

Cape Times (2009c) 'Pitch Perfect'. 29 June.

Carey, E. (2005) *Plaza of Sacrifices: Gender, Power and Terror in 1968 Mexico*. University of New Mexico: Albuquerque.

Carmichael, S. and Hamilton, C. V. (1968) *Black Power – The Politics of Liberation in America*. Pelican Books: London.

Carrasco, E. (1982) 'The *nueva canción* in Latin America'. *International Social Science Journal* 34(4): 599–623.

Caruth, C. (1996) *Unclaimed Experience: Trauma, Narrative, and History*. Johns Hopkins University Press: Baltimore.

Casellas, R. (1992) *Mexico 68: Confidencias de una Olimpiada*. Editorial Jus: México, DF.

Cerny, P. G. (1980) *The Politics of Grandeur: Ideological Aspects of de Gaulle's Foreign Policy*. Cambridge University Press: Cambridge.

Cervantes, L. (1998) 'En 68, todo para todos, nada para nosotros'. [WWW document]. URL http://www.geocities.com/athens/troy/2268/vaca28 [accessed 3 August 2008].

Chafer, A. and Godin, E. (eds.) (2009) *The French Exception*. Palgrave MacMillan: London.

Chávez Teixeiro, L. (2008) Personal communication with Hazel Marsh, 23 September.

Chifflet, P. (2005) *Idélogie sportive et service public en France: mythe d'un système unifié*. Presses universitaires de Grenoble: Grenoble.

Chomsky, N. (1992) *Deterring Democracy*. Vintage: London.

Cochrane, T. (2007) *Shared Emotions in Music*. PhD thesis, University of Nottingham, Nottingham. [WWW document]. URL http://etheses.nottingham.ac.uk/archive/00000286/ [accessed 21 April 2009].

Confederación Deportiva Mexicana (1965) *Memoria deportiva mexicana*. Confederación Deportiva Mexicana: Mexico, DF.

Corominas, J. (1991) *Diccionario Crítico Etimológico Castellano e Hispánico*. Gredos: Madrid.

Dane, B. (2006) 'Sleeve Notes' in J. Reyes *Mexico: Days of Struggle* [CD]. Smithsonian Folkways Recordings: Washington.

Dauncey, H. (1997) 'Choosing and Building the "Grand stade de France" – National Promotion through Sport and 'incompétence technocratique?' *French Politics and Society* 15(4): 32–40.

Dauncey, H. (1998) 'Building the Finals: Facilities and Infrastructure'. *Culture, Sport, Society* 1(2): 98–120.

Dauncey, H. (2004) 'Les Jeux Olympiques de Londres de 1948: "figure imposée" ou "vitrine"?' in P. Milza, F. Jéquier and Ph. Tétart (eds.) *Le Pouvoir des anneaux*. Vuibert: Paris, 183–198.

Dauncey, H. (2008) 'Londres 1908' in C. Boli (ed.) *Les Jeux Olympiques. Fierté nationale et enjeu mondial*. Musée national du sport/Editions Atlantica: Biarritz, 201–210.

Dauncey, H. and Hare, G. (eds.) (1999) *France and the 1998 World Cup: The National Impact of a World Sporting Event*. Frank Cass: London.

de Vaan, M. (2008) *Etymological Dictionary of Latin and the Other Italic Languages*. Brill: Leiden.

Delfante, Ch. (1963) 'Correspondance à propos des Jeux olympiques'. *Résonances* 114: 4–6.

Dériol, C. (1963) 'Le Dossier lyonnais des Jeux olympiques'. *Résonances* 113: 37–39.

Derrida, J. (1981) *Dissemination* (trans. B. Johnson). The University of Chicago Press: Chicago.

Derrida, J. (1994) *Specters of Marx* (trans. B. Magnus and S. Cullenberg). Routledge: New York and London.

Derrida, J. (1996) *Archive Fever: A Freudian Impression* (trans. E. Prenowitz). The University of Chicago Press: Chicago and London.

Doyle, K. (2006) *The Dead of Tlatelolco. 1 October*. [WWW document]. URL http://www.gwu.edu/~nsarchiv/NSAEBB/NSAEBB201/index.htm [accessed 24 September 2008].

du Preez, M. (2009) 'Cup Will Change How World Looks at Africa'. *Cape Argus*, 11 June.

Edwards, H. (1969) *The Revolt of the Black Athlete*. Free Press: New York.

El Día (1966) 'Puntualidad'. 9 June.

El Nacional (1967) 'Un Pueblo Maduro'. 4 May.

El Nacional (1968a) 'El Debate Mundial en Torno a la Olimpiada'. 29 February.

El Nacional (1968b) 'Continúan las Censuras al Hitlerista que Injurió a México en "Der Spiegal"'. 3 March.

El Nacional (1970) 'El Deporte, Expresión Vital del Mexicano' (editorial). 25 May.

El Universal (1963) 'No se Mostraron Complacidos los Soviéticos con la Elección Final'. 20 October.

El Universal (1966) 'Sección Editorial: Juegos Olímpicos'. 14 September.

Ernout, A. and Meillet, A. (2001) *Dictionnaire Etymologique de la Langue Latine: Histoire des Mots*, revised 4th edn. C. Klinksieck: Paris.

Estrada Nuñez, A. (1965) 'Campaña Nacional Para Crear una "Conciencia Olímpica"'. *Excélsior*, 29 August.

Evans, S. and Mazola, M. (2009) 'FIFA Gives SA 2010 Thumbs Up'. *Sunday Times*, 23 June.

Excélsior (1966) 'Foro de Excélsior'. 22 December.

Excélsior (1968a) 'Principio Unificador'. 25 February.

Excélsior (1968b) 'Decisión de los 32'. 27 February.

Eyerman, R. and Jamison, A. (1998) *Music and Social Movements: Mobilizing Traditions in the Twentieth Century*. Cambridge University Press: Cambridge.

Fairley, J. (1984) 'La Nueva Canción Latinoamericana'. *Bulletin of Latin American Research* 3(2): 107–115.

Fairley, J. (2000) 'An Uncompromising Song' in S. Broughton and M. Ellington (eds.) *World Music: the Rough Guide*, Vol. 2. Rough Guides: London, 362–371.

FIFA (2004) *Inspection Group Report for the 2010 FIFA World Cup*. FIFA: Zurich.

Foner, P. S. (ed.) (1995) *The Black Panthers Speak*. Da Capo Press: Cambridge.

Forsdick, C. (1999) 'Edward Said after Theory: The Limits of Saidian Counterpoint' in M. McQuillan, G. Macdonald, R. Purves and S. Thompson (eds.) *Post-Theory: New Directions in Criticism*. Edinburgh University Press: Edinburgh, 188–199.

Fourastié, J. (1979) *Les trente glorieuses, ou la révolution invisible de 1946 à 1975*. Fayard: Paris.

Franz, C. (2007) '"Una tristeza insoportable" (Ocho hipótesis sobre la mela-cholé de B.)'. *Letras Libres*, **64**: 38–41.

Frazer, C. (2006) *Bandit Nation: A History of Outlaws and Cultural Struggle in Mexico, 1810–1920*. University of Nebraska Press: Lincoln and London.

Freud, S. (1961a) *Beyond the Pleasure Principle* (trans. and ed. J. Strachey). Norton: New York and London.

Freud, S. (1961b) 'A Note Upon the "Mystic Writing Pad"' in J. Strachey (ed.) *The Standard Edition of the Complete Psychological Works of Sigmund Freud* (trans. J. Strachey), Vol. XIX. Hogarth: London, 225–232.

Fuentes, C. (2005) *Los 68: París-Praga-México*. Debate: México, DF.

Galeano, E. (1973) *The Open Veins of Latin America: Five Centuries of the Pillage of a Continent*. Monthly Review Press: New York and London.

García, L. (2008a) *Línea Abierta: Programa Especial de Cinco de Mayo – Judith Reyes*. 5 May [WWW document]. URL http://www.archivosderb.org/?q=en/node/395 [accessed 21 April 2009].

García, L. (2008b) Personal communication with Hazel Marsh, 28 September.

García Canclini, N. (2004) 'Aesthetic Moments of Latin Americanism' (trans. P. Legarreta). *Radical History Review* **89**: 13–24.

Gleeson, M. (2008) 'Filling Stadiums a Challenge, Says Jordaan'. *Mail and Guardian*, 22 November.

González de Alba, L. (1997a) *Los días y los años*. Biblioteca Era: México, DF.

González de Alba, L. (1997b) 'Para limpiar la memoria'. *Nexos* **20**(238): 45–49 .

Gravier, J.-F. (1947) *Paris et le désert français*. Le Portulan: Paris.

Green, D. (2003) *Silent Revolution: The Rise and Crisis of Market Economics in Latin America.* Latin American Bureau: London.

Guerra, V. (2008) *La canción de protesta no morirá mientras en México haya injusticias.* [WWW document]. URL http://setebc.wordpress.com/2008/07/23/ [accessed 3 August 2008].

Guttmann, A. (1984) *The Games Must Go On: Avery Brundage and the Olympic Movement.* Columbia University Press: New York.

Hamnett, B. (1999) *A Concise History of Mexico.* Cambridge University Press: Cambridge.

Harding, V. G. (1987) 'Beyond Amnesia: Martin Luther King and the Future of America'. *Journal of American History* **74**(2): 468–476.

Hartmann, D. (2003) *Race, Culture and the Revolt of the Black Athlete.* University of Chicago Press: Chicago, IL.

Hellman, J. A. (1983) *Mexico in Crisis.* Holmes and Meier: New York.

Hill, C. R. (1996) *Olympic Politics: Athens to Atlanta 1896–1996.* Manchester University Press: Manchester.

Hodges, D. and Gandy, R. (2002) *Mexico under Siege: Popular Resistance to Presidential Despotism.* Zed Books: London.

Horne, J. and Manzenreiter, W. (2006) 'An Introduction to the Sociology of Sports Mega-Events' in J. Horne and W. Manzenreiter (eds.) *Sports Mega-events: Social Scientific Analyses of a Global Phenomenon.* Wiley-Blackwell: Malden/Oxford, 1–29.

Jameson, F. (2003) 'The End of Temporality'. *Critical Inquiry* **29**: 695–718.

Jimenez, A. (2008) 'La "sacudida del 68" marcó el final de la "gran rectoría del Estado" en la cultura'. *La Jornada*, 13 September. [WWW document]. URL http://www.jornada.unam.mx/2008/09/13/index.php?section=cultura&article=a04n1cul [accessed 21 April 2009].

Killanin, D. and Rodda, J. (eds.) (1979) *The Olympic Games.* Macdonald and Jane's: London.

Kraul, C. (2004) 'Victims' Families Hopeful About 'Dirty War' Case'. *Los Angeles Times*, 27 July. [WWW document]. URL http://articles.latimes.com/2004/jul/27/world/fg-mexico27 [accessed 24 September 2008].

Kukawka, P. (1999) 'Les Jeux Olympiques d'hiver: enjeux et perspectives. Grenoble 1968 – Nagano 1998'. *Revue de Géographie Alpine* **87**(1): 99–104.

Laget, S. and Mazot, J.-P. (2000) *Marceau Crespin: à la Force des Poignets.* PPL: Mende.

L'Equipe (1962) 'Paris en concurrence avec Lyon pose sa candidature pour 1968'. 6 August, 6.

Le Progrès de Lyon (1962) 'Je suis convaincu que les Jeux Olympiques de 1968 seront organisés à Lyon, a déclaré M. Armand Massard, vice-président du Comité international olympique'. 21 July, 21.

Le Progrès de Lyon (1963a) 'Devant les principales personnalités lyonnaises, M. Pradel a plaidé le dossier de Lyon pour les J.O en 1968'. 5 July, 11.

Le Progrès de Lyon (1963b) 'Un magistral et précis exposé sur les chances et les possibilités des Jeux Olympiques 1968 a reçu l'unanime approbation des "responsables" sportifs et des élus'. 5 July, 12.

Lewis, O. (1964) *The Children of Sánchez.* Penguin: Harmondsworth.

Lipsitz, G. (2007) *Footsteps in the Dark: the Hidden Histories of Popular Music.* University of Minnesota Press: Minneapolis.

Llaven, Y. (2008) *La canción de protesta no morirá mientras en México haya injusticias.* [WWW document]. URL http://setebc.wordpress.com/2008/07/23/ [accessed 3 August 2008].

Logan, G. (2009) 'We Must Look Past Problems in South Africa'. *The Times*, 19 June.

Los Angeles Times (2007) 'The World – Mexico's Ex-leader Cleared in '68 Genocide'. 13 July. [WWW document]. URL: http://articles.latimes.com/2007/jul/13/world/fg-mexico13 [accessed 8 July 2009].

Mail and Guardian (2009) 'FIFA Hands Out Free Tickets to Confed Cup'. 17 June.

Manzoni, C. (2003) 'Reescritura como desplazamiento y anagnorisis en *El amuleto* de Roberto Bolaño'. *Hispamérica* **32**: 25–34.

Martín, G. (1998) *El Perfume de Una época*. Alfadil: Caracas.

Maslin, J. (2008) 'The Novelist in His Literary Labyrinth'. *The New York Times*, 12 November, C1.

Matthews, V. (1974) *My Race Be Won*. Charterhouse: New York.

Mexican Organising Committee (1969) *Official Report of the Organising Committee of the XIX Olympiad* (5 vols.). Mexican Organising Committee: Mexico City.

Michela, I. (1963) 'Les Lyonnais atterrés: le score plus déprimant que la défaite'. *Le Progrès de Lyon*, 19 October, 13–14.

Mkhize, T., Evans, S., Bradlow, B. and Kamaldien, Y. (2009) 'All Systems Go for 2010', *Sunday Times*, June 10.

Monsiváis, C. (1970) *Días de Guardar*. Ediciones Era: México, DF.

Moore, K. (1991a) 'A Courageous Stand'. *Sports Illustrated*, 5 August.

Moore, K. (1991b) 'The Eye of the Storm'. *Sports Illustrated*, 12 August.

Moore-Gilbert, B. (1997) *Postcolonial Theory: Contexts, Practices, Politics*. Verso: London.

Morris, N. (1986) '*Canto porque es necesario cantar*: the New Song Movement in Chile, 1973–1983'. *Latin American Research Review* **21**(1): 117–136.

Mratz, J. (2001) 'Today, Tomorrow, and Always: The Golden Age of Illustrated Magazines in Mexico, 1937–1960' in G. Joseph, A. Rubenstein and E. Zolov (eds.) *Fragments of a Golden Age: The Political Culture in Mexico since 1940*. Duke University Press: Durham, NC, 116–157.

MSNBC (2006) 'Ex-Mexico leader cleared of genocide charges'. 9 July. [WWW document]. URL http://www.msnbc.msn.com/id/13772086/ [accessed 24 September 2008].

Nail, S. (2009) 'Sound of SA football won't be silenced'. *Cape Argus*, 20 June.

News 24 (2008) 'Fifa gives Vuvuzelas thumbs up'. 11 July. [WWW document]. URL http://www.news24.com/News24/ Sport/SWC_2010/0,2-9-2188_2356051,00.html [accessed 23 December 2009].

New York Times (1968) 'Article'. 26 October, 7.

Nicolopolous, J. (1997) 'Another Fifty Years of the Corrido: A Reassessment'. *Aztlan: A Journal of Chicano Studies*. **22**(1): 115–138.

Paz, O. (1961) *The Labyrinth of Solitude* (trans. H. Lane). Grove Press: New York.

Paz, O. (1993) 'Posdata' in E. M. Santi (ed.) *El Laberinto de la Soledad*. Cátedra: Madrid, 363–415.

Pilcher, J. (2001) *Cantinflas and the Chaos of Mexican Modernity*. SR Books: Wilmington, DE.

Pittsburgh Courier (1968) 'Article'. 19 October, 45.

Ponce, R. (1998) 'El 68 y el golpe a "Excélsior" abrieron los espacios, dice el cartonista'. *Proceso*, 27 September, 16–20.

Poniatowska, E. (1971) *La Noche de Tlatelolco*. Ediciones Era: México, DF.

Poniatowska, E. (1975) *Massacre in Mexico* (trans. H. R. Lane). Viking: New York.

Poniatowska, E. (1998) *La Noche de Tlatelolco: Testimonios de Historia Oral*, 2nd edn. Ediciones Era: México, DF.

Pradel, L. (1963) 'A Propos des Jeux olympiques'. *Résonances* **115**: 41–43.

Pring-Mill, R. (1987) 'The Roles of Revolutionary Song – a Nicaraguan Assessment'. *Popular Music* **6**(2): 179–189.

Pron, P. (2008) *Archivo I: Entrevista a Roberto Bolaño (Göttingen, 2000)*. [WWW document]. URL http://patriciopron.blogspot.com/2008/07/un-rescate-una-entrevista-roberto-bolao.html [accessed 30 April 2009].

Quick, S. P. (1990) '"Black Knight Checks White King": The Conflict between Avery Brundage and the African Nations over South African Membership in the IOC'. *Canadian Journal of the History of Sport* **21**(2): 20–32.

Quiroz Trejo, J. (2000) *El Rock Mexicano y la Contracultura*. [WWW document]. URL http://www.uam.mx/difusion/revista/abr2000/quiroz.html [accessed 3 August 2008].

Real Academia Española (1992) *Diccionario de la Lengua Española*, 21st edn. RAE: Madrid.

Revueltas, J. (1978) 'Gris es toda teoría [II]' in A. Revueltas and P. Cheron (eds.) *México 68: Juventud y Revolución.* Ediciones Era: México, DF, 76–84.

Reyes, A. and Pérez, F. (1997) *Recordando a Judith Reyes.* [WWW document]. URL http://www.geocities.com/yellymar/ [accessed 13 January 2008].

Reyes, J. (1974 [1968]) *'La Cronología del Movimiento Estudiantil'* [LP]. Le Chant du Monde: Arles, France.

Reyes, J. (1974) *La otra cara de la patria.* Talleres Gráficos: Banjudal, Mexico.

Reyes, J. (2006 [1973]) *Mexico: Days of Struggle* [CD]. Smithsonian Folkways Recordings: Washington.

Reyes Matta, F. (1988) 'The New Song and its Confrontation in Latin America' in C. Nelson and L. Grossberg (eds.) *Marxism and the Interpretation of Culture.* University of Illinois Press: Urbana.

Rhône-Alpes (1995) *Jeux olympiques d'été 2004. Etude de faisabilité : document de synthèse.* Mission JO/Traces: Charbonnières-les-Bains.

Rivera Conde, S. (1999) 'El Diseño en la XIX Olimpíada: Entrevista al Arq. Pedro Ramírez Vázquez'. *Creación y Cultura* **1**(1): 13–38.

Roche, M. (2000) *Mega-events and Modernity: Olympics and Expos in the Growth of Global Culture.* Routledge: London.

Roche, M. (2006) 'Mega-events and Modernity Revisited' in J. Horne and W. Manzenreiter (eds.) *Sports Mega-events: Social Scientific Analyses of a Global Phenomenon.* Wiley-Blackwell: Malden/Oxford, 30–49.

Rodda, J. (1968a) 'After the Games are Over'. *The Guardian*, 1 November, 10.

Rodda, J. (1968b) 'Trapped at Gunpoint in Middle of Fighting'. *The Guardian*, 4 October, 2.

Rodríguez Kuri, A. (1998) 'El otro 68: Política y estilo en la organización de los juegos olímpicos de la ciudad de México'. *Relaciones* **76**(19): 109–129.

Rodríguez Kuri, A. (2003) 'Hacia México 68. Pedro Ramírez Vázquez y el Proyecto Olímpico' *Secuencia* **56**: 37–73.

SAFA (2010) *Africa's Stage SA 2010 Bid Book.* South African Football Association: Johannesburg.

Said, E. (1994) *Culture and Imperialism.* Vintage: London.

Sauzay, L. (1996) *Louis Pradel, Maire de Lyon 1957–1976. Conquête d'un Pouvoir, les Clés de l'enracinement Local.* Unpublished doctoral thesis, Institut d'études politiques de Lyon, Lyon.

Sauzay, L. (1998) *Louis Pradel, Maire de Lyon: Voyage au Coeur du Pouvoir Municipal.* Editions lyonnaises d'art et d'histoire: Lyon.

Scherer García, J. and Monsiváis, C. (1999) *Parte de Guerra, Tlatelolco 1968: Documentos del General Marcelino García Barragán: los Hechos y la Historia.* Nuevo Siglo/Aguilar: México, DF.

Scruggs, T. M. (2004) 'Music, Memory, and the Politics of Erasure in Nicaragua' in D. Walkowitz and L. Knauer (eds.) *Narrating the Nation: Memory and the Impact of Political Transformation in Public Spaces.* Duke University Press: Durham, NC and London, 255–275.

Segura Procelle, R. (1965) '"Cantinflas" Encabezará en Televisión una Cruzada Para Crear el Espíritu Olímpico'. *El Nacional*, 10 February, 4d.

Shaw, T. C. (2006) 'Two Warring Ideals: Double Consciousness, Dialogue, and African-American Patriotism Post 9/11' in J. Battle, M. Bennett and A. Lemelle (eds.) *Free at Last – Black America in the Twenty-First Century.* Transaction Publishers: London, 33–50.

Siempre (1964) 'Correspondencia'. 4 November, 5.

Smith, D. (2009) 'Footballers Upset as Noisy Fans Blow their Own Trumpets'. *Guardian*, 19 June.

Soldatenko, M. (2005) 'Mexico '68: Power to the Imagination!' *Latin American Perspectives* **32**(4): 111–132.

Sowetan (2004) 'Congratulations to Ourselves'. 14 May.

Steinberg, S. (2009) *Unfinished Events: Writing, Visual Culture, and the Durations of Mexico, 1968*. Unpublished doctoral dissertation, University of Pennsylvania, Philadelphia.

Stewart, M. (1997) *The Time of the Gypsies*. Westview Press: Boulder, Colorado.

Suárez, L. (1968) 'Ramírez Vázquez da Siempre el Balance Olímpico'. *Siempre*, 13 November, 28, 70.

Sunday Times (2009) 'Confederations Cup a Successful Rehearsal for FIFA 2010, Says Experts'. 29 June.

Taibo, P. I. II (1991) *68*. Planeta: México, DF.

Taibo, P. I. II (2004) [1991] *'68*. Seven Stories Press: New York.

Terret, T. (1990) 'Les retombées des Jeux Olympiques d'hiver: Grenoble 1968' in P. Arnaud (ed.) *Le Sport Moderne en Question: Innovation et Changements Sociaux*. AFRAPS: Grenoble, 45–53.

Terret, T. (2004) 'Lyon, the City which Never Hosted the Olympic Games' in I. Okubo (ed.) *Sport and Local Identity: Historical Study of Integration and Differentiation*. Academia Verlag: Sankt Agustin, 238–244.

Torres, C. R. (2007) 'Stymied Expectations: Buenos Aires Persistent Efforts to Host Olympic Games'. *Olympika: The International Journal of Olympic Studies* **16**: 43–75.

Tumblety, J. (2008) 'The Soccer World Cup of 1938: Politics, Spectacles, and "la Culture Physique" in Interwar France'. *French Historical Studies* **31**(1): 77–116.

Van Deburg, W. L. (1992) *New Day in Babylon*. University of Chicago Press: Chicago.

Velasco García, J. (2004) *El Canto de la Tribu*. Consejo nacional para la cultura y las artes: México, DF.

Velasco Polo, G. de (1978) 'Porqué los equipos mexicanos siempre pierden'. *El Heraldo de México*, 14 June, 7, 16.

Ville de Lyon (1963) *Jeux de la XIX Olympiade*. Association typographique lyonnaise: Lyon.

Volpi, J. (1998) *La imaginación y el poder: una historia intelectual de 1968*. Biblioteca Era: México, DF.

Vourron, Ph. (1962a) 'Le Colonel Crespin délégué à la Préparation Olympique: "J'ai été Séduit et Étonné par les Arguments de Lyon en Faveur de l'organisation des J.O. en 1968". *Le Progrès*, 19 April, 6.

Vourron, Ph. (1962b) 'Pour s'imposer en Indiscutable Favori à l'organisation des JO 1968 Lyon Devra Compter sur un Important Budget'. *Le Progrès*, 30 November, 8.

Waddell, T. and Schapp, D. (1996) *Gay Olympian*. Alfred Knopf: New York.

Wilson, J. (2009) 'Five Things we've Learned from the Confederations Cup'. *Guardian*, 29 June.

Yáñez, A. (1958) *Discursos por Jalisco*. Porrúa: México, DF.

Yacobazzo, M. (2009) 'Cuando Alcira fue Mima: Ronda de la niña sola'. *La Lupa*, supplement to *Brecha*, 9 January, III–IV.

Zea, L. (1968) 'Golpe Racista a México'. *Novedades*, 3 March.

Zermeño, S. (1978) *México: Una democracia Utópica. El Movimiento Estudiantil del '68*. Siglo XXI: México, DF.

Zolov, E. (1999) *Refried Elvis: The Rise of Mexican Counterculture*. University of California Press: Berkeley, London.

Zolov, E. (2004) 'Showcasing the "Land of Tomorrow": Mexico and the 1968 Olympics'. *The Americas* **61**(2): 159–188.

Zolov, E. (2005) 'The Harmonizing Nation: Mexico and the 1968 Olympics' in A. Bass (ed.) *In the Game: Race, Identity, and Sports in the Twentieth Century*. Palgrave Macmillan: New York, 191–220.

Television and Radio

Black Power Salute, 2008. Television documentary. Directed by Geoffrey Small. UK: BBC.

1968: Myth or Reality (2008). Radio. BBC Radio 4. 1 March to 31 August. [WWW document]. URL http://www.bbc.co.uk/radio4/1968/daybyday.shtml [accessed 28 July, 2009]

Archives

Archive of the International Olympic Committee (IOC/HA), Lausanne, Switzerland.
Archive of the Pentathlón Deportivo Militar Universitario (PDMU), Mexico City, Mexico.
Archivo del Congreso Nacional, Mexico City, Mexico.
Archivo General de la Nación (AGN), Mexico City, Mexico.
Archives Municipales de Lyon, Lyon, France.
Avery Brundage Collection, University of Illinois, Urbana-Champaign, USA.
Frederick J. Ruegsegger Papers University of Illinois, Urbana-Champaign, USA.
NAACP Collection, Library of Congress, Washington DC, USA.
United States Olympic Committee Archives, Colorado Springs, USA.

Interviews

Amdur, Neil (2005), sportswriter (telephone interview with Simon Henderson), November.
Bradley, Bruce (2004) Olympic water polo player (telephone interview with Simon Henderson), November.
Fosbury, Dick (2004) Olympic high jumper (telephone interview with Simon Henderson), 5 February.
Livington, Cleve (2004) Olympic rower (telephone interview with Simon Henderson), August.
Lipsyte, Robert (2005) *New York Times* sports correspondent (telephone interview with Simon Henderson), June.
Norman, Peter (2004) Olympic sprinter (telephone interview with Simon Henderson), April.
Oerter, Al (2004) Olympic discus thrower (telephone interview with Simon Henderson), November.
Ramírez Vázquez, P. (2001) Chairman of the Mexican Organising Committee (interviewed by Keith Brewster), 26 April, Mexico City.
Swagerty, Jane (2004) Olympic swimmer (telephone interview with Simon Henderson), November.
Young, George (2004) Olympic track star (telephone interview with Simon Henderson), September.

Index

Yáñez, Agustín, 119, 121
Year of Peace, 39
Young, George, 81
youth groups, 58–9

Zolov, Eric, 111, 114, 120, 121
Zuma, Jacob, 101